AF361570

The Philosophy of
John Henry Newman and Pragmatism

The Philosophy of John Henry Newman and Pragmatism

A Comparison

Marial Corona

Foreword by Frederick D. Aquino

The Catholic University of America Press
Washington, D.C.

Library of Congress Cataloging-in-Publication Data

Names: Corona, Marial, author. | Aquino, Frederick D., 1963– writer of foreword.

Title: The philosophy of John Henry Newman and pragmatism : a comparison / Marial Corona ; foreword by Frederick D. Aquino.

Description: Washington, D.C. : The Catholic University of America Press, [2023] | Based on author's doctoral dissertation: The pragmatism of J.H. Newman : his contributions for a commitment to truth in contemporary times. | Includes bibliographical references and index. |

Identifiers: LCCN 2023022353 (print) | LCCN 2023022354 (ebook) | ISBN 9780813236834 (cloth) | ISBN 9780813236841 (ebook)

Subjects: LCSH: Newman, John Henry, Saint, 1801 1890—Philosophy. | Pragmatism.

Classification: LCC BX4700.N45 C67 2023 (print) | LCC BX4700.N45 (ebook) | DDC 282.092—dc23/eng/20230607

LC record available at https://lccn.loc.gov/2023022353

LC ebook record available at https://lccn.loc.gov/2023022354

For Jaime Nubiola,

a mentor who has shown me

what is most important in life.

Contents

Foreword

Frederick D. Aquino

While John Henry Newman's writings have long received the attention of historians, theologians, and literary critics, they have largely been overlooked by philosophers. As Marial Corona notes in *The Philosophy of John Henry Newman and Pragmatism*, Newman has not been read or seen primarily as a philosopher, nor has his thought figured in the modern story of philosophy. However, his writings raise and tackle important philosophical issues. There has also been a growing interest in exploring the contours of his philosophical thought and showing with greater depth and precision its relevance to contemporary issues in philosophy. Thus, the time seems ripe for providing philosophical analysis, evaluation, and constructive appropriation of his thought.

Reading Newman philosophically can happen in various ways and with different goals in mind. One may be to identify, clarify, and evaluate the philosophical questions, issues, or proposals in his own writings (e.g., the indefectibility of certitude, the illative sense, real and notional assent, does the *Grammar of Assent* focus largely on the psychological or epistemological conditions of religious belief?). Or, one may seek to locate Newman within the history of philosophy. This kind of reading analyzes and evaluates Newman's conceptual engagement with a school of thought or the extent to which he was a forerunner to a particular tradition (e.g., pragmatism, common sense philosophy, personalism, the British Naturalist tradition). Still another reading may draw from or employ Newman's thought as a springboard for tackling contemporary problems (e.g., the rationality of religious belief, the role of properly formed dispositions in evaluating the force of evidence, and the cognitive function of the emotions).[1]

1.   See, for example, Basil Mitchell, *The Justification of Religious Belief* (New York: The Seabury Press, 1973), William J. Wainwright, *Reason and the Heart: A Prolegomenon to a Critique*

Newman's thought may also be approached as philosophically sugges-
tive but not fully developed.[2] As a result, the aim may be to articulate and
advance a view that Newman did not himself develop but that is clearly
related to or consistent with certain concepts in his writings. In the *Grammar
of Assent*, for example, Newman not only sought to show that there can be
appropriate certitude in matters of religion but in other aspects of life as well.
There are many propositions to which we unconditionally assent, though they
do not arise from demonstration or intuition. A relevant question, which
Corona takes up in her book, is whether Newman is an epistemic fallibilist.
Is his understanding of certitude compatible with the claim that a person
can know something without conclusive evidence or grounds to justify that
belief? It is doubtful that Newman had the contemporary debate between
infallibilism and fallibilism in mind when he, for example, wrote the *Grammar*.
Yet, the contemporary discussion may illuminate Newman's claim that we
can be "certain on premises which do not touch [reach] demonstration."[3] In
this respect, such a reading may explore how contemporary work in epistemology illuminates Newman's thought and how his thought contributes to
and advances the discussion.[4]

Notwithstanding the diversity of philosophical aims, we still want to
know how Newman's thought fares in light of critical philosophical analysis,
whether in his or our own context, or how his thought fits with and makes
sense in light of new pieces of information. There is a difference between

---

of Passional Reason (Ithaca, N.Y.: Cornell University Press, 1995), Mark Wynn, "The Relationship of Religion and Ethics: A Comparison of Newman and Contemporary Philosophy of
Religion," *Heythrop Journal* 46, no. 4 (2005): 435–49, and Frederick D. Aquino and Logan Paul
Gage, "On the Epistemic Role of Our Passional Nature," *Newman Studies Journal* 17, no. 2
(2020): 41–58.

2.   Newman himself described the *Grammar of Assent* as a "conversational essay" or
a "preliminary opening of the ground." He acknowledged that this work "may be full of
defects, and certainly characterized by incompleteness and crudeness, but it is something to
have started a problem, and mapped in part a country, if I have done nothing more" (*LD*,
xxv 131, 280). See also Jamie Ferreira, *Doubt and Religious Commitment: The Role of the Will in
Newman's Thought* (Oxford: Clarendon Press, 1980), 14–15.

3.   Newman, *LD*, xxiv 104. Bracketed phrase in the original.

4.   For example, Nicholas Wolterstorff's works on Locke and Reid unpack and
develop the philosophical insights of these writers on their own terms, though with contemporary work in epistemology in mind. See his *John Locke and the Ethics of Belief* (Cambridge:
Cambridge University Press, 1996) and *Thomas Reid and the Story of Epistemology* (Cambridge:
Cambridge University Press, 2006).

clarifying the philosophical position Newman held and determining whether it is coherent, plausible, true, or contributes to contemporary work in philosophy. We certainly want to avoid putting words in his mouth or misconstruing his thought. Instead, the hope is that a reading reflects consistently his thought while making the relevant adjustments and developments in light of new insights and pieces of information.

With this caveat in mind, Corona seeks to do justice to Newman's thought while locating it in the modern story of philosophy and drawing attention to the relevant comparative and constructive links with the pragmatist tradition. The tone of the book is refreshing and exploratory. She recognizes that Newman's appropriation of insights from different thinkers complicates attempts to reduce his philosophical approach to one school of thought. As a result, the aim is not to try to fit or force Newman into one philosophical tradition but to mine the corpus of his writings for fruitful insights into contemporary philosophical questions, issues, and problems. As intimated, the emergence of interest in Newman's philosophical thought is growing and promising. In this respect, Corona's proposal creates space for attending more fully to the nuances of Newman's philosophical thought, the lines of concurrence with the pragmatist tradition, and his place in and contribution to modern philosophy.

Acknowledgments

My acquaintance with Newman began in 2013 as I was looking for an author who could enlighten my reflection on the role of philosophy in higher education. His unfaltering decision to follow the truth wherever it led him, along with his insights into the quandaries his contemporaries faced, have been an invitation to delve into his thought and follow a similar path of study, conversion, and an ever-deepening coherence with the truth.

This book is largely based upon my doctoral dissertation titled "The Pragmatism of J. H. Newman, His Contributions for a Commitment to Truth in Contemporary Times," which I successfully defended at the University of Navarra on September 25, 2020. I used what I learned from my committee to add greater nuance to my exposition and enriched and reorganized its material after much reflection. A summary of chapters 1 and 3 was published in the winter 2020 issue of the *Newman Studies Journal*. Parts of chapter 4 rely on my master's thesis and a paper I presented at the conference of the Newman Association of America in 2019.

While there were some challenging moments, the research and writing of my dissertation and this book have been a thoroughly enriching, stimulating, and enjoyable experience. I am extremely grateful to Jaime Nubiola for directing my dissertation and providing invaluable encouragement and advice for its adaptation into book form. Although he left the ownership of both in my hands, he modeled the virtues of a committed academic and an authentic servant leader that I strive to emulate; I consider myself very blessed by his friendship and guidance.

Several conversations with Fred Aquino were fruitful for my research; I have benefitted not only from his acute scholarship but from his advice as I take my first steps in the academic world. Rosario Athié, Patricia Camarero, Ono Ekeh, Jorge López, Joe Milburn, and Fr. Juan Carlos Ortega also provided me with valuable advice as I advanced in my research. Fred Aquino,

Patricia Camarero, Jorge López, Fr. Sergio Sánchez Migallón, and Joe Milburn served on my committee and provided insightful feedback on my dissertation, which I did my best to incorporate into this book.

My doctoral studies were significantly enriched by the month I spent as a visiting scholar at the National Institute of Newman Studies. I am grateful to Elizabeth Huddleston, Bud Marr, and Ken Parker for the scholarly support they provided. I also had the opportunity to work as a visiting researcher at the University of St. Mary of the Lake, which has a significant collection of Newman scholarship. I am indebted to DeAnne Besetzny for her tireless and joyful attention to my bibliographic needs and to the late Fr. Thomas Baima for his invitation to work there. This text, and my work as a scholar, have been much improved by the thoughtful suggestions and editing skills of John Martino, Kira Howes, and Jessica Schubert.

I am beyond grateful to my community and my family for their constant encouragement and support during these years. Through their kindness and interest, they provided an ideal space for intellectual and spiritual growth.

Finally, I am grateful to Jorge López and Mary Schwarz, who generously read a draft of this book and offered valuable suggestions. Sharing one's work can be daunting, but through their constructive criticism and availability for numerous conversations, they allowed me to experience the crowning jewel of academic work: friendship.

Abbreviations

The abbreviations used for Newman's works are those listed by Joseph Rickaby in the *Index to the Works of John Henry Cardinal Newman* (London: Longmans, Green and Co., 1914) and followed by the *Newman Studies Journal*, with some additions. References to works included by Newman in his thirty-six-volume uniform edition, begun in 1868 and concluded in 1881, are always to that edition, the text of which is available in the National Institute for Newman Studies's Newman Reader (www.newmanreader.org).

Apo   *Apologia pro Vita Sua.* Edited by Wilfrid Ward. London: Oxford University Press, 1913.

AR   *Addresses to Cardinal Newman with His Replies (1879–81).* Edited by William Neville. London: Longmans, Green and Co., 1905.

AW   *Autobiographical Writings.* Edited by Henry Tristam. New York: Sheed & Ward, 1956.

Call   *Callista.* London: Longmans, Green, and Co., 1901.

Camp   *My Campaign in Ireland.* Aberdeen: A. King & Co., 1896.

Cons   *On Consulting the Faithful in Matters of Doctrine.* Edited by John Coulson. New York: Sheed & Ward, 1961.

DA   *Discussions and Arguments on Various Subjects.* London: Longmans, Green and Co., 1907.

Dev   *An Essay on the Development of Christian Doctrine.* London: Longmans, Green and Co., 1909.

Diff   *Certain Difficulties Felt by Anglicans in Catholic Teaching.* 2 vols. London: Longmans, Green and Co., 1900.

Ess   *Essays Critical and Historical.* 2 vols. London: Longmans, Green and Co., 1907.

GA   *An Essay in Aid of a Grammar of Assent.* London: Longmans, Green and Co., 1903.

HS   *Historical Sketches*. 3 vols. London: Longmans, Green and Co.,
          1909.

Idea   *The Idea of a University*. London: Longmans, Green and Co., 1907.

LD   *Letters and Diaries*. Edited by Charles Stephen Dessain, Ian
          Ker, and Thomas Gornall. 32 vols. Oxford: Clarendon Press,
          1978–2009.

LG   *Loss and Gain: The Story of a Convert*. London: Longmans, Green
          and Co., 1906.

Mix   *Discourses Addressed to Mixed Congregations*. London: Longmans,
          Green and Co., 1906.

OS   *Sermons Preached on Various Occasions*. London: Longmans, Green
          and Co., 1908.

PN   *The Philosophical Notebook of John Henry Newman: The Text*. Edited
          by Edward Sillem. Louvain: Nauwelaerts, 1970.[1]

Prepos   *Lectures on the Present Position of Catholics in England*. London:
          Longmans, Green and Co., 1908.

PS   *Parochial and Plain Sermons*. 8 vols. London: Longmans, Green and
          Co., 1907–08.

TP, i   *Theological Papers of John Henry Newman on Faith and Certainty*.
          Edited by Hugo de Achaval and Derek Holmes. Oxford: Clar-
          endon Press, 1976.

TP, ii   *Theological Papers of John Henry Newman on Biblical Inspiration and on
          Infallibility*. Edited by Derek Holmes. Oxford: Oxford University
          Press, 1979.

US   *Fifteen Sermons Preached before the University of Oxford*. London:
          Longmans, Green and Co., 1909.

VV   *Verses on Various Occasions*. London: Longmans, Green and Co.,
          1903.

---

1.   This is the second volume of Newman's *Philosophical Notebook*, which corresponds
to Newman's actual text. The first volume, subtitled "General Introduction," is not cited as
one of Newman's works, as it was written by Edward Sillem.

Introduction

Although John Henry Newman did not consider himself a philosopher and did not subscribe to any particular philosophical tradition, he did engage with the classical problems of truth, knowledge, and belief in a new and effective way. He stands out as a courageous witness of what it means to search for the truth and adhere to it. Not only did he make truth a personal and vital option, but he also reflected deeply on how people can know the truth, assent to it, and communicate it, engaging with these questions at length in several of his works. When one studies his legacy from a philosophical standpoint, one can identify truth as the focal point of his endeavors.

Newman's life spanned most of the nineteenth century, a time in which the illusions of modern philosophy, with its characteristic rationalism and liberalism, were quickly becoming manifest. He confronted the growing skepticism he encountered as a searching contradiction, and for more than sixty years he invested his heart and mind in resolving that contradiction. Newman reflected on the causes of the doubts that assailed his contemporaries and developed his philosophical thought as an attempt to find a way forward and offer them the intellectual resources needed to assent to truths in all fields of knowledge. His works reveal his concern for their quandaries and his keen ability to connect with believers and unbelievers alike.

While Newman's philosophical contributions have historically received little attention, this has changed in recent years.[1] Philosophers who have engaged with his thought have found that although he made valuable contributions to philosophy, Newman remains on its sidelines because his philosophical insights are not usually framed within an established tradition. Building

---

1. Examples of the growing interest in Newman as a philosopher include the winter 2019 issue of the American Catholic Philosophical Association, which is dedicated to Newman's philosophical legacy, or the fourth part of the 2018 *Oxford Handbook of Newman Studies*, which examines Newman's philosophical work.

upon the research of others, I argue that demonstrating a connection between Newman's thought and philosophical pragmatism is a feasible and worthwhile undertaking that can show the relevance of his philosophical endeavors.[2]

Although his philosophical papers remained unfinished and unpublished during his lifetime, Newman dealt with philosophical themes in several of his works.[3] In *The Idea of a University,* he used the following words to describe how a person knows reality:

> We know, not by a direct and simple vision, not at a glance, but, as it were, *by piecemeal and accumulation*, by a mental process, by going round an object, by the comparison, the combination, the mutual correction, *the continual adaptation of many partial notions,* by the employment, concentration, and joint action of many faculties and exercises of mind.[4]

This description of the individual's way of knowing reality served as the starting point for the research that has culminated in this book. My analysis relies primarily on Newman's texts that refer to his search for and commitment to the truth. Although I reference the vast array of his publications (thirty-one to be precise), my primary sources are Newman's *Oxford University Sermons* (1826–1843), *An Essay on the Development of Christian Doctrine* (1845), *The Idea of a University* (1852), *The Grammar of Assent* (1870), and his *Letters and Diaries* (1808–1890). The discussion of these texts highlights the nuances of

---

2.   To the best of my knowledge, the first mention of Newman in the context of pragmatism is found in Leslie Walker's book, *Theories of Knowledge*, published in 1911. Cyprus Mitchell wrote his master's thesis on this topic in 1913, and Wilfrid Ward, Newman's earliest biographer, gave a lecture in 1914 titled "Newman's Philosophy," in which he calls him a pragmatist. This connection was overlooked for most of the twentieth century but has recently been rediscovered. In 2014 Daniel Morris-Chapman dedicated a section of his doctoral thesis to "Newman and the Dawn of Pragmatism," in which he mentions thirteen authors who have studied this possibility. These historical connections between Newman and pragmatism will be discussed in chapter 2.

3.   These papers were published posthumously by Adrian Boekraad and Edward Sillem as *The Philosophical Notebook of John Henry Newman: The Text* (1970). William Myers published a second edition, which I found easier to read due to the absence of abbreviations and symbols. See William Myers, *The Thoughtful Heart: The Metaphysics of John Henry Newman* (Milwaukee: Marquette University Press, 2013).

4.   John Henry Newman, *The Idea of a University* (London: Longmans, Green and Co., 1907), 151 (hereafter, *Idea*) (emphasis added).

Newman's thought and showcases the compelling philosophical resources he offers. Newman does not provide ready-made answers to today's questions, but as we will see, the ways he analyzes and engages with the challenges of his time pave the way for creative and effective ways of dealing with the issues of today.

In a brief list of individuals who traveled a unique path and blazed an enriching trail for their contemporaries, the historian Lewis Mumford mentions both J. H. Newman and C. S. Peirce.[5] Across the Atlantic fifty years after Newman published *The Grammar of Assent*, Charles Sanders Peirce, the father of the pragmatic tradition, faced similar questions and sought to resolve them in ways that are reminiscent of Newman. My initial exploration of Newman's understanding of the Illative Sense revealed several affinities to Peirce's theory of Abductive Reasoning, which suggested that I could research Newman's commitment to the truth by using pragmatism as the starting point.

To conduct this study, I had to identify and adopt a specific understanding of pragmatism as a philosophical tradition. The perception of pragmatism varies widely in specialized and nonspecialized circles alike. In its colloquial sense, a pragmatic outlook can be predicated either as a compliment for a person who achieves results or as criticism of one who lacks principles. Among philosophers who are well acquainted with the history of philosophy but not with the pragmatic tradition, one potential pitfall is that of reducing pragmatism to a utilitarian attitude.[6]

While this understanding of pragmatism may be accurate in some cases, the conception that underpins this project is grounded in the writings of C. S. Peirce and follows a realist and objective interpretation of his thought, which

---

5.   See Lewis Mumford, *My Works and Days: A Personal Chronicle* (New York: Harcourt Brace Jovanovich, 1979), 244.

6.   Charlene Seigfried, a political theorist, explains that people are "resistant to embracing pragmatism because it recognises that we are all fallible, that truth is never had, but only worked toward." Quoted in Joe Humphreys, "Pragmatism: A Philosophy That's as Sensible as It Is Unpopular," *The Irish Times*, October 24, 2017, https://www.irishtimes.com/culture/pragmatism-a-philosophy-that-s-as-sensible-as-it-is-unpopular-1.3260684. In the context of erroneous philosophical theories, John Paul II asserted, "No less dangerous is *pragmatism*, an attitude of mind which, in making its choices, precludes theoretical considerations or judgements based on ethical principles. The practical consequences of this mode of thinking are significant. In particular there is growing support for a concept of democracy which is not grounded upon any reference to unchanging values: Whether or not a line of action is admissible is decided by the vote of a parliamentary majority." John Paul II, Encyclical Letter *Fides et ratio* (September 14, 1998), 89.

I discuss in chapter 1. Peirce argued that philosophy can provide a service to humanity by examining ideas in light of the effects they have upon behavior. By focusing on conceivable effects, Peirce did not deny the objectivity of truth, nor did he examine it solely from an abstract and theoretical standpoint. Precisely because Peirce believed that truth exists and that it can be known by individuals, he discussed the scientific method as an effective means for inquiry. Peirce saw the scientific method as a tool that facilitates communication and convergence among several individuals and their ideas. In defining truth as "the opinion which is fated to be ultimately agreed to by all who investigate,"[7] Peirce did not equate truth with consensus but identified it with the existing objective reality that is discovered through inquiry when carried out by a community of experts who build upon the findings of those who preceded them.

Peirce's pragmatism was popularized and taken in a new direction by William James. Two different strands of pragmatism can be discerned from their writings, with as many nuances as there are philosophers who have engaged with this tradition over the past 150 years. My analysis favors the Peircean account of pragmatism, which in recent years has been developed by Hilary Putnam, Susan Haack, and Cheryl Misak. The study of their contributions shows that pragmatism can help today's philosophers reclaim their intellectual responsibility towards the truth and tackle some of philosophy's more pressing problems. Their way of understanding the role of the community in the search for truth, along with Abductive Reasoning and fallibilism, has significantly enriched my exploration of truth, rationality, certainty, and assent. As will be seen throughout this book, delving into Newman's thought alongside that of the classical pragmatists allows us to appreciate their resourcefulness, to recognize their limitations, and to make use of the opportunities they afford to those committed to the truth.

It should go without saying that the harmony between Newman's philosophy and some pragmatic theses does not mean that Newman subscribes to *all* the claims held by pragmatist philosophers (this could not even be said of Peirce).[8] However, it does make it possible to place him within the pragmatic

7.   Charles S. Peirce, *Collected Papers*, ed. Charles Hartshorne and Paul Weiss (Cambridge, Mass.: Belknap Press, 1935), 5.407 (1878).

8.   Robert Westbrook speaks of pragmatism not as a coherent philosophical school, but as a quarrelsome family of thinkers that hold related positions on the "workmanlike" nature of knowledge and truth. See Robert Westbrook, *Democratic Hope: Pragmatism and the Politics of Truth* (Ithaca, N.Y.: Cornell University Press, 2005), 1.

tradition, specifically as its forerunner, since he preceded Peirce by half a century. On the other hand, Newman's insights provide an effective means for understanding the resources of pragmatism from a seldom-used vantage point and for appreciating its soundness and fruitfulness in a unique way.

While Newman was convinced of the human intellect's capacity to comprehend reality and rest in certitude and assent, he also acknowledged its limitations, especially when viewed from a purely rationalistic perspective. Buckley wrote that "no one celebrated the human intellect more wisely and more lyrically than Newman"[9] and, in the words of Peirce, "in order to reason well it is absolutely necessary to possess [...] a real love of truth."[10] Using Newman's and Peirce's commitment to truth as a framework, I have advanced the argument in this book as follows: In chapter 1, I explain why this project is a valuable contribution to philosophy, since Newman is seldom associated with pragmatism. In chapter 2 I explore Newman's philosophical profile through the lens of his relationships, as a basis for chapter 3, in which I examine five affinities between his thought and pragmatism. Finally, in chapter 4 I explore classic themes found in Newman studies from the perspective that is afforded by the comparison of his thought and pragmatism. After this broad overview of the project, I will now outline the contents of each chapter in more detail.

Chapter 1 begins with an exploration of Newman's biographical profile. This is important because truth was not only an academic interest for him; it was above all a vital commitment that guided his decisions and for which he sacrificed much. After a difficult period in 1834, he wrote: "I have not sinned against the light."[11] This self-awareness gave Newman clarity and strength to face the numerous trials that assailed him. The episodes from Newman's life and the excerpts from his writings that are particularly indicative of his philosophical commitments are highlighted in this chapter and organized into five periods: (1) Newman's formative period (1801–1833), in which he underwent what he called his first conversion and made important career decisions; (2) the years of the Oxford Movement (1833–1841), which were characterized

9. Michael Buckley, "The Winter of My Desolation: Conscience and the Contradictions of Atheism According to John Henry Newman," in *Newman and Truth* (Louvain: Peeters, 2008), 76.

10. Peirce, *Collected Papers*, 2.82 (1902).

11. John Henry Newman, *Autobiographical Writings*, ed. Henry Tristram (New York: Sheed & Ward, 1956), 127 (hereafter, *AW*).

by intense intellectual growth; (3) the period of his crisis and conversion (1841–1847), which centered around his reception into the Roman Catholic Church; (4) his first years in the Roman Catholic Church (1847–1864), in which he undertook several projects that provided him with the platform and focus for his philosophical reflection; and lastly, (5) the period in which he gathered the fruits of his labor (1864–1890) and developed the most systematic reflection of his philosophical insights.

This sketch of Newman's life is followed by a brief exposition of my understanding of pragmatism. This understanding is grounded in the contributions of the three classical pragmatists, Charles Peirce, William James, and John Dewey, and devotes particular attention to Peirce's thought. The chosen point of connection between Newman and pragmatism is based on Cheryl Misak's research about the commitments that pragmatists tend to share. These are a historical attitude towards objectivity, a fallibilist epistemology, and a commitment to keeping philosophy rooted in real-life experience.[12] I contrast these characteristics with Newman's philosophical thought, reaffirming that the study of Newman within the framework of pragmatism, thus understood, is a legitimate undertaking.

After considering crucial moments in Newman's life that were consequential for his philosophical development and expounding upon the understanding of pragmatism adopted in this book, chapter 2 delves into Newman's profile as a philosopher. It discusses the thinkers and ideas that shaped him, how he engaged with his contemporaries, and how his thought has been received in the twentieth and twenty-first centuries. This chapter begins by exploring Newman's acquaintance with five British thinkers who studied a broad range of subjects and shows how they enriched his thought and provided him with the various resources he used to develop his understanding of truth, inquiry, knowledge, and assent. After presenting Newman's understanding of the centrality of personal influence for moral and intellectual development, the chapter discusses how specific relationships shaped his

---

12.   See Cheryl Misak, introduction to *New Pragmatists* (Oxford: Oxford University Press, 2007), 2–4. Misak's synthesis of the commitments of pragmatism is also explained in Cheryl Misak, "The Impact of Pragmatism," in *The Cambridge History of Philosophy, 1945–2015*, ed. Kelly Becker and Iain Thomson (Cambridge: Cambridge University Press, 2019), 624–33. Another possible way of bringing Newman and Peirce into dialogue would have been a detailed study of their shared philosophical sources. While this was not the way I chose to approach this study, I examine the most significant source they shared, Richard Whately's logic, in chapter 2.

philosophical understanding. Chapter 2 focuses on three of his numerous friends and acquaintances: Richard Whately, Catherine Froude, and William Froude.[13] His work with Whately and his correspondence with the Froudes, which he maintained over four decades, show that his friendships kept him grounded in the real concerns of his contemporaries and allowed him to gradually develop and test his philosophical insights, which provided the stimulus for him to write *The Grammar of Assent*.

I then explore Newman's engagement with the philosophy of his day. The nuanced exposition of his response to rationalism, liberalism, skepticism, and fundamentalism identifies the elements in each of these positions that Newman rejected, as well as those he understood as valuable developments and thus incorporated into his works. Chapter 2 concludes with a discussion of how Newman's philosophical insights have been received by philosophers who ascribe to pragmatism, phenomenology, and personalism in the twentieth and twenty-first centuries. This exploration includes some recognized affinities between Newman and these traditions and thus shows the contemporary relevance of Newman's philosophical thought.

Chapter 3 studies five affinities between Newman's philosophy and pragmatism. As will be seen, the recognition of these affinities does not imply that there are no points of divergence, but it shows significant connections that can be made between Newman's philosophy and pragmatist philosophy, further revealing the benefits of this comparison for research and action. The chapter begins by arguing that Newman and the classical pragmatists are well acquainted with the methods of inquiry in the natural sciences, subscribe to a realist epistemology, and reconnect to the Aristotelian tradition, which helps them overcome a reductive conception of reason and opens fresh avenues for the understanding of knowledge, inquiry, and truth. The second affinity that is identified relates to Newman's and Peirce's understanding of the unity of knowledge: both place the human subject who possesses knowledge (or advances the sciences) as the axis of their considerations, and grounded in this perspective, both present the unity of knowledge as something that is not only possible but desirable, while respecting the inherent characteristics unique to each science.

Third, the search for truth as a collective pursuit through time is developed as another affinity between Newman and pragmatism. Newman placed

---

13. For an in-depth study of how Newman's friendships were a driving force in the development of his thought and personality, see Edward Short, *Newman and His Contemporaries* (New York: T&T Clark, 2011).

great emphasis on the efficacy of individuals working together, balancing each other's views, and contributing to a common pursuit. For his part, unlike the individualistic rationalism that characterized modern philosophy, Peirce wrote that truth can only be sought within a community of inquirers. Fourth, the chapter explores how Newman and the pragmatists recognized the crucial role that difficulties and errors play in the pursuit of truth and how they saw these as building blocks in the edifice of knowledge. In this regard, Newman maintained that truth can only be discovered through a laborious process of inquiry: a thesis that finds ample resonance in Peirce's pragmatism. Fifth, I show the clear affinity between Newman's Illative Sense and Peirce's Abductive Reasoning. Both thinkers present this faculty as an individual's natural inheritance, which nevertheless requires training. They also acknowledged that both the Illative Sense and Abductive Reasoning demonstrate that the person's mind is naturally attuned to truth.

Finally, chapter 4 discusses the benefits of studying Newman's contributions from the standpoint of pragmatism. To do this, I identify and analyze four resources Newman offers to strengthen one's commitment to truth: (1) liberal education, (2) personal influence, (3) conscience, and (4) fallibilism and pluralism. Liberal education is presented as the essential means Newman identifies for enriching the individual's intellectual abilities. He did not describe liberal education based on its contents; instead, he discussed a method that prioritizes leisure, inquiry, dialogue, and community. This understanding led Newman to develop his theory of personal influence and his understanding of conscience. It also prompted him to advocate for the efficacy of personal witness over an authoritarian style of governance. Newman believed that only personal influence can bring the individual to real assent and allow him to internalize the truth, discern the appropriate course of action to attain his goals, and own his decisions. Within this context, Newman was a firm defender of personal conscience as a privileged means for knowing the truth.

Further, Newman understood that truth is gradually discovered through time, and thus, it can never be possessed in full by any one person at any given moment. Consequently, he offered a fallibilist understanding of the interplay between inquiry, error, and truth, which can be perceived as a *via media* between fundamentalism and skepticism because it helps the person uphold her commitment to truth amidst ever-developing conditions. Newman's recognition of each person's unique history and path allows for the study of his philosophical commitments within the framework of pluralism; pluralism here is understood as the belief that there are distinct ways—better and worse ways—to internalize and deal with reality. One hundred and fifty years after Newman engaged with these resources, they continue to serve as an efficacious aid for those who seek to live a coherent life committed to the truth.

Even though Newman did not associate himself with any particular philosopher during his lifetime and did not seek to form a school or tradition as Peirce did, both left countless philosophical insights scattered throughout their works. Although not systematically presented, their philosophical principles have a strong internal coherence and provide avenues for the person to grow in her self-understanding and the understanding of the world around her.

As will be seen, Newman's and Peirce's coherence shine forth more clearly when considered side by side. A superficial understanding of pragmatism, along with Newman's Catholic commitments, often make scholars hesitant to associate him with this philosophical tradition, as his defense of dogma is considered incompatible with Peirce's account of truth. I analyze the nuances of Newman's and Peirce's understanding of truth and argue that their points of convergence are more than sufficient for a fruitful dialogue that leads to a clearer understanding of pragmatism and serves as a framework for an incisive exploration of Newman's philosophical principles. Maintaining this viewpoint does not exclude the possibility of studying Newman's philosophy in relation to other schools of thought. Instead, it adds one more avenue of research and provides a broader reach to his insights. Although Newman never sought to be considered a forerunner of pragmatism (the term *pragmatism* was coined seventeen years after his death), studying his philosophy in the context of pragmatism is a fruitful endeavor, as this book attempts to show.

In 1851 Newman said in a lecture that "nothing would be done at all, if a man waited till he could do it so well, that no one could find fault with it."[14] I came across these words at the beginning of my research, and they have accompanied me every step of the way. If my research provokes those who encounter it to question and enhance their commitment to the truth while they challenge and seek to improve its arguments, then I will have been successful; I can at the very least say that it has done so for me.

---

14. John Henry Newman, *Lectures on the Present Position of Catholics in England* (London: Longmans, Green and Co., 1908), 403 (hereafter, *Prepos*).

Chapter 1

Focusing the Lens

It is helpful to begin this study of Newman's affinity with pragmatism by discussing his biographical profile. Edward Sillem, the editor of his *Philosophical Notebook*, noted that Newman's philosophy originated "not from his reading of the works of other philosophers, but in his own life and experience [...] in studying his philosophy we have to ever be going from his life to his ideas, and from his ideas back to his life."[1] The brief profile I sketch in this chapter is not meant to present a detailed or strictly chronological account of Newman's life but rather to highlight some episodes in each stage of his journey that portray his deep coherence and commitment to the truth, which he considered his greatest duty. These episodes also shed light on Newman's philosophical commitments and provide a valuable context for them.

A review of *The Grammar of Assent*, published seventeen years after Newman's death, identifies his commitment to truth as the anchor that unified his life:

---

1.   Edward Sillem, *The Philosophical Notebook of John Henry Newman: General Introduction to the Study of Newman's Philosophy* (Louvain: Nauwelaerts, 1969), 93. This study also takes Newman's historical context into great consideration. As the editors of the *Oxford Handbook of John Henry Newman* note, "without historical analysis, Newman's life, thought, and writings become strangely disembodied, escaping from the sort of contextualizing that is needed to see and read him through the eyes of his contemporaries." Frederick Aquino and Benjamin King, eds., introduction to *The Oxford Handbook of John Henry Newman* (Oxford: Oxford University Press, 2018), 2.

> The world has borne witness to the honesty and singleness of purpose which ever guided [Newman] in his religious inquiries, and to the marvellous intellectual power which he manifested in his long and arduous search after truth. The thousand claims upon his affections, the friendships, habits, customs, and associations of years [...] did not avail in the least to avert his eye from the steadfast contemplation of the truth. He kept resolutely to his course, though he clearly foresaw that it would end in the surrender of all that he held dearest upon earth.[2]

After providing a succinct sketch of Newman's life, I will enounce the understanding of pragmatism I adopt in this work as a basis for the development of the affinities between Newman's philosophy and the pragmatic tradition. In 1878—eight years after Newman published *The Grammar of Assent*, in which he gave an account of the conditions needed to hold a proposition with certainty—Peirce published the paper "How to Make our Ideas Clear." This paper gave rise to pragmatism, understood by him as a philosophical method that delineates the conditions needed for inquiry to lead to truth.[3] In this paper, Peirce suggested that philosophy can find a way forward from Cartesian rationalism by examining ideas in relation to their consequences in human behavior. His discussion on the clarity and distinctness of ideas led him to develop the pragmatic maxim, the earliest formulation of which is as follows: "Consider what effects, that might conceivably have practical bearings, we conceive the object of our conception to have. Then, our conception of these effects is the whole of our conception of the object."[4]

---

2.   John Toohey, "The *Grammar of Assent* and the Old Philosophy," *The Irish Theological Quarterly* 2, no. 8 (1907): 467.

3.   Although Newman and Peirce were contemporaries, there is no evidence that Newman ever heard of Peirce. Peirce, however, was familiar with Newman's work. He included *The Grammar of Assent* in a list of books every scientist should have, and he cited it twenty-seven times in the entries he prepared for *The Century Dictionary*. Moreover, both Newman and Peirce recognized that Richard Whately's *Elements of Logic* played an important role in their education; Newman wrote some sections of this work, and Peirce read it enthusiastically at the beginning of his career. See Jaime Nubiola, "John Henry Newman y Charles S. Peirce: Conexiones y Afinidades" (paper, V Jornadas "Pierce en Argentina," Academia Nacional de Ciencias Buenos Aires, August 23–24, 2012).

4.   Peirce, *Collected Papers*, 5.402 (1878).

Since its beginnings, pragmatism has not been a uniform theory or set of doctrines but has developed as a workmanlike account of knowledge, justification, inquiry, and truth. While Peirce, James, and Dewey are considered classical pragmatists, each philosopher identified with this tradition emphasizes diverse interests or nuances. Throughout the decades, the method that has united pragmatists has been that of taking seriously lived human experience and theorizing from that basis—from its richness and its deficiencies—to identify and develop resources that are rooted in actual social practices. Stated in a very succinct way, pragmatic philosophy aims to justify the objective dimension of human inquiry.

Through a brief review of the historical development of pragmatism, common elements within the claims of pragmatist philosophers come to light. In 2007 Cheryl Misak identified three of these as central to pragmatist philosophers: a historical attitude towards objectivity, a fallibilist epistemology grounded in anti-foundationalism, and a commitment to keeping philosophy rooted in real-life experience.[5] Although these commitments can be nuanced or subject to discussion, they provide a suitable standpoint for studying Newman's philosophy in dialogue with pragmatism. After a sketch of Newman's life and my understanding of pragmatism, which form the foundation of this project, chapter 1 concludes with an analysis of Newman's philosophical principles contrasted with these three commitments of pragmatism, in order to determine whether he indeed has a place among the forerunners of this tradition.

A Sketch of Newman's Life

The Formative Period (1801–1833)

John Henry Newman was born to a pious Anglican family on February 21, 1801, the first of six children. Due to his father's bankruptcy and untimely death in 1824, he became the pillar of his household at a young age. From his early years as a student, first in the Great Ealing School and then in Trinity College, Newman developed foundational qualities for his life's calling: receptivity, resilience, responsibility, and openness to friendship. Although he faced challenges—first in failing the first examinations for his bachelor's degree and then, shortly after obtaining that degree, in having to take on his younger

---

5. See Misak, introduction to *New Pragmatists*, 2–4.

brother's tuition—he managed to grow not only intellectually but also in terms of piety and self-giving.

In his autobiography, Newman identified a moment when he was fifteen years old as his first conversion: "A great change of thought took place in me. I fell under the influences of a definite Creed and received into my intellect impressions of dogma, which, through God's mercy, have never been effaced or obscured."[6] He had come across the works of Thomas Scott (1747–1821), whom he described as the writer who left the deepest impression on him by virtue of his unworldliness and vigorous independence of mind; Newman tried to emulate these qualities for the rest of his life. In Scott's *Essays,* he found the two maxims that shaped him as a young man: "Holiness rather than peace" and "growth the only evidence of life."[7]

In June 1817, Newman enrolled at Oxford's Trinity College for his undergraduate courses, which he undertook with passion. He spent an average of twelve hours per day studying for his final examinations, but he severely underperformed due to his lack of experience. This setback did not discourage him but taught him important lessons for his future career. Before returning to Oxford for his graduate studies in 1821, he told his parents that he would pursue a fellowship at Oriel College, along with Holy Orders. After he was elected fellow in 1822, he continued to tutor young men while preparing for his priestly ordination, which he received in 1825. In 1826 he preached the first of fifteen sermons on the relationship between faith and reason, which would come to be known as the *Oxford University Sermons,* the last of which he preached in 1843.[8]

During these years Newman was influenced by Oriel's leading intellectuals, known as the Noetics, who promoted religious liberalism. He learned much from his conversations with the students he tutored and with his own mentors, particularly Richard Whately (1787–1863), Edward Hawkins (1789–1882), and Joseph Blanco White (1775–1841). By 1830, however, their paths

6.   John Henry Newman, *Apologia pro Vita Sua,* ed. Wilfrid Ward (London: Oxford University Press, 1913), 107 (hereafter, *Apo*).

7.   Newman's understanding of growth as the only evidence of life shows his natural affinity with Peirce's pragmatic maxim, which is built upon "conceivable effects." See Peirce, *Collected Papers,* 5.402 (1878).

8.   The theological and philosophical contributions that Newman made from the pulpit are exceptional in number and depth. In his nineteen years as an active clergyman of the Church of England, he preached over 1,270 sermons.

diverged as Newman moved away from their liberal outlook. A journal entry from 1824 reveals Newman's intellectual struggle and development. As he wrestled with the principles related to Baptism and tried to discern the position held by the Church Fathers, he wrote, "I am always slow in deciding a question; and last night I was so distressed and low about it that the thought even struck me I must leave the Church. I have been praying about it before I rose this morning, and I do not know what will be the end of it. I think I really desire the truth, and would embrace it wherever I found it."[9]

In 1832 he was invited to continental Europe by his dear friend Hurrell Froude (1803–1836), who was advised to leave England to recover his health, and his father Robert Froude (1771–1859).[10] Newman's diary entries and letters reveal the vitality of his mind and the continuous awakening of his soul that took place during this trip. The highlight of his travels were his visits to Athens and Rome—the latter serving to mitigate his bias against Roman Catholicism. It was Sicily, however, that provided the setting for a turning point in his life. After Robert's and Hurrell's return to England in April, Newman decided to visit Sicily one more time, where he fell gravely ill with typhoid fever. While many were dying, Newman was confident that he would live, as he realized that God had work for him to do. His illness and recovery lasted several weeks, and on June 13 he was able to begin his return to England. On the ship that took him home, he wrote his famous poem "Lead Kindly Light":

> Lead, Kindly Light, amidst th'encircling gloom,
> Lead Thou me on!
> The night is dark, and I am far from home,
> Lead Thou me on!
> Keep Thou my feet; I do not ask to see
> The distant scene; one step enough for me.

9.   *AW*, 202 (1824). "Would embrace it wherever I found it"; Newman's internal process and his clear commitment to truth cohere with the way Peirce described following the path of inquiry fifty-four years later: "This ground seems to hold for the present. Here I will stay *till it begins to give way.*" Peirce, *Collected Papers*, 5.589 (1898).

10.   Newman also developed a deep friendship with another of Robert's sons, William Froude (1810–1879), and his wife Catherine (1810–1878), for whom he would write *An Essay in Aid of a Grammar of Assent.* James Anthony Froude (1818–1894), the youngest of Robert's sons, became a historian and left a telling account of Newman in his *Short Studies on Great Subjects.*

> I was not ever thus, nor prayed that Thou
> Shouldst lead me on;
> I loved to choose and see my path; but now
> Lead Thou me on!
> I loved the garish day, and, spite of fears,
> Pride ruled my will. Remember not past years![11]

Newman's experiences during this six-month journey away from Oriel's Common Room reinforced his awareness of the dangers of liberalism and his decision to fight it. With the realization that he had a mission, he arrived home on July 9, 1833, to witness the beginning of the Oxford Movement.

The Oxford Movement (1833–1841)

During his Mediterranean trip, Newman corresponded with like-minded individuals who became the core of the Oxford Movement: John Keble (1792–1866), William Palmer (1803–1885), Arthur Perceval (1799–1853), Hugh James Rose (1795–1838), and Edward Pusey (1800–1882). He considered the "Assize Sermon," preached by Keble on July 14, 1833, to be the beginning of the Movement. While acknowledging Newman's judgment, Juan Velez points out that one could also consider the beginning of the Movement to be January 22, 1832, when Newman delivered his sermon, "Personal Influence, the Means for Propagating the Truth."[12] In this sermon, Newman explained that while doctrinal truths are often blurred by secular reason, they are not overcome if personal witness upholds them:

> The warfare between Error and Truth is necessarily advantageous to the former [...]. Truth is vast and far-stretching, viewed as a system; and, viewed in its separate doctrines, it depends on the combination of a number of various, delicate, and scattered evidences; hence it can scarcely be exhibited in a given number of sentences. [...] How, then, after all, has it maintained its ground among men, and subjected to its dominion unwilling minds? [...] It has been upheld in the world not as a system, not by books, not by argument, nor

---

11. John Henry Newman, *Verses on Various Occasions* (London: Longmans, Green and Co., 1903), 156 (hereafter, *VV*).

12. See Juan Velez, *Passion for Truth: The Life of John Henry Newman* (Charlotte, N.C.: TAN Books, 2011), 169.

by temporal power, but by the personal influence of such men as have already been described, who are at once the teachers and the patterns of it.[13]

The initial meeting of the Oxford Movement was held among men of personal influence, as Newman had suggested. Although Rose and Palmer wanted to formally constitute a society, Newman opposed this idea because he feared it would stifle each individual's zeal.

Three episodes from this period illustrate Newman's intellectual coherence: his development of the *Via Media* along with the publication of the *Tracts for the Times,* his study of the Christological heresies from the early Church, and his reaction to the establishment of an Anglican bishopric in Jerusalem. Prepared by these events, the turning point in Newman's faith journey was the publication of *Tract* 90, which brought the Oxford Movement to a halt and launched his journey toward the Catholic Church.

Newman intended for the *Tracts,* which developed the theses of the Oxford Movement, to be published by each author without the sanction of an association, because he believed that "individuals who are seen and heard, who act and suffer, are the instruments of Providence in all great successes."[14] In his *Apologia,* he recorded an inspiration that became a foundational idea for the Movement: "Deliverance is wrought, not by the many but by the few, not by bodies but by persons."[15] Newman held this principle of individual ownership for the *Tracts* throughout his career and definitively expressed it in the *Grammar,* where he described assent as "a free act, a personal act for which the doer is responsible."[16] He explained to Perceval:

As to the Tracts every one has his own taste. You object to some things, another to others. If we altered to please every one, the effect would be spoiled. They were not intended as symbols *è cathedrâ,* but as the expression of individual minds; and individuals, feeling strongly, while on the one hand, they are incidentally faulty in mode

13.   John Henry Newman, *Fifteen Sermons Preached before the University of Oxford* (London: Longmans, Green and Co., 1909), 89–92 (1832) (hereafter, *US*).

14.   John Henry Newman, *Letters and Diaries,* ed. Charles S. Dessain, Ian Ker, and Thomas Gornall (Oxford: Clarendon Press, 1978), iv 68 (1833) (hereafter, *LD*).

15.   *Apo,* 135.

16.   John Henry Newman, *An Essay in Aid of a Grammar of Assent* (London: Longmans, Green and Co., 1903), 232 (hereafter, *GA*).

or language, are still peculiarly *effective*. No great work was done by a system; whereas systems rise out of individual exertions. Luther was an individual. The very faults of an individual excite attention; he loses, but his cause (if good and he powerful-minded) gains. This is the way of things: we promote truth by a self-sacrifice.[17]

The advocates of the Oxford Movement wrote ninety *Tracts* in eight years. Newman wrote twenty-nine of them, including the first and the last, holding fast to his heroic stance of promoting truth through self-sacrifice. While the *Tracts* were the vehicle by which the Oxford Movement gained popularity in England, Newman's sermons at St. Mary's developed its essence by detailing the spiritual and moral consequences of the principles expressed in the *Tracts*.

In his effort to bring forth the Catholicity of the Church of England, Newman built upon the doctrine of the *Via Media* proposed by the Anglican Divines. This doctrine distinguished the Anglican Church from Protestantism and from the Roman Church, but in Newman's opinion it failed to deliver a positive theology. Newman developed what he understood to be the essential doctrines of Anglicanism as a *via media*—dogma, the sacramental system, and opposition to the Church of Rome—in *Tracts* 38 and 41 and complemented them with the *Lectures on the Prophetical Office of the Church*. This endeavor led him to his first contact with a Roman Catholic theologian. Newman's correspondence with Fr. Jean-Nicolas Jager (1790–1868), from the University of Paris, gave him some initial insights into the theory of the development of doctrine, which would become the intellectual tool that enabled his acceptance of Roman Catholicism.

When the *Tracts* drew significant controversy, Newman retreated into what he expected to be a less polemical area of study: the Christological heresies. Through this study he learned that in the early Church, the deciding factor between heresy and sound doctrine was communion with the other Churches and with the See of Rome, both of which were severed by the Anglican Church in the sixteenth century. He understood the words of St. Augustine, "*Securus judicat orbis terrarum!*" to be a decisive blow to Anglicanism and the branch theory of the Church he maintained at the time. He explained, "For a mere sentence, the words of St. Augustine, struck me with a power which I never had felt from any words before[. . . .] By those great words of

17.   *LD*, iv 307–8 (1834).

the ancient Father [...] the theory of the *Via Media* was absolutely pulverized."[18] Newman took note of these discoveries but continued to perform his duties as an Anglican cleric, determined to be guided not by imagination but by reason. Two years later, as he translated the works of St. Athanasius, he once again felt a strong pull towards Rome. He would say of this period, "The ghost [of Antiquity] had come a second time."[19]

What brought his journey to its breaking point was, however, a political event. Newman had been interested in the proper relation between Church and state since his youth. Velez explains that Newman "opposed Parliament's control over the Anglican Church, and, at the same time, he considered the loss of Church prerogatives as an abuse. In some sense, he held an inconsistent position that favored government patronage of the Anglican or Established Church while objecting to State interference."[20] The main problem Newman perceived was that in order to secure financial support from the state, the Church gave up her adherence to dogma and thus betrayed her mission. When the government decided to appoint a bishop for Jerusalem to increase England's presence in the Middle East, even though no Anglicans lived there at the time, Newman judged that the Church had effectively become a vehicle for the advancement of England's political ends.

Up to this moment, Newman had been silent about his disagreements with the Anglican bishops. At this time, however, he published his objection to the Jerusalem bishopric, preached four sermons on the state of the Church, and wrote a formal protest to the Archbishop of Canterbury. Although his efforts regarding this political decision were fruitless, they accelerated the conversion of many of his acquaintances and proved decisive for him as well. He concluded the fifth part of his *Apologia* by saying, "As to the project of a Jerusalem Bishopric, I never heard of any good or harm it has ever done, except what it has done for me; which many think a great misfortune, and I one of the greatest of mercies. It brought me on to the beginning of the end."[21]

---

18.   *Apo*, 213. Newman translated Augustine's adage as "The multitude may not falter in their judgement." The significance he gives to the bishops' collective judgement is highly consistent with the pragmatist notion of truth as the long-run agreement of the community of inquirers. See Susan Haack, "Descartes, Peirce and the Cognitive Community," *Monist* 65, no. 2 (1982): 158.

19.   *Apo*, 235.

20.   Velez, *Passion for Truth*, 104.

21.   *Apo*, 241.

Although these events did not happen in a strict chronological order, they do outline Newman's conversion. This journey reached its climax with the publication of *Tract* 90, which was the culmination of Newman's efforts to remain in the Anglican Church.[22] By 1840 he could only justify his position as an Anglican cleric if the Thirty-nine Articles were taught from a Catholic perspective, which he recommended in *Tract* 90. As he foresaw, *Tract* 90 was not well received by the bishops. Some of his friends had tried to persuade him not to go forward with its publication, but he firmly believed that his primary loyalty was to truth itself. When asked to suppress *Tract* 90, he replied that he could not. However, on the condition that it not be censured by the bishops, he agreed to discontinue the publication of the *Tracts*.

The Oxford Movement had intended to show the Catholicity and Apostolicity of the Church of England, and thus prove that it was the legitimate continuation of the Church of the Fathers. With *Tract* 90, Newman realized this was not the case and chose semiretirement in Littlemore, hoping to remain in the Anglican Church by bringing to life the third note of the Church, that is, holiness: "Under these circumstances I turned for protection to the Note of Sanctity, with a view of showing that we had at least one of the necessary Notes, as fully as the Church of Rome."[23]

Newman's life in Littlemore is discussed in the next section. Regarding the fate of *Tract* 90, Newman thought the storm would pass if he kept silent. In May 1842, however, the Bishop of Oxford condemned the Tractarian doctrines as heretical. As the Oxford Movement began with the publication of the first *Tract*, it ended with their suspension. Twenty years later, Newman recognized, "I was on my death-bed, as regards my membership with the Anglican Church, though at the time I became aware of it only by degrees."[24]

Crisis and Conversion (1841–1847)

In his *Apologia*, Newman asserted that his first doubts regarding Anglicanism surfaced in 1839 as he studied the Christological controversies. He cited a letter from that year to explain the timeframe of his conversion: "If I had

22.   It is significant that Newman signed this *Tract* on January 25, the feast of the conversion of St. Paul.

23.   *Apo*, 248. The Nicene Creed identifies the four notes of the Church: unity, holiness, catholicity, and apostolicity.

24.   *Apo*, 245.

my will, I should like to wait till the summer of 1846, which would be a full seven years from the time that my convictions first began to fall on me. But I don't think I shall last so long."[25] Indeed, he did not; he asked to be received into the Catholic Church in October 1845. The prospect of being moved by feelings and causing scandal and undue suffering to his friends led Newman to move slowly. Furthermore, he was haunted by the fear of being in error: "I had been deceived greatly once; how could I be sure that I was not deceived a second time? I then thought myself right; how was I to be certain that I was right now?"[26] The process of his conversion led him to reflect upon the nature of certitude:

> He who made us, has so willed that in mathematics indeed we should arrive at certitude by rigid demonstration, but in religious inquiry we should arrive at certitude by accumulated probabilities [...]. And thus I came to see clearly, and to have a satisfaction in seeing, that, in being led on into the Church of Rome, I was proceeding, not by any secondary or isolated grounds of reason, or by controversial points in detail, but was protected and justified [...] by a great and broad principle.[27]

Three events can be identified as the formal steps Newman took while seeking to uphold his commitment to truth in this crucial stage of his life: his resignation as Vicar of St. Mary's, his drafting of the *Essay on the Development of Christian Doctrine*, and his resignation of his fellowship. It was only after taking these gravely pondered steps that he asked to be received into the Catholic Church and began to discern what place he would occupy within her.

Since 1840 Newman had been troubled about his post as Vicar of St. Mary's Church, because he no longer considered himself suited to act as a public representative of the Anglican faith. However, he knew that resigning the pulpit would mean opening the door for liberalism to be preached in the University Church. He discussed the issue at length with Pusey, who convinced him to remain as Vicar until August 1843. When Oxford's environment became more antagonistic towards him on account of *Tract* 90,

---

25. *LD*, x 610 (1845).
26. *Apo*, 318.
27. *Apo*, 292.

Newman spent more and more time in Littlemore where he owned a plot of land. He turned the stables into cottages and made a place of study and prayer for himself and those who wished to join him in a life of greater discipline and devotion. He moved there permanently in September 1841, and others soon joined him. Newman was not seeking to establish a monastery, but he allowed others who felt called to a similar lifestyle to come and live with him, with the express condition that if they desired to leave the Anglican Church, they would wait a significant amount of time before doing so. He had a strong sense of duty and could not bear the incoherence of swaying anyone under his care away from the Church. As a means of renewal for the Anglican Church, he began a project to publish the lives of the English saints. He resigned its editorship within a few months, however, as those he consulted felt that the narratives led their readers towards Rome.

The conversion of William Lockhart (1820–1892), a young man sent by his family to Newman to keep him from defecting to the Roman Church, ultimately precipitated his resignation from his post at St. Mary's. As was his custom, Newman had asked Lockhart to sign an agreement that he would remain in the Anglican Church for three years, but he announced his conversion within a year. Newman saw this event as sufficient reason to resign from St. Mary's. He explained, "After that, I felt it was impossible to keep my post there, for I had been unable to keep my word with my Bishop."[28]

By the summer of 1843, Newman was convinced that the Anglican Church was in schism but still harbored reservations about the Church of Rome: "I could not go to Rome, while I thought what I did of the devotions she sanctioned to the Blessed Virgin and the Saints."[29] His difficulty was not with the doctrines themselves but with what he considered extreme forms of their expression not found in the early Church. His study on the Christological controversies had given him an initial insight into the development of doctrine, and his continued reflection made him realize that perhaps here lay the key to understanding the contemporary Roman practices he did not see in the Apostolic Church: "so, I determined to write an essay on Doctrinal Development; and then, if, at the end of it, my convictions in favour of the Roman Church were not weaker, to make up my mind to seek admission into her fold."[30]

28.   *Apo*, 272.
29.   *Apo*, 278.
30.   *Apo*, 318–19.

Newman undertook this endeavor with a firm conviction of its relevance: "I must do my best and then leave it to a higher power to prosper it."[31] For many years, he had acted seeking the spiritual good of others; however, he wrote the *Essay on Development* to clarify ideas for himself with no intent to publish it. His research gave him the decisive reassurance for his conversion. He narrated, "Before I got to the end, I resolved to be received [into the Roman Catholic Church]. [... M]y own duty seemed clear [...] in my case it was, 'Physician, heal thyself.' My own soul was my first concern [....] I wished to go to my Lord by myself, and in my own way, or rather His way."[32]

On October 8, 1845, with his characteristic discretion, Newman invited Fr. Dominic Barberi (1792–1849) to Littlemore and asked to be received into the Catholic Church. His love for the truth prevailed over his many prejudices, the modest comfort of his life, and the separation from his dear friends. Aware that Newman's conversion was imminent, Fr. Barberi wrote, "A little more still and we shall see happy results from Littlemore. When the learned and holy Superior of Littlemore will come, then I hope we shall see the beginning of a new era. Yes, we shall see again the happy days of Augustine, of Lanfanc, and Thomas."[33] Fr. Barbieri's excitement was not an isolated incident. Shortly after Newman's conversion, Pope Gregory XVI sent him a silver crucifix with a relic of the Holy Cross as a congratulatory gift. But for Newman, his passage to the Roman Church was not a victory. He shared with his sister Jemima (1807–1889) the non-triumphalist way in which he saw his conversion:

> I have a good name with many; I am deliberately sacrificing it. I have a bad name with more; I am fulfilling all their worst wishes and giving them their most coveted triumph. I am distressing all I love, unsettling all I have instructed or aided. I am going to those whom I do not know, and of whom I expect very little. I am making myself an outcast, and that at my age. Oh, what can it be but a stern necessity which causes this.[34]

31. *Apo*, 318.

32. *Apo*, 310, 324.

33. Barberi to John Dalgairns, September 22, 1845, quoted in Denis Gwynn, "Father Dominic Barberi and Littlemore," in *Newman and Littlemore* (Oxford: Salesian Fathers, 1945), 41.

34. *LD*, x 595 (1845). The stern necessity of which he speaks is the necessity of following his conscience.

Along with his budding community, he remained in Littlemore until February 1846, when they moved into the Old Oscott College at the invitation of Bishop Nicholas Wiseman (1802–1865). Shortly thereafter, Bishop Wiseman suggested to Newman that he go to Rome to prepare for the priesthood. While in Rome, Newman visited several religious communities to discern where God was calling him. St. Philip Neri's Oratory seemed to be the right choice, since it provided a sense of continuity with the pastoral and intellectual ministry he had carried out in the Anglican Church. He was granted permission to start the first Oratory in England, provided that he adapt the rule to fit England's apostolic needs. Newman did not have any projects in mind at the time, but in the following decades he would decisively and passionately embrace those given to him by the bishops.

Newman received Holy Orders in the Catholic Church in May 1847, underwent a brief novitiate with the Oratorians, and returned to England in December. Even though some friends had insinuated that it would be better if he were not to return, Newman always saw his place as being among the English people. While he acknowledged that his presence would unsettle many, he found comfort in the realization that "St. Paul must have unsettled all the good and conscientious people in the Jewish Church. Unsettling might be a blessing."[35]

Newman's first writing project as a Catholic was the novel *Loss and Gain,* in which he tells the story of Charles Reding. Although a fictional character, Reding bears many similarities to Newman. This novel provides an insight into Newman's thoughts about his conversion:

> It was Sunday morning about seven o'clock, and Charles had been admitted into the communion of the Catholic Church about an hour since. He was still kneeling in the church of the Passionists before the Tabernacle, in the possession of a deep peace and serenity of mind, which he had not thought possible on earth. It was more like the stillness which almost sensibly affects the ears when a bell that has long been tolling stops, or when a vessel, after much tossing at sea, finds itself in harbour. It was such as to throw him back in memory on his earliest years, as if he were really beginning life again. But there was more than the happiness of childhood in his heart; he seemed to feel a rock under his feet; it was the *soliditas Cathedrae Petri.*[36]

35.   *LD,* x 103 (1844).
36.   John Henry Newman, *Loss and Gain: The Story of a Convert* (London: Longmans, Green and Co., 1906), 430 (hereafter, *LG*),

Projects in the Catholic Church (1847–1864)

Newman spent half of his life in the Anglican Church and the other half in the Catholic Church. If the Oxford Movement clearly characterizes his Anglican years, it is harder to identify any one project as a highlight from the Catholic period. The amount of secondary literature could point to his leadership at the University of Dublin, on account of which he wrote *The Idea of a University*. However, in itself, the University of Dublin was an undertaking marked by frustration and failure.

Newman's ministerial life as a Catholic priest was characterized by times of intense activity and times of silence and retreat. Even though he did not seek publicity and was faithfully obedient to the Episcopacy, he was immersed in controversy more often than not. To continue with the development of his profile from the perspective of his commitment to truth, I will now discuss four of Newman's projects: the foundation of the Oratory, the establishment of the Catholic University, his editorship of *The Rambler*, and the publication of the *Apologia*. As the events explored in the previous sections, these did not occur in a strictly sequential way.

From the beginning of his time at Oxford, Newman was highly sought as a mentor by young men, whom he aided with great solicitude. He also developed a deep friendship with some of his peers, which can be glimpsed in his correspondence: he left over twenty thousand letters that have been compiled into thirty-two volumes. Further, his life in community was semi-formalized during his years in Littlemore. It is no wonder then that the communities of the Oratorian fathers provided him with an attractive model for living his vocation: "As a model for the English Oratorians, Newman had in mind something akin to that of celibate Fellows in Oxford colleges who cultivated an intellectual life and, as clergymen, exercised pastoral care; this had been his way of life at Oriel, St. Mary's, and Littlemore."[37] Newman realized that the Oratory could meet a critical need by providing educated and pastoral priests for the Church in England and, in his adaptation of the rule, called for schools to prepare young Catholics for university studies.

The Oratory of England was formally established on February 1, 1848. The original founding members, all of them converts, were soon joined by the Wilfridians, a community that had formed around William Faber (1814–1863). Newman not only faced much suspicion from cradle Catholics who doubted the authenticity of his conversion, he also had to deal with the

---

37. Velez, *Passion for Truth*, 516.

internal division brought on by Faber. Within two years, the group had split into two independent houses. Although the division eased the tension, the relationship between both Oratories would be a source of great suffering for Newman. As a way of elucidating the rift between the two Oratories, Ian Ker identified

> [a] contrast between Newman's view of the necessity for adaptation and change if the Oratory was to remain true to St Philip's original inspiration, and Faber's idea that a real Oratory was one that imitated as exactly as possible the sixteenth-century Philip Neri and his Oratory. [...] Did loyalty to the past mean development or revival? Did fidelity to the tradition imply growth or imitation? It was one of Newman's deepest convictions that to cling to the literal letter of the past was to lose its essential spirit, and therefore to betray it.[38]

As has been mentioned, the notion of development was pivotal for Newman's conversion, and it continued to occupy a central place in his thought.

Three years after Newman established the Oratory, Archbishop Paul Cullen (1803–1878) approached him with the prospect of establishing a Catholic University in Dublin. From 1851 to 1858, Newman dedicated much of his time and energy to this project, crossing St. George's Channel fifty-six times. Cullen's first request was that he write a series of lectures to persuade the Irish people to support the project. Newman devoted himself wholeheartedly to this task, and within a year he completed nine discourses on the scope and nature of university education. These discourses, still discussed today, were the longest-lasting fruit of the University. In these, Newman argued that science and religion should not be at odds with one another. Speaking of the educated man, he stated:

> If he has one cardinal maxim in his philosophy, it is, that truth cannot be contrary to truth; if he has a second, it is, that truth often seems contrary to truth; and, if a third, it is the practical conclusion, that we must be patient with such appearances, and not be hasty to pronounce them to be really of a more formidable character.[39]

---

38. Ian Ker, *John Henry Newman: A Biography* (Oxford: Oxford University Press, 2010), 441.

39. *Idea*, 461. Newman's understanding of the harmony between scientific and religious truths anticipates Peirce's "natural classification" of the sciences. See Charles S. Peirce,

Grounded in the conviction that truth is the object of knowledge, Newman explained that "when we inquire what is meant by truth, I suppose it is right to answer that truth means facts and their relations [. . .]. Knowledge is the apprehension of these facts, whether in themselves, or in their mutual positions and bearings."[40] Knowledge thus understood is the mark of the person with a "truly great intellect, [able to take] a connected view of old and new, past and present, far and near, and which has an insight into the influence of all these one on another."[41] These excerpts from the *Idea* show that according to Newman's understanding, knowledge is not a mere accumulation of data but presupposes a philosophical mind, and only thus understood does it constitute the purpose of university education.[42]

Although Newman applied himself to recruiting professors and students, his relationship with the Irish bishops was complicated. Further, the tension created by dividing his time between the Birmingham Oratory (where he habitually spent seven months of the year) and the University in Dublin led him to resign as Rector of the University in 1857 and to fully retreat by the end of 1858.

As he settled back into Birmingham, Newman realized that the situation of the Catholic Church in England was quite different from eight years prior, when he had started traveling to Ireland:

The English Catholic community had been revitalized and enormously strengthened, intellectually by the wave of conversions from the Oxford Movement and numerically by the influx of Irish immigrants. The restoration of the hierarchy had given it a new status [. . .]. But the phenomenal growth of a tiny, despised sect into a major religious body brought with it new strains and tensions. The clash with the London Oratory turned out to be the prelude for Newman of a much larger conflict, in which similar principles were at stake, although the issue was no longer the nature of the

"Adirondack Summer School Lectures" (MS 1334, 1905), p. 8, The Charles S. Peirce Papers, Harvard University Library Photographic Service. Although quotations from Peirce's manuscripts were not retrieved directly from the collection itself, the transcriptions have been corroborated across multiple sources.

40.   *Idea*, 45.

41.   *Idea*, 134.

42.   In his sixth discourse Newman defines philosophy as "thought or Reason exercised upon Knowledge." *Idea*, 139.

Oratory, but the nature of the Church itself, the problem became not how to be an Oratorian, but how to be a Catholic in the nineteenth century.[43]

Newman's work in the University, through which he advocated for the laity to hold leadership positions, led him to reflect more generally on the role of the laity in the Church. This reflection was central to his next apostolic undertaking: *The Rambler's* editorship, which Newman assumed in 1859. Although he accepted this project at the behest of his own archbishop, William Ullathorne (1806–1889), Newman was soon rejected by most of the English Episcopate when he advocated for consulting the laity on some ecclesial matters.

His essay *On Consulting the Faithful in Matters of Doctrine* maintains that "the body of the faithful is one of the witnesses to the fact of the tradition of revealed doctrine, and because their *consensus* through Christendom is the voice of the Infallible Church."[44] It ignited much controversy, and Newman was accused of heresy. The Holy See asked for clarification, but this communication did not reach Newman in a timely manner, and when it did, it caused him great distress. A moving letter he wrote in 1861 to Maria Giberne (1802–1885) offers a glimpse into the state of his soul:

> As for me, my writing days are for the present day over. The long cares I have had, the disappointments of religious hopes, and the sense of cruelty in word and deed on the part of those from whom I deserved other things—a penance which I have had in one shape or another for thirty years—at length have fallen on my nerves—and though I am otherwise well, I am sent here to be idle.[45]

Charles Kingsley's (1819–1875) accusations of untruthfulness brought him out of his silence in 1864. Working fifteen hours per day for three months, Newman wrote his reply, in which he narrates the history of his religious opinions, defending the fact that he "loved honesty better than name, and truth better than dear friends."[46] The *Apologia* signaled a new beginning in Newman's public life, as his reputation was restored in England and abroad.

43.   Ker, *Biography*, 463.

44.   John Henry Newman, *On Consulting the Faithful in Matters of Doctrine*, ed. John Coulson (New York: Sheed & Ward, 1961), 63 (hereafter, *Cons*).

45.   *LD*, xx 38 (1861).

46.   *Apo*, 82.

Gathering the Fruits (1864–1890)

Newman was aware that he would not be fully understood in his lifetime and on several occasions was disheartened by what he called hopeless misrepresentations of his work. After many misunderstandings, he resolved in 1865 not to worry about pleasing anyone other than God. He wrote:

> I have always preached that things which are really useful, still are done, according to God's will, at one time or another—and that, if you attempt at a wrong time, what in itself is right, you perhaps become a heretic or schismatic. What I may aim at may be real and good, but it may be God's will it should be done a hundred years later. [...] Of course it is discouraging to be out of joint with time, and to be snubbed and stopped as soon as I begin to act.[47]

In the final years of his life, however, Newman received recognition from various fronts as well as the opportunity to reconnect with dear friends like Pusey and Keble. He remained active until 1886 and died as a well-respected cardinal in the Catholic Church on August 11, 1890.

To conclude this sketch of Newman's life from the perspective of his commitment to the truth, I will briefly discuss three of his works: *An Essay in Aid of a Grammar of Assent*, the *Letter to the Duke of Norfolk*, and the *Select Treatises of St. Athanasius*. These works express his most systematic treatment of topics that deeply interested him throughout his life: faith and reason, conscience, and the Church Fathers. Afterwards, I will highlight the honors he received from the Anglican Church and from the Catholic Church.

During his first years at Oxford, Newman became well acquainted with Aristotle's *Logic* and Butler's *Analogy of Religion*. His interest in philosophy deepened once he entered the Catholic Church, and from 1858 onward he kept a philosophical notebook. The relative peace that followed the publication of his *Apologia* was crowned with the publication of *The Grammar of Assent*, which he had pondered for over thirty years. If the *Essay on Development* and the *Apologia* may be considered a first and second justification, respectively, of Newman's religious beliefs, then the *Grammar* could be a third. In this work, he develops his views on assent, certitude, and belief in a philosophical way.

---

47. *LD*, xix 179–80 (1859). See also *AW*, 260–61 (1865); *LD*, xxv 279 (1871); Ker, *Biography*, 650.

In 1868 he disclosed his desires for the future of his intellectual work: "I have my own subject, one I have wished to do all my life [...] one, which, if I did, I should of course think it the best thing I have done."[48] He was referring to the exposition of his philosophy of knowledge, which he articulated in *The Grammar of Assent*, in continuity with his *Oxford University Sermons*. Setting the course for his argument took him three years; he later acknowledged that he wrote or rewrote a significant part of the *Grammar* over ten times. Once published, it sold out in one day, and two more editions would be printed before the end of the year. In this work, Newman displays his deep acquaintance with the human heart, his commitment to stand by experience, and his refined analysis.[49]

The same year in which Newman published the *Grammar*, the dogma of papal infallibility was defined, and the defense of its Catholic sense provided him with a new intellectual challenge. Although three times he declined the invitation to assist the Council as an advisor and intended to stay away from controversy, when William Gladstone (1809–1898) published a pamphlet criticizing the Council's decrees, Newman resolved to manifest his thoughts. His response took the form of a letter to the Duke of Norfolk, Henry Fitzalan Howard (1847–1917), a Catholic layman who had been his student at the Oratory. The "letter" was 150 pages long, and Newman described it as the toughest essay he ever had to write.[50] In this work, he articulated his view of the conscience and advanced a minimalist interpretation of the dogma of papal infallibility.

The positive reception of the *Letter to the Duke of Norfolk* took Newman by surprise. Although he had no shortage of critics, he was increasingly respected by both Anglicans and Roman Catholics. The Anglicans showed their appreciation first. Samuel Wayte (1819–1898), the President of Trinity College, offered Newman an Honorary Fellowship in 1877. Newman's response discloses the depths of his affection: "Trinity College is ever, and ever has been, in my habitual thoughts. Views of its buildings are at my bed side and bring before me morning and evening my undergraduate days, and those good friends, nearly all now gone, whom I loved so much during them,

---

48.   *LD*, xxiv 112 (1868).

49.   Newman's grounding in experience is seamlessly coherent with Peirce's pragmatic maxim, which is also built upon experience. See Peirce, *Collected Papers*, 5.402 (1878).

50.   See *LD*, xxvii 158 (1874).

and my love of whom has since their death ever kept me in affectionate loyalty to the college itself."[51]

As Newman received this award from an Anglican institution, his elevation to the Cardinalate was under consideration in Rome. Newman accepted this honor because he anticipated that it would be apostolically fruitful: "I knew many would become Catholics, as they ought to be, if only I was pronounced by Authority to be a *good* Catholic."[52] He chose a phrase from St. Francis de Sales as his motto: "*Cor ad Cor Loquitur*," and he traveled to Rome one last time in April 1879. On May 12, he delivered his famous address known as the "Biglietto Speech" in which he identified his life's work as a fight against liberalism in religion. His words after the initial formalities reveal his tireless commitment to the truth:

> In a long course of years I have made many mistakes. I have nothing of that high perfection which belongs to the writings of Saints, namely, that error cannot be found in them; but what I trust I may claim throughout all that I have written is this—an honest intention, an absence of private ends, a temper of obedience, a willingness to be corrected, a dread of error, a desire to serve the Holy Church, and, through the Divine mercy, a fair measure of success.[53]

Newman returned to Birmingham as a fellow of an Oxford College and a cardinal of the Roman Church; the two halves of his career having come together in an astonishing way. At last free from controversy, he prepared a uniform edition of his works, which he finished in 1881 with the publication of the *Select Treatises of St. Athanasius*. His study of the Church Fathers had launched his intellectual journey and now marked its conclusion. Newman's profoundest appreciation for them is summed up in these lines: "The Fathers made me a Catholic [...] I do not wish to say more than they suggest to me, and will not say less."[54]

---

51. *LD*, xxviii 279 (1877).

52. *LD*, xxix 161 (1879).

53. John Henry Newman, *Addresses to Cardinal Newman with His Replies (1879–81)*, ed. William Neville (London: Longmans, Green and Co., 1905), 63–64 (hereafter, *AR*). Newman's willingness to be corrected harmonizes well with Peirce's understanding of the role of the community in the search for truth. See Peirce, *Collected Papers*, 5.265 (1868).

54. John Henry Newman, *Certain Difficulties Felt by Anglicans in Catholic Teaching* (London: Longmans, Green and Co., 1901), ii 24–25 (hereafter, *Diff*).

A Sketch of Pragmatism

Having provided an overview of Newman's life as a framework for the upcoming analysis, I will now focus on pragmatism. The understanding of pragmatism I embrace is built upon contributions of the three classical pragmatists, Charles Peirce, William James, and John Dewey, with particular attention to Peirce's thought. Further, it incorporates insights offered by contemporary expositors of Peircean pragmatism, such as Hilary Putnam, Susan Haack, and Cheryl Misak.[55]

This review begins with the thought of Charles Sanders Peirce (1839–1914), the first philosopher to propose pragmatism as a principle of inquiry and an account of meaning. One of Peirce's central convictions, shared by all pragmatists, is that Descartes' method of universal doubt is not an appropriate foundation for knowledge. In reference to Cartesian doubt, Peirce wrote in one of his earliest papers, "Now without wishing to return to scholasticism, it seems to me that modern science and modern logic require us to stand upon a very different platform from this."[56]

Peirce maintained that all thought is relational and that there is no immediate or intuitive knowledge. Further, he argued that all knowledge is built upon our interaction with the external world through signs, in a three-way (triadic) relationship, in contrast with Descartes' two-way (dualist) relationship. Although Peirce revised his theory of signs several times, its three essential elements and their correlation remained consistent: "I define a sign as anything which is so determined by something else, called its Object, and so determines an effect upon a person, which effect I call its interpretant, that the latter is thereby mediately determined by the former."[57]

The relationship Peirce recognized between inquiry and truth (built upon his theory of signs) is central to his conception of pragmatism. He dismissed Descartes' foundational doubt as "paper doubt" and argued that inquiry must be grounded in the external world, since "there are real things, whose characters

---

55. While I believe that the main ideas of Peircean pragmatism are compatible with Newman's thought, not all Peircean theses are relevant or congruent with Newman's philosophy; thus, I am selective about those ideas from Peirce and other pragmatists with which I choose to engage. While undoubtedly limited, I have attempted to provide a consistent and fair interpretation of pragmatism as understood by Peirce and some of his followers.

56. Peirce, *Collected Papers*, 5.265 (1868).

57. Charles S. Peirce, *The Essential Peirce: Selected Philosophical Writings*, ed. Nathan Houser and Christian Kloesel (Bloomington: Indiana University Press, 1992), 478 (1908).

are entirely independent of our opinions about them."[58] Moreover, inquiry is sparked by a genuine doubt, since "there must be a real and living doubt, and without this all discussion is idle."[59] This meaningful interplay between the external world, surprise, doubt, inquiry, and truth is generally held by pragmatists who choose, as a matter of principle, to ground their philosophy in real-life experience.

Peirce held that the only path that leads from inquiry to truth is the scientific method, since it gets its data from the external world and remains accountable to reality. He understood that the essence of scientific work entails a meaningful engagement with evidence: showing how beliefs accommodate themselves to evidence or revising them until they do. This understanding of inquiry led him to describe truth as "the opinion which is fated to be ultimately agreed to by all who investigate."[60] With this definition, Peirce claims that genuine inquiry involves a collective effort and the willingness to revise a hypothesis for as long as there is a motive to do so; when these two elements are present, inquiry results in truth. In upholding these principles, Peirce did not maintain that truth is determined by the community, but rather, that truth is that to which the community is led through inquiry. This is why Peirce can be understood as "a traditional and systematic philosopher [...] one dealing with the modern problems of science, truth, and knowledge from his valuable personal experience as a logician and as an experimental researcher in the bosom of an international community of scientists and thinkers."[61]

While he began his research in dialogue with Peirce, William James (1842–1910) soon departed from Peirce's pragmatism. Whereas Peirce, who worked as a scientist for many years, focused the development of pragmatism in the realm of the natural sciences, James, a psychologist, broadened the application of the pragmatic maxim to metaphysical questions and the

58. Peirce, *Collected Papers*, 5.384 (1877).

59. Peirce, *Collected Papers*, 5.376 (1877).

60. Peirce, *Collected Papers*, 5.407 (1878). Cheryl Misak explains that Peirce's account of truth "must be understood primarily in terms of what is deserving of belief. On Peirce's account, truth is what would be best, were we to inquire as far as we could on a matter and were we to arrive at a belief that really would stand up to all experience and argument. [...] A belief is such that it resigns in the face of good evidence against it." Misak, "The Impact of Pragmatism," 625.

61. Jaime Nubiola, "Abduction or the Logic of Surprise," *Semiotica* 153, no. 1 (2005): 119. Peirce's formal education in the natural sciences (particularly in chemistry) and the thirty years he conducted research in mathematics and astronomy shaped his philosophical views.

human sciences. He stated explicitly that the pragmatic maxim "should be expressed more broadly than Mr. Peirce expresses it. The ultimate test for us of what a truth means is indeed the conduct it dictates or inspires."[62] James understood pragmatism as "a method only. However, the general change of that method would mean an enormous change [...]. Science and metaphysics would come much nearer together, would in fact work absolutely hand in hand."[63] This understanding led him to engage the metaphysical questions that Peirce left aside and to attempt to show that pragmatism offers satisfactory answers by framing them in terms of their effect on human behavior. Through this widening of the pragmatic maxim, pragmatism lost the objectivity that Peirce had secured by grounding it in the natural sciences.

James used psychological states as a justification for certain beliefs. After the publication of his work "The Will to Believe" he realized that the title should have been "The Right to Believe," as his intention was not to discuss the volition behind belief but rather the possibility of holding a belief with partial evidence.[64] James' understanding of psychological states as evidence in the process of inquiry informed his novel conception of truth, in which the person is not only an observer of reality, but an active cocreator:

> The knower is not simply a mirror floating with no foothold anywhere, and passively reflecting an order that he comes upon and finds simply existing. The knower is an actor, and coefficient on one side, while on the other he registers the truth which he helps to create. Mental interests, hypotheses, postulates, so far as they are bases for human action [...] help to make the truth which they declare.[65]

62. William James, "Philosophical Conceptions and Practical Results," *University Chronicle* 1, no. 4 (1898): 291.

63. William James, *Selected Papers on Philosophy* (London: Dent & Sons, 1918), 202.

64. See Michael Bacon, *Pragmatism: An Introduction* (Cambridge: Polity, 2012), 32. Newman had a similar objective in writing the *Grammar*, but as "much as he shared James's taking seriously religious experience, [Newman] always retained something that James had abandoned: he retained a respect for notional apprehension and notional assent and thus a respect for the rational side of religion. He wanted not only experience, but truth as well." John Crosby, "What Newman Can Give Catholic Philosophers Today," *American Catholic Philosophical Quarterly* 94, no. 1 (2019): 9.

65. William James, "Remarks on Spencer's Definition of Mind as Correspondence," *Journal of Speculative Philosophy* 12, no. 1 (1878): 17.

If the knower creates truth, then reality is not universal but particular to each person. This understanding led James to embrace a conception of the world characterized by a plurality of goods that cannot be brought together in a unitary way. His conception of pluralism is the source of his break from Peirce's pragmatism, which, while characterized by pluralism and fallibilism, upholds the objectivity of truth.

In 1907 James published his work *Pragmatism, a New Name for Some Old Ways of Thinking*, in which he compiled eight lectures that clarified his views of the pragmatic movement. As a response, Peirce drafted an article in which he presented his most thorough account of pragmatism:

> Pragmatism is, in itself, no doctrine of metaphysics, no attempt to determine any truth of things. It is merely a method of ascertaining the meanings of hard words and of abstract concepts. [...] All pragmatists will further agree that their method of ascertaining the meanings of words and concepts is no other than that experimental method by which all the successful sciences [...] have reached the degrees of certainty that are severally proper to them today; this experimental method being itself nothing but a particular application of an older logical rule, "By their fruits ye shall know them."[66]

With this explanation, Peirce distanced himself from James, and divergent strains of pragmatism developed. Nevertheless, through a careful study of the developments of the "pragmatic century" (as Richard Bernstein called the twentieth century), common elements within pragmatism can be discerned, as will be seen in the upcoming pages.

Before commenting upon these common elements, I will discuss the thought of John Dewey (1859–1952), the third and last philosopher who is considered a classical pragmatist. Like Peirce, Dewey believed in the self-correcting nature of empirical investigation when carried out within a community of inquirers. He suggested that the scientific method has ample bearings upon everyday life and that the principles of pragmatism—flexibility, open-mindedness, and readiness to be swayed by the discoveries of fellow inquirers—ought to be adopted by all sciences, including education, sociology, and politics. Thus, like James, Dewey widened the scope of pragmatism, arguing that philosophy ought to deal with the ordinary problems of

---

66. Peirce, *Collected Papers*, 5.464–65 (1907).

individuals, instead of burying itself in elusive abstract questions. Like Peirce, Dewey held that the most pressing philosophical questions concern the relationship between thought and action, and between privately held beliefs and the external world:

> Philosophy recovers itself when it ceases to be a device for dealing with the problems of philosophers and becomes a method, cultivated by philosophers, for dealing with the problems of men. Emphasis must vary with the stress and special impact of the troubles which perplex men. Each age knows its own ills, and seeks its own remedies. One does not have to forecast a particular program to note that the central need of any program at the present day is an adequate conception of the nature of intelligence and its place in action.[67]

Another element of the process of inquiry in which Dewey adopted Peirce's stance is the role of the community: "No scientific inquirer can keep what he finds to himself or turn it to merely private account without losing his scientific standing. [...] Every new idea and theory has to be submitted to this community for confirmation and test."[68] By making recourse to a community of inquirers, Dewey overcame the subjectivity of Descartes' rationalism.

Dewey coined the term "warranted assertability" as the goal of inquiry, a term he preferred to those such as *knowledge* or *belief.* Even though he did not equate warranted assertability with truth, he adopted Peirce's account when he spoke of truth: "The best definition of truth from the logical standpoint which is known to me is that of Peirce: 'The opinion which is fated to be ultimately agreed to by all who investigate is what we mean by the truth, and the object represented by this opinion is the real.' "[69] The pragmatic understanding of the relationship between inquiry, community, and truth is central to Dewey's conception of democracy as a method of social inquiry.

Although the background of Willard Quine's (1908–2000) thought is not the study of the classical pragmatists, in 1951 he described his position as a shift toward this tradition. He argued that an individual's belief system

---

67.   John Dewey, "The Need for a Recovery of Philosophy," in *Creative Intelligence: Essays in the Pragmatic Attitude* (New York: Holt, 1917), 65–66.

68.   John Dewey, *Individualism Old and New* (London: Allen & Unwin, 1931), 143. Thus understood, the notion of community is central to Newman's thought. See *Idea*, 101, 145–46.

69.   John Dewey, *The Later Works of John Dewey, 1925–1953*, ed. Jo Ann Boydston (Carbondale, Ill.: Southern Illinois University Press, 2008), 12:343.

resembles an interconnected web, in which mathematics and logic are at the center and progressively lead into the theoretical sciences. In this web, all beliefs are subject to revision and must be adjusted when faced with contrasting evidence. This metaphor brings out three central characteristics of Quine's account of knowledge: naturalism, holism, and fallibilism. Based on these characteristics, Quine asserted that pragmatism identifies an order within reality, because it is anchored in the external world. The second metaphor he used in his study of knowledge is that of a cord woven together from different threads. This metaphor implies that any belief can be preserved when faced with doubt if one has the willingness to revise other beliefs.[70]

After Quine's work, the next milestone in the development of pragmatism corresponds to Richard Rorty's (1931–2007) *Philosophy and the Mirror of Nature* published in 1979, which signaled a renewed interest in pragmatism in the American philosophical scene. Two opposing versions of the pragmatic understanding of truth and objectivity were solidified. One version, grounded in Peirce, focuses on inquiry and attempts to grasp the individual's aspirations for objectivity; the other version, grounded in James and taken to its extreme by Rorty, discards objectivity.

A crucial principle in Rorty's pragmatism is that "we understand knowledge when we understand the social justification of belief, and thus have no need to view it as accuracy of representation."[71] Rorty argued that philosophy is not meant to account for nature but to provide the necessary tools to cope with its demands. In this approach, he followed James' conception of the knower as a coefficient actor and claimed that "our only usable notion of objectivity is agreement, rather than mirroring."[72] This led him to conclude that there is no certainty, no objectivity, and no truth, but only agreement with others and solidarity within a community.

Susan Haack (b. 1945), one of Rorty's strongest critics, dedicated much of her career to bringing Peirce's account of pragmatism to the forefront of

70. Two similarities with Newman's thought come to light. First, Newman also used the metaphor of the woven cord in his account of knowledge. See *LD*, xxi 146 (1864); *GA*, 288. Second, Quine's understanding of holism is reminiscent of Newman's theory of knowledge, which maintains that all of its branches are interconnected and have multiple bearings on one another. See *Idea*, 99.

71. Richard Rorty, *Philosophy and the Mirror of Nature* (Princeton: Princeton University Press, 1979), 170.

72. Rorty, *Philosophy and the Mirror of Nature*, 337.

philosophical research. She argued that Rorty distorted the classical pragmatists' insights to such a degree that he should not even be considered a pragmatist philosopher. In 1998 she published a constructed dialogue between Peirce and Rorty, which she composed by weaving together statements from their writings. This dialogue shows how contrasting their notions of pragmatism are: Peirce upheld the objectivity of truth and set it as the goal of inquiry, while Rorty argued that inquiry can only aspire to a consensus that will always be relative to its circumstances.[73]

In her effort to elaborate on Peirce's account of inquiry, Haack explored the notion of good standards of inquiry as evidence for belief. In her account of justification, she included the notions of community and development and argued that a belief is justified if it stems from well-evidenced and mutually supporting premises. To explain her understanding of good evidence, she used the analogy of a crossword puzzle: "How reasonable one's confidence is that a certain entry in a crossword puzzle is correct depends on: how much support is given to this entry by the clue and any intersecting entries that have already been filled in; how reasonable, independently of the entry in question, one's confidence is that those other already filled-in entries are correct; and how many of the intersecting entries have been filled in."[74]

Haack also studied truth, inquiry, and fallibilism, sharing Peirce's conception of truth as the final opinion that everyone would agree upon, were inquiry to continue indefinitely. The conditional, "were inquiry to continue," is telling: the fact that the fullness of truth cannot be possessed by an individual at any given moment does not imply that inquiry does not yield truth or that one cannot advance in knowledge of it. She summarized her position by suggesting

> that we [avoid thinking] of pragmatism as a party one must either join or oppose, or as a brand one might "export." In brief: I see the classical pragmatist tradition [...] as an extraordinarily fertile one,

73.   See Susan Haack, "We Pragmatists: Peirce and Rorty in Conversation," in *Manifesto of a Passionate Moderate* (Chicago: University of Chicago Press, 1998), 31–47.

74.   Susan Haack, *Evidence and Inquiry: A Pragmatist Reconstruction of Epistemology* (Oxford: Blackwell, 1993), 82. Haack's notion of good evidence resembles Newman's analogy of a "cable which is made up of a number of separate threads, each feeble, yet together as sufficient as an iron rod; [representing] an assemblage of probabilities separately insufficient for certainty, but, when put together, irrefragable." *LD*, xxi 146 (1864). Newman made use of this image to illustrate the legitimate and sufficient conditions for assent.

and moreover, as in some ways ahead not only of its own time but also of ours. It is high time to focus less on squabbling over who owns its legacy, and more on exploring the wealth of insight that classical pragmatism bequeathed us.[75]

Without being as close a follower of Peirce as Haack, or a manifest detractor like Rorty, Hilary Putnam (1926–2016) is one of pragmatism's most significant contemporary proponents. He suggested that the heart of pragmatism lies in its insistence on the supremacy of the agent's point of view and labels his epistemic position *direct realism*, describing it as the middle ground between a metaphysical realism in which there is only one true account of reality and Rorty's irresponsible relativism. Putnam used the notion of direct realism to argue for the pluralism espoused by other pragmatist philosophers.

Putnam's direct realism also led him to hold a fallibilism similar to that of Peirce. He observed that "fallibilism does not require us to doubt *everything*, it only requires us to be prepared to doubt *anything*—if good reason to do so arises."[76] His understanding of objectivity implied grounding oneself in reality as one perceives it, and from that starting point, working out, through conversation with others, better or worse approaches to the relevant questions that it poses. These questions are analyzed and discerned by a community of inquirers, which Putnam considered an essential element of pragmatism—one that is indispensable for overcoming modern rationalism. The notions of anti-foundationalism, community, development, and fallibilism emerge once more as common threads when the pragmatic method is followed.

For his part, Jürgen Habermas (b. 1929) shared a similar approach to Peirce and Dewey regarding truth and knowledge, although he has not always been seen as a pragmatist philosopher. When asked what he considered to be the greatest strengths of pragmatism, Habermas answered that he finds them in "the combination of fallibilism with anti-skepticism, and a naturalist approach to the human mind and its culture that refuses to yield to any kind of scientism."[77] Following Peirce and the pragmatic tradition,

---

75. Susan Haack, "Five Answers on Pragmatism," *Journal of Philosophical Investigations* (Tabriz) 12, no. 24 (2018): 11.

76. Hilary Putnam, *Pragmatism: An Open Question* (Oxford: Blackwell, 1995), 21.

77. Jürgen Habermas, "Reflections on Pragmatism," in *Habermas and Pragmatism*, ed. Mitchell Aboulafia, Myra Bookman, and Catherine Kemp (London: Routledge, 2002), 228.

Habermas maintained that truth is tied to the external world, since it exists independently of human understanding. Furthermore, he believed that knowledge is legitimized through social interaction:

> Reaching understanding cannot function unless the participants refer to a single objective world, thereby stabilizing the intersubjectively shared public space with which everything that is merely subjective can be contrasted. This supposition of an objective world that is independent of our descriptions fulfills a functional requirement of our processes of cooperation and communication. Without this supposition, everyday practices [...] would come apart at the seams.[78]

To account for the diversity of opinions characteristic of today's culture, Habermas made recourse to pluralism in traditions and values while retaining universally valid moral norms, which, he argued, emerge from rational discourse under ideal conditions. He understood the law to be local and described it as the application of a universal moral norm to the particular situation of a particular person.[79]

Another twentieth-century philosopher, Richard Bernstein (b. 1932), argued that "much of the best philosophic thinking of our century can be understood as variations [*sic*] on pragmatic themes [that] have had a strong influence on the range of cultural and social disciplines."[80] A central topic in Bernstein's philosophical research is that of pluralism, which he studied to overcome Rorty's rejection of truth and objectivity. He developed the concept of engaged fallibilist pluralism in contrast to what he identified as fragmenting, flabby, or polemical pluralisms, understanding it as "an orientation wherein we acknowledge what is different from us, but seek to understand and critically engage it [since] it is always possible to move beyond and enlarge our limited horizon."[81] He argued that engaged pluralism requires us

---

78. Jürgen Habermas, "Richard Rorty's Pragmatic Turn," in *Rorty and His Critics* (Malden: Blackwell, 2000), 41.

79. See Jürgen Habermas, *Truth and Justification*, trans. Barbara Fultner (Cambridge: Polity, 2003), 101. These considerations recall Newman's Illative Sense, which aims at the assent to truth in particular circumstances. See *LD*, xxix 115 (1879).

80. Richard Bernstein, *The Pragmatic Century: Conversations with Richard J. Bernstein*, ed. Sheila Davaney and Warren Frisina (Albany: State University of New York Press, 2012), 4.

81. Richard Bernstein, *The Abuse of Evil: The Corruption of Politics and Religion since 9/11* (Cambridge: Polity, 2005), 34–35.

to develop certain habits of inquiry, including openness, imagination, fairness, and willingness to change our ideas.[82]

A second theme worth highlighting in Bernstein's philosophical project is his methodology:

> Bernstein moves back and forth between different philosophers, reading them against each other in an attempt not merely at criticisms but to show how they lend mutual support and indeed strengthen each other's arguments. [...] By interweaving the ideas and insights of members of different philosophical traditions, Bernstein argues for the transformation of ourselves and of our societies. This is achieved not by reference to an objective perspective, but through pluralist and self-reflective conversation. This proposal is pragmatist in holding that, through dialogue, we can reach a situated but non-relativist consensus.[83]

The last philosopher I will discuss in this sketch of pragmatism is Cheryl Misak (b. 1961). While focusing on Peirce, Misak attempts to show that the actual distance between those who consider themselves Peircean pragmatists and those who do not, is not as large as often believed. In her 2007 anthology of essays on pragmatism, she identified three commitments that pragmatists tend to share. Although these commitments can be challenged or may be nuanced, they are helpful for this investigation, since they offer a framework for an understanding of pragmatism with which Newman can enter into conversation. As Misak understands them, these commitments are as follows:

1. standards of objectivity evolve over time, but being historically situated does not compromise their objectivity;
2. knowledge has no certain foundations and is fallible; and
3. philosophy is connected with first-order inquiry and real-life experience.[84]

---

82. These traits resemble the habits that Newman recalled when he described philosophy as a virtue. See *Idea*, 74–75.

83. Bacon, *Pragmatism*, 141. Bernstein's call for a self-reflective and pluralist conversation in philosophy is reminiscent of Newman, who speaks of the University as an assemblage of learned men who consult, respect, and aid one another and, in this way, transmit knowledge that can transform the students. See *Idea*, 101, 148.

84. See Misak, introduction to *New Pragmatists*, 2–4.

These commitments will be further analyzed and explained in relation to Newman's philosophical principles in the following section.

Rooted in Peirce's notion of truth, Misak argues that truth must be understood in the context of our lives, not as something that stands apart from them. In this way, she holds a realist approach that grounds knowledge in the external world. In an essay written for Misak's anthology *New Pragmatists*, Jeffrey Stout indicated that "philosophers who believe that classical pragmatism was on to something important [...] have recently renewed the effort to provide accounts of inquiry that are both recognizably pragmatic in orientation and demonstrably hospitable to the cognitive aspiration to get one's subject matter right."[85] In the upcoming pages, Newman will be studied in conversation with philosophers who identify with this particular conception of pragmatism, which has withstood the test of time and continues to bear fruit.

Commitments of Pragmatism to Which Newman Subscribes

In the preceding review of the development of pragmatism as a way of thinking, common elements in pragmatist philosophers' claims came to light. Misak has identified three of these as descriptive of pragmatism: a historical attitude towards objectivity, a fallibilist epistemology grounded in anti-foundationalism, and a commitment to keeping philosophy rooted in real-life experience. In this section, I study Newman's philosophical principles in contrast with these three claims, as understood by Misak, to evaluate if indeed he should have a place among the forerunners of this tradition.

The first commitment entails adopting a historical attitude towards objectivity and truthfulness. In Misak's words, "Standards of objectivity come into being and evolve over time, but [...] being historically situated in this way does not detract from their objectivity."[86] Bernard Williams (1929–2003) made a helpful distinction between truth and truthfulness, which sheds light on this principle. He defined truth as a formal concept, and as such, an objective and timeless reality. In contrast, he believed that truthfulness is rooted in history as the way in which finite human beings can apprehend and conceptualize truth at any given moment.

---

85.   Jeffrey Stout, "On Our Interest in Getting Things Right: Pragmatism without Narcissism," in *New Pragmatists* (Oxford: Oxford University Press, 2007), 7.

86.   Misak, introduction to *New Pragmatists*, 2.

Furthering this argument, Ian Hacking (b. 1936) referred to truth as a condition for truthfulness and referred to truthfulness as that which individuals can predicate about a subject. Truthfulness thus understood is analogous to objectivity. This led Hacking to state that "the fact that the methods of argument we now regard as canonical have a history, and once did not exist even for the wisest of the ancients, does not make them any less objective standards."[87] This claim is reminiscent of Peirce, who understood science as "a living historic entity" and "a living and growing body of truth"[88] discovered by a community of experts who build on one another's discoveries, correct one another, and, as a community, advance towards truth:

> Science is to mean for us a mode of life whose single animating purpose is to find out the real truth, which pursues this purpose by a well-considered method, founded on thorough acquaintance with such scientific results already ascertained by others as may be available, and which seeks cooperation in the hope that the truth may be found, if not by any of the actual inquirers, yet ultimately by those who come after them and who shall make use of their results.[89]

This idea that standards of objectivity evolve over time is often traced back to Hegel's *Phenomenology of Spirit*. For his part, Wilfrid Ward (1856–1916), in one of the first commentaries ever written on Newman's theory of development, stated that "the idea of the gradual deepening of thought in the synthesis of aspects of objective reality is certainly common to Newman's idea of development and Hegel's conception of evolution."[90] Although it is improbable that Newman read Hegel's *Phenomenology*, this similitude within their notion of development is worth noticing.[91]

Newman had a deep awareness of man's historical existence and insisted to his readers that historical context is essential for grasping the flexible and nuanced nature of human discourse. As early as 1834 he alluded to the notion

---

87.   Ian Hacking, "On Not Being a Pragmatist: Eight Reasons and a Cause," in *New Pragmatists* (Oxford: Oxford University Press, 2007), 39.

88.   Peirce, *Collected Papers*, 1.44 (ca. 1896), 6.428 (1893).

89.   Peirce, *Collected Papers*, 7.54 (ca. 1902).

90.   Wilfrid Ward, "Newman's Philosophy," in *Last Lectures* (London: Longmans, Green and Co., 1918), 93.

91.   It is improbable because Newman did not read German, and the *Phenomenology* was only translated into English in 1910.

of truth evolving over time, writing that "the greater part of the theological and ecclesiastical system [...] was developed at various times according to circumstances. [...] Our Creeds, our Liturgies, our canons are for the most part developed and determined by a definite period after the Apostles."[92] Newman grappled with the theme of development in the following decade, as it was the theoretical background for his main objection to the Church of Rome. He expounded on these principles in his 1843 sermon "The Theory of Developments in Religious Doctrine," the last sermon he preached in Oxford. In this sermon, he connected his theory of development with his previous distinction of implicit and explicit knowledge.

Speaking specifically of religious truths, Newman affirmed that "even centuries might pass without the formal expression of a truth, which had been all along the secret life of millions of faithful souls."[93] In saying so, he upheld that historicity does not detract from truthfulness or objectivity. To make his claim more precise, he exclaimed, "Its half sentences, its overflowings of language, admit of development; they have a life in them which shows itself in progress; a truth, which has the token of consistency; a reality, which is fruitful in resources; a depth, which extends into mystery: for they are representations of what is actual, and has a definite location and necessary bearings and a meaning in the great system of things."[94] In these lines, Newman refers to truth, consistency, reality, and actuality and establishes that precisely because of these characteristics, historical development is admitted in the commitment to truth, thus showing how he upheld a historical attitude towards objectivity.

This principle of the historicity or development of ideas was of vital importance for Newman. As he studied the Church Fathers, he grew in the conviction that the Roman Catholic Church held the truth. However, he had to intellectually work out what for many years he had understood to be innovations or corruptions in her practice. Once he could formulate a solid and coherent theory of development, he was ready to ask to be received into her bosom. He began writing his *Essay on Development* in the Anglican Church and took this momentous step once he obtained the necessary reassurance for his conversion.

In the first chapter of this essay, Newman not only dealt with religious doctrines but with the development of ideas in general. He argued that "there is no one aspect deep enough to exhaust the contents of a real idea, no one

92.   *LD*, iv 180 (1834).
93.   *US*, 323 (1843).
94.   *US*, 318 (1843).

term or proposition which will serve to define it."[95] He then went on to explain that the multitude of facets through which an idea presents itself, the collision of opinions it causes, and its change over time, provide evidence for its truthfulness, not for the contrary. Speaking specifically of the history of ideas in philosophy, he explained that

> its vital element needs disengaging from what is foreign and tempo-rary, and is employed in efforts after freedom which become more vigorous and hopeful as its years increase. Its beginnings are no measure of its capabilities, nor of its scope. At first no one knows what it is, or what it is worth. [...] From time to time it makes essays which fail, and are in consequence abandoned. It seems in suspense which way to go; it wavers, and at length strikes out in one defi-nite direction. In time it enters upon strange territory; points of controversy alter their bearing; parties rise and around it; dangers and hopes appear in new relations; and old principles reappear under new forms. It changes with them in order to remain the same. In a higher world it is otherwise, but here below to live is to change, and to be perfect is to have changed often.[96]

With these words, Newman described his positive understanding of the historicity of ideas and explained how being historically situated does not compromise their objectivity. He concluded his *Essay on Development* by stating seven notes to discern healthy developments from corruption and decay.

In his 1855 novel, *Callista*, Newman mentioned the theme of develop-ment once again, this time applying it to the conversion of a fictional char-acter living in the third century. Callista's conversion, like his own, was not a sudden event but a slow and steady development. Newman narrated, "While she was continually differing from herself, in that she was changing, yet it was not a change which involved contrariety, but one which expanded itself in (as it were) concentric circles, and only fulfilled, as time went on, the promise of its beginning."[97] The seven notes he had established for discerning a healthy

---

95. John Henry Newman, *An Essay on the Development of Christian Doctrine* (London: Longmans, Green and Co., 1909), 35 (hereafter, *Dev*).

96. *Dev*, 40.

97. John Henry Newman, *Callista* (London: Longmans, Green and Co., 1901), 291 (hereafter, *Call*).

development are present in Callista's story: preservation of type, continuity of principles, assimilative power, logical sequence, anticipation of its future, conservative action on its past, and chronic vigor.

In her discussion on Newman's theory of truth, Jane Garnett explores his recognition that "persuasiveness of argument—whether in the past or the present—grows within a historical tradition the terms of articulation of which themselves change over time."[98] What has been explained so far, along with Garnett's understanding, shows that like most pragmatist philosophers Newman held a historical attitude towards objectivity.

A second claim closely associated with pragmatism is that "knowledge has no certain foundations. All beliefs, no matter how strongly held, are fallible."[99] Since Descartes wrote his *Discourse on Method* in 1637, his foundationalism has been understood, upheld, and criticized from numerous angles. The interpretation of foundationalism I assume is not the moderate contemporary version, but the Cartesian-minded foundationalism encountered by Newman and by the classical pragmatists: "At the heart of the foundationalist agenda is the desire to overcome the uncertainty generated by our human liability to error and the inevitable disagreements that follow. Foundationalists are convinced that the only way to solve this problem is to find some means of grounding the entire edifice of human knowledge on invincible certainty."[100]

Both strains of classical foundationalism, empirical and theoretical, claim that only what is grounded empirically or logically can be accepted. This was an insufficient position for Newman, since he wanted to protect the right of any individual to believe beyond empirical and logical proof. Specifically, Newman rejected the strain of foundationalism upheld by Locke and Hume, which claims that for knowledge to be valid, it must be grounded in the immediacy of sense experience. Newman wrote in his *Philosophical Notebook*, "Another remark to be made is (against all *my* lifelong convictions), their obstinate assumption that all things must be reduced to *one* principle."[101] Although the rejection of foundationalism by most pragmatist philosophers is broader than Newman's, it encompasses the nuances he opposed.

<hr>

98. Jane Garnett, "Joseph Butler," in *The Oxford Handbook of John Henry Newman* (Oxford: Oxford University Press, 2018), 141.

99. Misak, introduction to *New Pragmatists*, 2.

100. Stanley Grenz and John Franke, *Beyond Foundationalism: Shaping Theology in a Postmodern Context* (Louisville: John Knox Press, 2001), 30.

101. John Henry Newman, *The Philosophical Notebook of John Henry Newman: The Text*, ed. Edward Sillem (Louvain: Nauwelaerts, 1970), 91 (hereafter, *PN*).

In contrast to Descartes and Locke, pragmatist philosophers argue that knowledge is justified, not because of its ultimate foundations, but because of its practical success in enabling individuals to cope with the world. Peirce argued that there is no intuitive or immediate knowledge, but that all knowledge is inferential: "We must begin, then, with a process of cognition, and with that process whose laws are best understood and most closely follow external facts. This is no other than the process of valid inference."[102]

Peirce derived his anti-foundationalist stance from his insights on inquiry. He believed that individuals are immersed in a context of inquiry, where their decision concerns what to believe from their present situation, not what to believe as if they were starting from scratch or from infallible foundations. This notion of inquiry governed by the scientific method (which understands science to be intrinsically self-correcting) allowed Peirce to embrace a fallibilist epistemology while avoiding skepticism. In this context, it is relevant to note Putnam's observation: "[The fact that] one can be both fallibilistic and antisceptical is perhaps the basic insight of American Pragmatism."[103]

In contrast to Locke, Newman argued that *"there is no ultimate test of truth besides the testimony born to truth by the mind itself* [...] this phenomenon, perplexing as we may find it, is a normal and inevitable characteristic of the mental constitution of a being like man on a stage such as the world."[104] Newman understood rationality as a natural practice that requires no justification beyond the cognitive exercises in which individuals do in fact engage; through his philosophical project, he solved the paradox introduced by the possibility that a proposition can be accepted as true without a doubt, even though it cannot be demonstrated.[105] His project is further elucidated by the fact that he chose to call his epistemological work a "Grammar":

102. Peirce, *Collected Papers*, 5.267 (1868).

103. Putnam, *Pragmatism: An Open Question*, 21. As Peirce would do a century later, Newman developed his theory of knowledge based on the way individuals actually think and inquire, not on a general and abstract notion of human rationality. Blehl explains that Newman's "philosophy of mind is one which acknowledges various roads to truth, arising out of different first principles and methods of investigation proper to each individual area of intellectual activity, but each converging and needing the completion of other areas of thought, if one is to attain a comprehensive grasp of reality." Vincent Blehl, "The Intellectual and Spiritual Influence of J. H. Newman," *The Downside Review* 111, no. 385 (1993): 251.

104. *GA*, 350 (emphasis added).

105. See Frederick Aquino, "Philosophical Receptions of the *Grammar of Assent*, 1960–2012," in *Receptions of Newman* (Oxford: Oxford University Press, 2015), 64; Joe Milburn, "Newman's Skeptical Paradox," *American Catholic Philosophical Quarterly* 94, no. 1 (2019): 108.

Grammar is not simply description of practice, but description of the norms generated in practice. Genuine description cannot be *a priori*, and prescription cannot be arrived at without regard to description. Newman does not attempt to say *a priori* what should be practised; nor does he evaluate the norms he abstracts. [...] The description he aims at is clearly meant to allow him to correct illegitimate usage, so it is description of norms [...] rather than merely empirical generalization.[106]

In *The Grammar of Assent,* Newman asserted that "any philosophical theory [does not have] the power to force on us a rule,"[107] and sought to overcome the unnecessary intellectual restriction that modern philosophy had placed upon reason: a strict epistemic foundationalism or evidentialism. He wanted to avoid grounding certitude on intuition, as well as admitting that there are internal marks that distinguish true certitudes from false ones.

The foundationalists Newman opposed held that propositions that do not satisfy required criteria must be rejected as irrational or dogmatic. Contrary to their claims that knowledge must be grounded in indubitable foundations and that assent must be proportional to evidence, Newman maintained that the combination of informal and formal inference is the basis for assent. Furthermore, he argued that assent is not relative to evidence and is not given in degrees. Ker explains, "Since he rejects foundationalism, the problem for Newman [...] is how to judge between differing systems of belief. [...] Newman's resolution [...] lay in the recognition that a rational resolution of disputes between rival traditions does not depend on a neutral standpoint. Instead, one can always re-examine and revise one's first principles or antecedent assumptions in light of one's evolving understanding and appeal to tradition."[108]

With this understanding, Newman moved away from the classical foundationalist tradition of modern philosophy towards a non-foundationalist account of knowledge, placing the final judgment about the validity of an inference in the Illative Sense, not in logical correctness. Thus, Newman's

---

106. Jamie Ferreira, *Scepticism and Reasonable Doubt: The British Naturalist Tradition in Wilkins, Hume, Reid and Newman* (Oxford: Clarendon Press, 1986), 231–32.

107. *GA,* 179.

108. Ian Ker, "Newman's Standing as a Philosopher," *Proceedings of the American Catholic Philosophical Association* 78 (2004): 71.

understanding of certitude does not require the exclusion of every doubt but is instead grounded in an assemblage of probabilities. He explained, "My argument is in outline as follows: that that absolute certitude which we were able to possess [...] was the result of an assemblage of concurring and converging probabilities, [...] that probabilities which did not reach to logical certainty, might create a mental certitude."[109] For Newman, the truth of a proposition is perceived through the *accumulation* of probabilities, not through the corroboration of its foundations. Therefore, Newman's theory of knowledge provides a rigorous account of certainty, which is compatible with fallibilism when considered as an attempt to account for the fact of human knowledge, along with its profound limitations.[110]

The third and final claim Misak identifies as central to pragmatism is the commitment "to keeping philosophy connected to first order inquiry, to real examples, to real-life expertise."[111] Peirce's pragmatic maxim aimed to bring to the forefront of philosophical research the relationship between concepts and practical endeavors. He wrote that the fundamental hypothesis of the scientific method is that "there are real things whose characters are entirely independent of our opinions about them."[112] This realization led him to ground inquiry in the external world, rather than in the subject. In the application of the pragmatic maxim to the concept of truth, Peirce focused on practices of inquiry and invited the community of experts to journey towards objectivity: "Remembering, then, that philosophy is a science based upon everyday experience, we must not fall into the absurdity of setting down as a datum and starting-point of philosophy any abstract and simple idea [...]. We must not begin by talking of pure ideas—vagabond thoughts that tramp the public roads without any human habitation—but must begin with men and their conversation."[113]

Likewise, in his first lecture on pragmatism, James grounded pragmatism in everyday life and articulated the consequences this brings about: "I know that you, ladies and gentlemen, have a philosophy, each and all of you, and that the most interesting and important thing about you is the way in which

---

109. *Apo*, 122.

110. See Brandon Dahm, "The Certainty of Faith: A Problem for Christian Fallibilists?," *Journal of Analytic Theology* 3, no. 1 (2015): 130–46.

111. Misak, introduction to *New Pragmatists*, 4.

112. Peirce, *Collected Papers*, 5.384 (1877).

113. Peirce, *Collected Papers*, 8.112 (ca. 1900).

it determines the perspective in your several worlds. [...] For the philosophy which is so important in each of us is not a technical matter; it is our [...] sense of what life honestly and deeply means."[114] Contemporary pragmatists who understand philosophy not as a strictly academic endeavor but as an instrument for the critical and reasonable reconstruction of our daily practices find this connection with real-life experience one of the most appealing traits of pragmatism. In this regard, Misak writes, "The hope is that the new pragmatists can connect our philosophical concepts of truth, rationality and norms to the practices which are so central to human life—science, ethics and politics."[115]

This goal is highly compatible with Newman's conception of philosophy; in fact, it is highly compatible with his entire academic and pastoral career. His philosophical project emphasized the personal aspect of knowledge and belief and offered a philosophical account of knowledge as it is formed and given in everyday experience. Unlike the British empiricists that preceded him, Newman did not ground his insights in formulas or theories. Instead, he based them on the real people he encountered and walked with throughout his life. He had a deep knowledge of the human mind and heart, which he matured through decades of study and ministry, allowing himself to be affected by his contemporaries' quandaries, questions, and concerns. His philosophical project was not an isolated endeavor, but one carried out in dialogue with others and with reality itself, as his twenty thousand letters attest.

In the *Grammar* Newman explicitly stated his concern with real life: "My aim is of a practical character [in regards] to the truth of things, and to the mind's certitude of that truth."[116] His objective was not to devise an epistemological system a priori, but to justify how it is that individuals do in fact attain certitude and reach assent. To leave no doubt about this, he exclaimed:

> Life is not long enough for a religion of inferences; we shall never have done beginning, if we determine to begin with proof. We shall ever be laying our foundations; we shall turn theology into evidences, and divines into textuaries. We shall never get at our first principles. Resolve to believe nothing, and you must prove your proofs and

114. William James, *Pragmatism, a New Name for Some Old Ways of Thinking* (London: Longmans, Green and Co., 1907), 3–4.

115. Misak, introduction to *New Pragmatists*, 5.

116. *GA*, 344.

analyze your elements, sinking further and further [...] till you come to the broad bosom of scepticism. [...] Life is for action. If we insist on proofs for everything, we shall never come to action: to act you must assume.[117]

Newman not only believed that life was for action, he also maintained that philosophy begins with facts: "Let us take things as we find them: let us not attempt to distort them into what they are not. True philosophy deals with facts. We cannot make facts. All our wishing cannot change them. We must use them," and he held that "truth means facts and their relations."[118] Newman's robust realism and deep interest in the connection between thought and human practice is one more reason we can comfortably place him in dialogue with pragmatism.

As not all pragmatists share a common set of doctrines, but rather understand pragmatism to be "a philosophical family—often a contentious family—of thinkers holding distinct yet related positions on the 'workman-like' nature of knowledge, meaning and truth,"[119] it is unnecessary to reconcile Newman with every pragmatic principle to justify his place among the forerunners of pragmatism. His consonance with these three central claims of pragmatism seems to be enough.

117. *GA*, 94–95.
118. *US*, 231 (1839); *Idea*, 45.
119. Westbrook, *Democratic Hope*, 1.

Chapter 2

Newman as a Philosopher

The editor of his *Philosophical Notebook* described Newman's philosophical project as "something it can never be, that is to say, something *too* personal. [...] Instead of presenting his ideas and developing them objectively and systematically for their own sake, he is ever present himself in all he has to say."[1] Thus, the biographical profile sketched in the preceding chapter provides a suitable framework for analyzing his philosophical ideas. Newman was likely familiar with the adage pronounced by another English clergyman, "No man is an island, entire of itself; every man is a piece of the continent, a part of the main."[2] He intensely lived out this principle throughout his career, grappling with others' ideas and learning from them.

Although he read extensively and philosophy was central to his interests, Newman's philosophical mind was not dominated by any one influence. While he nourished and challenged his ideas with the thought of other British theologians, scientists, and philosophers, he was never the disciple of any one of them. His independent spirit led him to use what he found valuable in other systems and develop his own proposals. In 1868, as he undertook his last major project, *The Grammar of Assent*, he considered different avenues for discussing the nature of faith, belief, assent, and certitude. He concluded that the only approach "likely to do good, is *philosophical*."[3]

---

1.   Sillem, *Philosophical Notebook*, 1.

2.   John Donne, *Devotions upon Emergent Occasions* (Ann Arbor, Mich.: University of Michigan Press, 1959), 108. First published in 1624.

3.   *LD*, xxiv 74 (1868). William Clarke's (1827–1878) review of *The Grammar of Assent*,

Newman's conviction that "the human mind is made for truth"[4] is the cornerstone of his project and of my analysis. His deep introspection into the gradual unfolding of truth in his own mind was the hermeneutical key for his research, which was characterized by his ability to bring together seemingly opposed truths even when he could not exactly explain how they cohered. Early in his career, Newman understood that "each mind pursues its own course and is actuated in that course by tenthousand [*sic*] indescribable incommunicable feelings and imaginings."[5] His lifelong study of the operations of reason led him to develop the notion of the Illative Sense as a way to give an account of the incommensurability of the human mind. In this sense, "Newman was a distinctly modern thinker, that is, a thinker who was dealing with the 'turn to the subject' that is commonly taken to be the signature of the modern period. For he is not only interested in what is objectively true [...] but also in the way in which objective truth is 'lived,' is owned by the subject, is absorbed into the existence of the subject."[6]

Because of his personalist bent, Newman advocated a comprehensive approach to knowledge as a way to avoid subjectivity: "In knowledge, we begin with wholes, not with parts. We see the landscape, or the mountain, or the sky. We perceive men, each individually being a whole. Then we take to pieces, or take aspects of, this general & vague object, which is before us."[7]

---

written a couple of weeks after its publication, shows the appreciation Newman's contemporaries had for his philosophical work:

> The powerful grasp of Dr. Newman's mind appears very vividly and distinctly in its pages. The experience of a long life has perfected what was always one of the clearest notes of his intellect, his wonderful appreciation of points of view different from his own. [...] It is almost a paradox to say it, but it seems as if the acceptance of the most dogmatic of creeds has made him less dogmatic. The more intense his own convictions, the more generous and liberal he is to those whom he considers in the unfortunate position of rejecting them. His own labours and sufferings, the persecutions he has endured, so doubly painful to a mind intensely sensitive, the troublous journey by which he won his way to his present faith, have refined and softened a character always remarkable for its intense sympathy. (William Clarke, "Review of *An Essay in Aid of a Grammar of Assent*," *The Athenaeum*, no. 2212 [1870]: 379)

4.   *GA*, 221.

5.   *LD*, ii 60 (1828).

6.   Crosby, "Newman and Philosophers Today," 8.

7.   *PN*, 8.

Accordingly, in this project Newman's thought is taken as a whole, giving due importance to its historical and cultural context without trying to fit it into a foreign mold of interpretation. Newman often offered complex and multi-faceted ideas that completed one another and thus cannot be studied in isolation. To grasp all aspects of Newman's philosophy, one should follow the editor's suggestion in Newman's *Philosophical Readings*: "We in turn must take Newman's mind where we find it, rather than remove it to an alien setting."[8] Moreover, one can see that Newman's mind gives paramount importance to real assent and actual practices.

Another characteristic of Newman's philosophy is its deeply personal nature. He studied living people more than the writings of philosophers and refused to be guided by theories about how men ought to think, when he knew that these conflicted with the way they actually think. In this vein, I approach Newman as a living person, and the way he thinks is at the center of my analysis—hence the ample recourse to his published works and his *Letters and Diaries*. This comprehensive approach to his texts avoids two pitfalls: dealing with him as one would deal with a systematic author—which he is not—and taking isolated ideas out of context. In his *Autobiographical Writings,* Newman admits to his "habit, or even nature, of not writing & publishing without a call [...] or invitation, or necessity, or emergency."[9] Newman thought and wrote for others: for people he knew and cared about. His approach resulted in an unsystematic exposition characterized by a dearth of strict definitions.

In addition to the occasional nature of his work, Newman's engagement with philosophers in different schools of thought complicates the attempt to ground his philosophical approach in one single tradition. The *Grammar* portrays his acquaintance with the British naturalists; however, a few scholars reject every trace of empiricism from his thought while others treat him as merely an empiricist. I believe Newman incorporates some insights from Locke, Hume, and Mill—particularly from their epistemology—and uses them to show that reason does not operate any differently in matters of religion than it does in morality, philosophy, or history. Thus, he overcomes some constraints of the empirical tradition and allows for the possibility of certainty and assent. Newman's congeniality with empiricism was limited by

8.   James Collins, "Newman and Philosophy," in *Philosophical Readings in Cardinal Newman* (Chicago: Henry Regnery Company, 1961), 4.

9.   *AW*, 272–73 (1874).

his all-encompassing realism, which is expressed in his conviction that "true philosophy deals with facts. We cannot make facts. All our wishing cannot change them. We must use them."[10]

Although Newman was always in dialogue with his predecessors and contemporaries, he is one of the most personal, or independent philosophers in history; that is, personal but not isolated:

> [Newman] considered that knowledge is an intellectual possession of the truth which is the more intimately our own when held in union with other people who share it with us, for he thought that other people act upon our minds at a deeper level than things, methods or arguments. He sought objective truth by the method of dialogue, in and through the experience of inter-subjectivity [...] that is to say in the intercourse of man with man, and the action of mind on mind.[11]

To sketch Newman's philosophical profile, this chapter begins by identifying five British thinkers whose work Newman engaged with. This exposition is followed by a profile of his friendship with three of his contemporaries who were an impetus for his philosophical development. His insights into the philosophy of his day are then discussed to show how he engaged with different ideas and valued what they had to offer. Finally, this chapter presents three philosophical doctrines that have claimed him as their own in the twentieth and twenty-first centuries, to deepen the historical understanding between his philosophy and pragmatism.

This chapter offers a glimpse into the diverse and often contradictory interpretations of Newman's writings. To account for these differences, John Crosby appeals to Newman's capacity to harmonize apparent opposites.[12] In this regard, Newman himself explained that "seeming contradictions arise from the want of depth in our minds to master the whole truth."[13] Among other objectives, this project attempts to offer a deeper look at Newman's rich understanding of truth.

---

10.   *US*, 231 (1839).

11.   Sillem, *Philosophical Notebook*, 8.

12.   See John Crosby, "John Henry Newman on Personal Influence," in *Personalist Papers* (Washington, D.C.: The Catholic University of America Press, 2004), 241.

13.   John Henry Newman, *Parochial and Plain Sermons* (London: Longmans, Green and Co., 1907), v 48 (1836) (hereafter, *PS*).

Engagement with His Predecessors

Although Newman's philosophical principles have been interpreted in diverse and often contradictory ways, his thought presents a unique synthesis. As he contended in his *Apologia*, his intellectual position had an organic and coherent development. James Froude's testimony is a good starting point for illustrating Newman's philosophical profile and discerning its foundations:

> Newman's mind was world-wide. He was interested in everything which was going on in science, in politics, in literature. Nothing was too large for him, nothing too trivial, if it threw light upon the central question, what man really was, and what was his destiny. [...] Newman had read omnivorously; he had studied modern thought and modern life in all its forms, and with all its many-coloured passions.[14]

Even though he read extensively, Newman was shaped by his Oxford education and his engagement with primarily British thinkers.[15] I have deliberately chosen the term *thinkers*, since the contemporary understanding of the division of the sciences was uncommon in Newman's time. He understood philosophy not as a constricted discipline but as a habit that informed the whole mind.

To develop and clarify his own views, Newman contrasted his thought with that of other philosophers, mainly from the empiricist tradition. In this respect, Ian Ker maintains that Newman can be regarded as an empiricist in the general sense, since he had an empirical and undogmatic approach to truth and knowledge, which prioritized an informal over a formal model of reasoning. However, fitting his thought into a strictly empiricist mold distorts

14. James Froude, *Short Studies on Great Subjects* (London: Longmans, Green and Co., 1894), 4:278–80. James Froude was an Oxford student who regularly attended Newman's sermons at St. Mary's and who would go on to become a well-respected historian.

15. See Fergus Kerr, " 'In an Isolated and, Philosophically, Uninfluential Way': Newman and Oxford Philosophy," in *Newman and the Word* (Louvain: Peeters, 2000), 173. Pattison's widely cited epigram offers an insight into what some interpret as a limitation in the sources of Newman: "How different the fortunes of the Church of England might have been, if Newman had been able to read German!" Mark Pattison, *Memoirs* (London: Macmillan, 1885), 210. Although Newman never read Kant, he was acquainted with his thought through the works of Samuel T. Coleridge and William Hamilton. See Johannes Artz, "Newman in Contact with Kant's Thought," *The Journal of Theological Studies* 31, no. 2 (1980): 518–19.

it and discards its originality, since he overcame the common empiricist stance and offered new philosophical insights.[16] To give a balanced assessment of Newman's philosophy, one must give central consideration to his own description of his intellectual trajectory: "I like going my own way."[17]

In the tenth of his *University Sermons*, in which he spoke about habits of the mind, Newman described the person's search for truth as a night battle.[18] James Collins explains: "Groping around for a more appropriate metaphor to convey the philosophers' condition, he called it a night battle in which the footing is terribly slippery and where the darkness does not enable us to distinguish friend and foe with any ease."[19] A relevant aspect of Newman's genius lies in the fact that he dialogued with friends and foes alike and derived a profoundly original and compelling theory of knowledge from these encounters. The cast of philosophers to whom he paid attention is unconventional. His appropriation of insights from diverse thinkers, who often held conflicting views, makes the assessment of his philosophical roots a difficult task. Although the importance attributed to each of his sources varies widely, a few names do appear regularly. I have selected five British thinkers to shed light upon his philosophical profile and present them here in chronological order according to the year of their birth: Francis Bacon (1561–1626), John Locke (1632–1704), Isaac Newton (1643–1727), Joseph Butler (1692–1752), and David Hume (1711–1776).[20]

16.   See Ker, "Newman's Standing as a Philosopher," 75. Some scholars, such as Collins and Kerr, claim that Newman was simply an English empiricist. However, the position I take is that of Richardson, who maintains that "to associate his descriptive approach with empirical experience does not make him an empiricist. His use of certain phraseology common to the empiricism of his day is the result of it being more appropriate to express his realist position as opposed to that of idealism." Laurence Richardson, *Newman's Approach to Knowledge* (Herefordshire: Gracewing, 2007), 39. See also James Cameron, "The Night Battle: Newman and Empiricism," *Victorian Studies* 4, no. 2 (1960): 102. Aquino argues that Newman appropriated and transformed the British Naturalist tradition, particularly its epistemological and methodological aspects. Frederick Aquino, "The British Naturalist Tradition," in *The Oxford Handbook of John Henry Newman* (Oxford: Oxford University Press, 2018), 154.

17.   *LD*, xxiv 213 (1869).

18.   See *US*, 201 (1839).

19.   Collins, "Newman and Philosophy," 14.

20.   The main sources for this exposition are Aquino, "The British Naturalist Tradition"; Johannes Artz, "Newman as Philosopher," *International Philosophical Quarterly* 16, no. 3 (1976): 263–87; Collins, "Newman and Philosophy"; John Cronin, "Cardinal Newman: His Theory of Knowledge" (PhD diss., The Catholic University of America, 1935); Basil

At the beginning of his education at Oxford, Newman delved into the study of mathematics, physics, and natural philosophy. He valued these subjects for the rigor and depth they conveyed. Two diary entries from 1822 show his enthusiasm:

> I lay great stress on the attention I have given to mathematics, on account of the general strength it imparts to the mind [...] I think (since I am forced to speak boastfully) few have attained the facility of comprehension which I have arrived at from the regularity and constancy of my reading, and the laborious and nerve-bracing and fancy-repressing study of Mathematics, which has been my principal subject.[21]

One of the first book collections he acquired was *The Works of Francis Bacon*. He cited it relatively often throughout his career: there are twenty-four references to Bacon and his method in *The Idea of a University* and three in *The Grammar of Assent*. In the *Grammar*, Newman referred to Bacon as "our own English philosopher," and in the *Idea* he called him "the most orthodox of Protestant philosophers."[22] Amidst his compliments and references, one can identify three principles that Newman held in common with Bacon.

First, both clearly distinguished the sacred and natural domains, although Bacon's subject was modern science and Newman's was religious truth. Second, both recognized that each science required a suitable method of investigation and that the inductive methods, so profitable for the experimental sciences, should not be applied to philosophy and theology. Third, Newman referred to Bacon's recognition of the laws of nature to support his epistemological principles. Although Newman did not advocate for the use of Bacon's inductive method to ascertain how the person knows, he promoted Bacon's realism:

> We are accustomed in this day to lay great stress upon the harmony of the universe; and we have well learned the maxim so powerfully inculcated by our own English philosopher, that in our inquiries

---

Mitchell, "Newman as a Philosopher," in *Newman after a Hundred Years* (Oxford: Clarendon Press, 1990), 223–46; Richardson, *Newman's Approach to Knowledge*; Sillem, *Philosophical Notebook*.

21. *AW*, 61 (1822).

22. *GA*, 350; *Idea*, 319.

into its laws, we must sternly destroy all idols of the intellect [...].
So also is it in that microcosm, the human mind. Let us follow
Bacon more closely than to distort its faculties according to the
demands of an ideal optimism, instead of looking out for modes
of thought proper to our nature, and faithfully observing them in
our intellectual exercises.[23]

In his private notes from 1863, Newman described a good philosopher
as someone who "demands and exercises perfect liberty of thought within
the bounds of experience [and who] has the power of boundless speculation,
which he carries by his originality in abstracting, generalizing and applying."[24]
After this description, he identified Bacon as an exemplar of these characteristics and stated that time would tell which of his doctrines are fruitful and
which are not.

Newman regarded Bacon and Locke as the leading English philosophers:
the former for his study of the external world and the latter for his study of
man's inner life. Locke is by far the most disputed (and most commented
upon) of Newman's sources; that Newman engaged with his thought is
beyond question, but there is much debate about his level of adherence to
Locke's principles. Newman read Locke's *Essay Concerning Human Understanding* in 1818 and, throughout his life, addressed similar questions in a
similar language. Following Newman's recognition in the *Grammar*, Frederick
Copleston's assessment is that Newman regarded Locke with admiration and
respect but disagreed with him on substantial aspects.[25] In Newman's own
words: "I have so high a respect both for the character and the ability of
Locke, for his manly simplicity of mind and his outspoken candour, and there
is so much in his remarks upon reasoning and proof in which I fully concur,
that I feel no pleasure in considering him in the light of an opponent."[26]

Newman and Locke built their analysis of knowledge upon realism. Both
identified the individual as the starting point of their philosophy, acknowledged the reality of individual things, rejected the theory of innate ideas,

---

23.   *GA*, 350–51.

24.   John Henry Newman, *Theological Papers of John Henry Newman on Faith and Certainty*,
ed. Hugo M. De Achaval and Derek Holmes (Oxford: Clarendon Press, 1976), 118 (hereafter,
TP, i).

25.   See Frederick Copleston, *A History of Philosophy* (New York: Doubleday, 1946),
8:512.

26.   *GA*, 162.

and understood knowledge as the relation between a knowing subject and a particular object apprehended through the senses. Newman believed that Locke stood more firmly on human ground than other empiricists, and therefore chose him as a foil for his theory of knowledge. Despite these areas of agreement, three significant points of divergence should also be recognized.

First, Newman opposed Locke's account of rationality, because it proceeds from an a priori view of reasoning and not from observation. He wrote in the *Grammar*, "We must take the constitution of the human mind as we find it, and not as we may judge it ought to be."[27] In his reply to Richard Hutton (1826–1897), who sought to clarify this principle, Newman explained, "I accuse Locke and others of judging of human nature, not from facts, but from a self-created vision of optimism by the rule of 'what they think it ought to be'. This is arguing, not from experience, but from pure imagination."[28]

Second, Locke limited rationality to the boundaries of formal inference and ignored those aspects that depend on the multiform reality of the individual, while Newman's view of intellectual abstraction demanded that knowledge not be reduced to pure sense data: "When I speak of Knowledge, I mean something intellectual, something which grasps what it perceives through the senses; something which takes a view of things; which sees more than the senses convey; which reasons upon what it sees, and while it sees; which invests it with an idea."[29]

The third and clearest disagreement between them relates to degrees of assent: Locke thought they are possible, while Newman maintained they are not. One of Newman's objectives in the *Grammar* was to disprove Locke's thesis. The possibility of offering unconditional assent to truths that are not self-evident and of achieving moral certainty through a probabilistic process of reasoning is central to Newman's theory of knowledge and incompatible with Locke's.[30] Although Newman found Locke's conclusions unsatisfactory, he engaged with him as a respected interlocutor against whom he measured

27.   *GA*, 216. See Aquino, "The British Naturalist Tradition," 161.

28.   *LD*, xxv 115 (1870).

29.   *Idea*, 113. See Michele Marchetto, "The Philosophical Relevance of John Henry Newman," *Louvain Studies* 35, no. 3 (2011): 321.

30.   See Richardson, *Newman's Approach to Knowledge*, 80; Aquino, "The British Naturalist Tradition," 163; Reginald Naulty, "Newman's Dispute with Locke," *Journal of the History of Philosophy* 11, no. 4 (1973): 453.

his own ideas. For this reason, Locke is an important contextual figure for Newman's philosophy.

Despite their differing theories of knowledge, Newman admired Locke's commitment to the pursuit of truth, which is a characteristic that he also found in Isaac Newton, the third person I discuss in this profile. As to Bacon and Locke, Newman was exposed to Newton during his first months at Trinity College. He recalled that his early reading of Newton's *Observations on the Prophecies* made him "most firmly convinced that the Pope was the Antichrist predicted by Daniel, St. Paul, and St. John. My imagination was stained by the effects of this doctrine up to the year 1843."[31] Not only did Newton shape Newman's religious convictions for two decades, more importantly, he provided him with clarity regarding the nature of the knowledge yielded by the experimental sciences. Throughout his career, Newman firmly opposed the unequivocal application of the scientific method to philosophical and theological realities; however, his scientific knowledge helped him to deepen and elucidate his humanistic investigations.

In his *Essay on Development,* Newman illustrated his notion of antecedent probability with Newton's laws of gravity, observing that there are many realities we take for granted without relying on an explanation or on reason. In the *Grammar,* he referred to Newton's theory of the limit when developing his doctrine of informal inference. In his *Idea*, he noted that Newton did not make his great scientific discoveries in a university setting, arguing that universities are not the most conducive places to the advancement of science. Further, he identified Newton as a model of a thinker with a truly great intellect, who held an integrated view of past and present, and far and near.[32]

One of Newman's central claims was that certainty could be attained through mental operations other than formal inference. In his discussion on the theory of knowledge, he often referred to Newton's intellectual journey. He explained the following in his personal notes:

> Newton had ascertained his great discoveries, before he had *proved* them true; and he had great difficulty in proving them. He was obliged to invent a calculus in order to prove them [...]. He had a sort of presentiment of their truth, the result of his genius, and believed them before he knew them. It was his prudentia which

31.   *Apo*, 110.
32.   See *Dev*, 101; *GA*, 320–21; *Idea*, xiii, 134.

made them credible to him, presenting to him a proof of their credibility, which he could not communicate to another. So he went about to invent a scientific proof of their truth.[33]

Newton was not the only source from which Newman developed his understanding of scientific knowledge and his notion of probability. Another great thinker, Joseph Butler, informed his reflections on these matters. From Butler, Newman learned to recognize the limitations of human knowledge and acquired the principles of analogy and probability. He related the following in his *Apologia*:

> It was at about this date [1825], I suppose, that I read Bishop Butler's *Analogy* [...]. If I may attempt to determine what I most gained from it, it lay in two points [...]. First, the very idea of an analogy between the separate works of God leads to the conclusion that the system which is of less importance is economically or sacramentally connected with the more momentous system [...]. Secondly, Butler's doctrine that Probability is the guide of life, led me, at least under the teaching to which a few years later I was introduced, to the question of the logical cogency of Faith, on which I have written so much.[34]

Butler's doctrine of analogy was the means by which Newman understood that an order of things exists beyond what is sensibly perceived. He explained in his *University Sermons* that the material and invisible systems act as "two independent witnesses in one and the same question; an argument contained by implication, though not formally drawn out, in Bishop Butler's *Analogy*."[35] However, the central doctrine Newman acquired from Butler is that of probability. He explained that this principle

---

33. *TP*, i 25.

34. *Apo*, 113–14. A third principle Newman held in common with Butler is that of the unity of the person. He wrote, as an objection to Mill's *Logic*, "I can't quite stomach the idea, as expressing a fact, that I have no consciousness of Self, as such, as distinct from a bundle of sensations. Bishop Butler speaks of consciousness as indivisible and one—this is my idea of man—of no unity have we practically experience, but of self." *TP*, i 39. See also Garnett, "Joseph Butler," 136.

35. *US*, 31 (1830). Studies on Newman's sources either frame his theory of knowledge within the bounds of Butler's *Analogy* or maintain that he used it only as a starting point. See James Robinson, "Newman's Use of Butler's Arguments," *The Downside Review* 76, no. 244 (1958): 163; Cronin, "Newman's Theory of Knowledge," 30; Sillem, *Philosophical Notebook*, 170.

runs through very much that I have written, and has gained for me many hard names. Butler teaches us that probability is the guide of life. The danger of this doctrine, in the case of many minds, is, its tendency to destroy in them absolute certainty, leading them to consider every conclusion as doubtful, and resolving truth into an opinion, which it is safe indeed to obey or to profess, but not possible to embrace with full internal assent.[36]

Their point of disengagement was that, unlike Butler, Newman believed that probability can result in certitude. He wrote, "I use probable in opposition to demonstrative, not to certainty" and explained that left to himself, he would be tempted to adopt Butler's view and understand credibility as probability upon which it is safe to act.[37] Since people do not seek evidence for every fact they accept in daily life, Newman maintained that Butler's principle could only be held when it was understood empirically; he believed that "probability does in some sense presuppose and require the existence of truths which are certain."[38] Here lies the epicenter of his disagreement with William Froude, which prompted him to write *The Grammar of Assent*. In a letter to Newman, Froude wrote:

> For myself, in every province of thought and action, I am content to take as my motto the words "Ever learning and never able to come to a knowledge of the Truth." So long as I am able honestly to claim for myself the former characteristic, I am ready to submit contentedly to the reproach (if anyone choose to consider it a reproach) implied in the latter—as a condition inherent in imperfect faculties—I will not bury the talent in the earth on the plea that the Master "is a hard one and gathers when he has not strawed."[39]

A central theme in Newman's philosophical project was the rebuttal of this expression of skepticism. He challenged it by distinguishing between certitude as a property of the mind that cannot be qualified by degrees and certainty as a quality of propositions that can.[40] He contrasted probability

36.   *Apo*, 120–21.
37.   *LD*, xi 293 (1846). See *LD*, xv 456 (1853).
38.   *GA*, 237.
39.   Froude to Newman, December 29, 1859, quoted in *LD*, xix 271.
40.   Although this is a common understanding among Newman scholars, it is not a

with formal reasoning, not with demonstration or certitude, since informal inference may yield certitude in concrete matters. Despite their disagreements, Newman recognized the influence Butler had on him. In a letter he wrote fifty-five years after having read Butler's *Analogy* he asserted, "Without of course comparing myself with Bishop Butler, I may say that I am of his school."[41]

Although Newman referred to David Hume as someone whose "depth and subtlety all must acknowledge,"[42] his philosophical project deeply contrasts with Hume's skepticism. He owned Hume's *Essays and Treatises on Various Subjects* but rarely cited them. Aside from two passages—one in the *University Sermons* and one in *The Idea of a University*—Newman's quotations of Hume are limited to his *Essay on Miracles*, where he rejected Hume's view of the impossibility of the supernatural. He considered Hume acute but dangerous. While most literature studied in this section mentions Hume as one of Newman's sources, it devotes little attention to him.

The one exception is Cameron, who wrote, "The thesis I want here to maintain, namely, that there are many striking parallelisms between the thought of Newman and that of Hume, and that this far-reaching similarity represents a certain affinity in spirit and method—though not in conclusions—between the two writers, is not a thesis which is in any way tied to the possibility of demonstrating the literary dependence of Newman upon Hume."[43] In the *Grammar,* Newman's strong tendency towards self-analysis shines through; this resembles Hume's philosophical style, which begins from the self as the only indubitable certainty.[44] A further point of contact between Newman and Hume is their criticism of Locke, as Hume's project is coherent with Newman's aim to develop a broader account of the rationality of belief than Locke's.

The thinkers discussed in this section share similar terminology and belong to the same epoch; however, they differ in their specific disciplines and

---

distinction to which Newman systematically adhered, as he often used both terms interchangeably. For example, in the following instance he used them in the opposite way: "We differ in our sense and our use of the word *'certain'. I use it of minds*, you of propositions." *LD*, xxix 114 (1879) (emphasis added).

41.   *LD*, xxix 207 (1879).

42.   *US*, 195 (1839).

43.   Cameron, "The Night Battle," 102.

44.   See Artz, "Newman as Philosopher," 269. Artz makes this affirmation in light of Newman's early realization "of two and two only absolute and luminously self-evident beings, myself and my Creator." *Apo*, 108.

approaches to knowledge. Locke and Hume serve as sources for Newman by standing as foils to his ideas, while Bacon, Newton, and Butler provided mathematical or religious insights that Newman incorporated into his theory of knowledge. Newman greatly benefitted from his dialogue with others, and through this dialogue, he devised a new approach to overcome the a priori rationalist theories of knowledge.

Engagement with His Contemporaries

Newman not only dialogued with thinkers who preceded him. The thirty-two volumes that compile his letters witness to his engagement in the debates of his time and show that he understood that intellectual achievement is rarely individualist but more often results from conversations within a community.[45] His engagement with his contemporaries is also seen in his academic works, as he composed them not as ends in themselves but as expressions of his pastoral heart:

> The importance of the pastoral dimension in Newman's career cannot be overestimated [...] humdrum parochial concerns determined the kind of man he was and, more to the point here, the kind of books he wrote. [...] A pastor deals not with abstractions but with practical, concrete situations, with real people in all their individuality, not with belief as a speculative phenomenon but with the particular parishioner who has trouble believing.[46]

Newman's correspondence was aimed at accompanying like-minded individuals. But he also cultivated the friendship of people with whom he had significant differences of opinion. Often his interlocutors were his contemporaries as a collective. On some occasions, however, they were individuals: he wrote his *Apologia* as a reply to Charles Kingsley, his *Grammar of Assent* as

45. See Robert Barron, "John Henry Newman among the Postmoderns," *Newman Studies Journal* 2, no. 1 (2005): 20. Toward the end of his career Newman exclaimed, "What I trust that I may claim all through what I have written, is this—an honest intention, an absence of private ends, a temper of obedience, a willingness to be corrected, a dread of error." *AR*, 63. His willingness to be corrected is evident in the study of how he engaged with his contemporaries.

46. Marvin O'Connell, "Newman: The Victorian Intellectual as Pastor," *Theological Studies* 46, no. 2 (1985): 335.

part of a forty-year dialogue with William Froude, and his *Letter to the Duke of Norfolk* as a rebuttal to William Gladstone.

To continue the sketch of Newman's philosophical profile, I will focus on his relationship with three of his contemporaries. The first is Richard Whately, the professor with whom he worked during his first years at Oxford. Whately was a teacher and close friend to Newman, and Newman acknowledged his influence time and again. The other two are Catherine and William Froude, a married couple with whom he exchanged dozens of letters on the nature of certitude and assent for over forty-one years.

Upon his arrival to Oriel College in 1822 and because of his shy temperament, Newman was placed under the tutelage of Richard Whately, an extroverted professor who enjoyed mentoring introverted young men. Newman narrated in his diary:

> They determined on putting their unformed probationer [Newman] into his hands [Whately's]. If there was a man easy for a raw bashful youth to get on with it was Whately—a great talker, who endured very readily the silence of his company, original in his views, lively, forcible, witty in expressing them, brimful of information on a variety of subjects [...] free and easy in manners, rough indeed and dogmatic in his enunciation of opinion, but singularly gracious to undergraduates and young masters who, if they were worth anything, were only too happy to be knocked about in argument by such a man.[47]

At that time, Whately was the leading figure of the Noetic school. The school's cardinal principle was that reasoning in all subjects is carried out using the same process, which can be clearly manifested as a syllogism.[48] Along with Whately, the Noetic school was a profoundly formative influence for Newman; however, after 1829 he came to regard it as representative of the religious liberalism he so deeply opposed.

When their acquaintance began, Whately was immersed in the subject of logic and introduced Newman to this work: "It was not long before Mr. Whately succeeded in drawing him out, and he paid him the compliment of

---

47. *AW*, 66 (1825). Although this text refers to Newman in the third person, it is part of the third chapter of his "Autobiographical Memoir" published in 1874.

48. See Richard Whately, *Elements of Logic* (New York: Sheldon & Company, 1848), 208.

saying that he was the clearest-headed man he knew."[49] One of Newman's first projects for Whately consisted in turning a series of his manuscripts on logic into an article for the *Encyclopaedia Metropolitana*. Once this article was published, Newman continued to adapt Whately's manuscripts for his famous work, *Elements of Logic*.[50]

In its preface, Whately was generous in his recognition of Newman: "I cannot avoid particularising the Rev. J. Newman, Fellow of Oriel College, who actually composed a considerable portion of the work as it now stands, from manuscripts not designed for publication, and who is the original author of several pages."[51] Newman replied to this great compliment by writing Whately:

> Much as I owe to Oriel, in the way of mental improvement, *to none, as I think, do I owe so much as to you.* I know who it was that first gave me heart to look about me after my election, and taught me to think correctly, and (strange office for an instructor) to rely upon myself. Nor can I forget, that it has been at your kind suggestion, that I have been since led to employ myself in the consideration of several subjects, which I cannot doubt have been very beneficial to my mind.[52]

Logic and rhetoric formed the core of these subjects. Newman acquired Whately's understanding of logic as a method for analyzing the mental processes that must take place if reasoning is to be considered valid. He also inherited Whately's distinction (which was uncommon at the time) between the process of reasoning and the analysis of that process. Through his work with Whately, Newman not only developed a solid philosophical framework, but he also improved his writing skills, which were of invaluable benefit to him.

---

49.   *AW*, 66 (1825).

50.   *Elements of Logic* was printed in nine editions from 1826 to 1848, each one selling out faster than the last. Most Victorian logicians learned from it, and some launched their careers by reviewing it. George Boole (1815–1864) recommended it as the best treatment of logic, Augustus De Morgan (1806–1871) praised it as restoring logical study, and Charles Peirce was introduced to logic through its pages. See Jared Neumann, "Richard Whately's *Elements of Logic* and Its Popular Discontents," ResearchGate, accessed March 9, 2021, https://www.researchgate.net/publication/325177432_Richard_Whately's_Elements_of_Logic_and_Its_Popular_Discontents (this paper has since been removed from ResearchGate).

51.   Whately, *Elements of Logic*, 6.

52.   *LD*, i 307 (1826) (emphasis added).

Newman and Whately initially agreed on the scope and limitations of logic. As Newman's thought continued to mature, however, he realized that Whately was misusing logic by strictly identifying it with reason. Newman agreed with Whately that reasoning can be expressed as a syllogism, but he disagreed with his belief that this is a necessary condition for the validity of the reasoning process. For Newman, formal reasoning was one of the many avenues of reason, but not the only one.

In 1838 Whately published his work *Easy Lessons on Christian Evidences* for young people who did not have the benefit of an education. He intended to provide them with evidence for their religious beliefs, in a way that sparked their interest and offered a rational conviction; in doing so, he effectively reduced belief to the logical conclusion of a syllogistic process.[53] Newman responded to Whately through the four sermons on faith and reason he preached between 1839 and 1840. In these sermons, he developed his views on implicit reasoning from antecedent probabilities and expanded the theoretical framework he inherited from Whately. He did not directly reject Whately's understanding of logic; he merely expanded it because he found it insufficient: "It was never Newman's way to abandon one habit of thought for another; his new perceptions always grew out of his earlier insights."[54]

After six years of intense collaboration around the *Elements of Logic,* Newman realized that Whately and himself would need to part ways, as their views had clearly diverged. He recalled that after the first edition of the *Elements of Logic* in 1826, "[Whately's] hold upon me gradually relaxed. He had done his work towards me or nearly so, when he had taught me to see with my own eyes and to walk with my own feet."[55] Beyond the specific disagreements in their understanding of logic, theology, and politics, Newman's difficulties with Whately reflected his determination to avoid the extremes of fideism and rationalism, since he saw both as unjustifiable theories of knowledge. Their formal break happened in 1829, and although they took different paths, Newman continued to respect him. In 1836 he wrote of Whately, "Whatever his errors, [he] is openhearted, generous and careless of

---

53. See Richard Whately, *Easy Lessons on Christian Evidences* (London: John Parker, 1838), 5.

54. Gillian Evans, " 'An Organon More Delicate, Versatile and Elastic': John Henry Newman and Whately's Logic," *The Downside Review* 97, no. 328 (1979): 191.

55. *Apo*, 114.

money." Sixteen years later he recollected, "thinking that I would dedicate my first book to him with some inscription as this if I could express it without rudeness, 'To R. Whately etc, who by teaching me to think, has taught me to differ from him', or 'to think for myself.' "[56]

Another decisive influence in Newman's thought, established through dozens of letters, is that of Catherine and William Froude. Through his life-long correspondence with them, Newman delved into the conflict between religion and philosophical naturalism when the latter restricts all knowledge to the purview of the scientific method and its demonstrable conclusions. Newman met William in 1828 at Oriel College, where Newman tutored him in mathematics and classics, and met Catherine in 1836. Catherine and Newman began corresponding three years before she married William. Newman sincerely appreciated William because he held intellectual honesty above every other virtue and Catherine because she had the utmost respect for the truth.

A close intellectual friendship between the three of them was strengthened through more than four decades of correspondence, in which they carried on a philosophical dialogue about the nature of evidence and belief. Although raised in the Anglican Church, William had left the faith of his youth. He adopted a growing scientific agnosticism that constricted him to a narrow understanding of doubt and certainty. Newman saw Froude, a brilliant engineer, as the archetype of scientists who embraced the rationalist views of Thomas Huxley (1825–1895), who maintained that for "the improver of natural knowledge [...] scepticism is the highest of duties; blind faith the one unpardonable sin."[57]

Their relationship deepened after the publication of *Tract* 90, and Newman confided in the Froudes his growing uneasiness with the Church of England. In 1844, as the truth of the Roman Church dawned on him, Newman admitted to the Froudes that his doubts had started in 1839, and although he tried to set them aside, they returned time and again. In a letter addressed to the Froudes he reflected, "If the doubt come from Him [God], He will repeat the suggestion [...] fancies, excitements, feelings go and never return—truth comes again and is importunate."[58] Through their correspondence he matured his ideas: "I am not writing with a purpose so much as

---

56.   *LD*, v 251 (1836), xv 178 (1852).
57.   Thomas Huxley, *Lectures and Lay Sermons* (London: Dent & Sons, 1910), 53.
58.   *LD*, x 201 (1844).

finishing a subject I may not otherwise get myself to work out."[59] Catherine encouraged him in his discernment by saying, "Even if you did in the end leave the Church, I might be quite sure you would not do so without a *call* so to do, and surely after the life you have led, you are not likely to mistake a call."[60] William and Catherine were part of the small circle of friends that remained with Newman after his conversion. Unlike many Tractarians, they saw in Newman's momentous decision not inconsistency or betrayal but a response to a divine call.

After his priestly ordination in the Catholic Church, Newman continued his correspondence with the Froudes, encouraged by his desire to enlighten influential scientists and intellectuals with the truths of Roman Catholicism. In 1848 he wrote to Catherine:

Oh that I were near you, and could have a talk with you!—but then I should need great grace to know what to say to you—This is one thing that keeps me silent, it is, dear friend, because I don't know what to say to you. If I had more faith, I should doubtless know well enough; I should then say, "Come to the Church, and *you will find* all you seek." I *have myself* found all I seek—"I have all and abound"— my every want has been supplied.[61]

Catherine asked to be received in the Roman Catholic Church in March 1857, and four of her five children followed. William bore this trial with much patience and gentleness. He continued to correspond with Newman due to his desire to discover the truth, which he believed lay somewhere between Newman's thought and his own. As they continued their dialogue, on December 29, 1959—a few days after Newman received the Froudes' eldest son, Hurrell, into the Catholic Church—William wrote a lengthy letter in which he stated his position of explicit universal doubt:

More strongly than I believe anything else, I believe this. That on no subject whatever [...] is my mind, (or as far as I can tell the mind of any human being) capable of arriving at an absolutely certain conclusion. [...] That though any probability however faint, may in its place make it a duty to *act as if* the conclusion to which it points

59.   *LD*, x 244 (1844).
60.   *LD*, x 51 (1843).
61.   *LD*, xii 223 (1848).

were absolutely certain, yet that even the highest attainable probability does not justify the mind in discarding the residuum of doubt;
and that the attempt [...] to enhance or intensify the sense of the
preponderance of the probabilities in either scale, is distinctly an
immoral use of faculties.[62]

After receiving this letter, Newman expressed deep gratitude to William,
as it allowed him to better understand his position. Although Newman
disagreed with William, he received his words with respect and allowed
himself to be challenged by William's arguments. He replied to William on
January 2 after pondering his letter for a couple of days:

> Now that I know clearly where to find you, I don't suppose that
> I'm going to argue, or indeed I can. The line you draw out in your
> letter is familiar to me [...] I shall keep your letter before me to use.
> Still I have long meditated on its subject. I think it a fallacy—but I
> don't think it is easy to show it to be so. It is one of various points
> which I have steadily set before me, as requiring an answer, and an
> answer from me. [...] I am habitually praying to God to direct me
> whether to take up the line of subjects on which it lies, or to devote
> my remaining years to some other undertaking. [...] In truth I think
> there is a far deeper philosophy on the subject than yours, if I could
> develop it.[63]

62.   *LD*, xix 270 (1860). The exchange of letters that followed over the subsequent
three weeks is quoted at length because it clearly portrays Newman's commitment to truth
and the genesis of *The Grammar of Assent*. Leggett discusses the honesty and complexity of
William's position: "For [him] doubt was not so much an opportunity as an experience, and
one which shaped his approach to scientific practice, just as that scientific practice contributed to his doubts. [...] He developed the conviction that experimenters were under a moral
obligation to doubt and not to extend the limits of their knowledge through either approximation or pride." Don Leggett, "William Froude, John Henry Newman and Scientific Practice in the Culture of Victorian Doubt," *The English Historical Review* 128, no. 532 (2013):
575–77. In 1859 William wrote to Newman: "Our 'doubts' in fact appear to me as *sacred*, and
I think deserve the be cherished as *sacredly* as our beliefs." *LD*, xix 270 (1860). In 1875 he
wrote to another colleague: "The only way to truth as far as my judgement carries me, is by
doubting and fumbling, and correcting errors where one can." Quoted in Leggett, "Froude,
Newman and Scientific Practice," 587.

63.   *LD*, xix 272–73 (1860).

On January 15, William replied elaborating on his position and inviting Newman to contest his views. Their exchange of clearly differing opinions reveals their intellectual humility and mutual appreciation. They made themselves vulnerable to one another with a desire to be corrected and to allow for a clearer view of truth to emerge:

> My dear Newman, I did not intend to let so many days pass without thanking you for your very kind letter [...]. I most heartily wish, (and I have heard others who think much as I do, express the same wish with equal heartiness) that you would really and fully work out this question—it is indeed one which you more than anybody else have been felt by those who know you, to be competent to examine fully.[64]

On January 18, Newman candidly answered and asked William to assist him by providing constructive criticism for his arguments, as he formally embarked upon the intellectual journey that led him to publish *The Grammar of Assent* ten years later. At the time, he wrote:

> It is a cause of great sadness to me, when I look back at my life, to consider how my time has been frittered away, and how much I might have done, had I pursued one subject. [...] Should I be led to pursue the subject of this letter (which would be by very slow marches) I should ask your leave to put various points before you, as iron girders are sent to the trying house.[65]

Thus unfolded a new chapter in their correspondence, which inspired the central arguments of the *Grammar*. Surprisingly, William's response to the *Grammar* is unknown, because after its publication their letters turned to more personal matters. Catherine died in July 1878, and William traveled to South Africa to mourn her loss. During this trip, he wrote one last letter to Newman reinstating his position. This letter reached Newman while he was in Rome waiting to be made a cardinal in the Catholic Church. He immediately began drafting his response, a summary of the principles he had discussed in the *Grammar*, but never sent it because he received word that William had passed away. He had begun this letter by expressing to his lifelong friend that his

64. *LD*, xix 283 (1860).
65. *LD*, xix 284–85 (1860).

"first and lasting impression is that in first principles we agree together more than you allow."[66]

Although Newman corresponded with hundreds of people, the length and depth of his conversation with the Froudes is remarkable, not only in terms of its fruits but in terms of their mutual perseverance in maintaining a cordial and constructive argument for over four decades. How Newman valued William despite their long-standing differences is beautifully summed up in the 1871 dedication of a collection of essays:

> To you, my dear William, I dedicate these miscellaneous compositions, old and new, as to a true friend, dear to me in your own person, and in your family [...] as one, who, amid unusual trials of friendship, has always been fair to me, never unkind; as one, who has followed the long course of controversy, of which these Volumes are a result and record [...]. Whatever may be your judgment of portions of their contents, which are not always in agreement with each other, you will, I know, give them a ready welcome, when offered to your acceptance as the expression, such as it is, of the author's wish, in the best way he can, of connecting his name with yours.[67]

Engagement with Some Philosophical Doctrines of His Time

In the fourth of his *University Sermons*, delivered in 1831, Newman denounced the dangers he saw in rationalism for the first time. From then forward, one can note a certain antirationalism as a thread that runs through his work. He continued to engage with this theme up to the publication of *The Grammar of Assent*: his crowning effort to overcome skepticism without falling into rationalism. In his later years, Newman did not directly speak of rationalism but of what he understood to be its most significant consequence: liberalism.

Newman had a broad focus when he spoke of liberalism. He referred to the personal and social consequences of the aggrandizement of reason that seeks to exclude every other faculty or sense. Then, in his writings, ratio-

---

66. *LD*, xxix 112 (1879).

67. John Henry Newman, *Essays Critical and Historical* (London: Longmans, Green and Co., 1907), i v (hereafter, *Ess*).

nalism can be understood as a principle of liberalism. In this section, I will consider Newman's criticism of rationalism and then discuss how he dealt with liberalism, skepticism, and fundamentalism.

Newman described rationalism as "a certain abuse of Reason; that is, a use of it for purposes for which it never was intended, and is unfitted."[68] A central thesis in his philosophical project is that reason plays an important, but not exclusive, role in the process of knowledge; he actually judged that reason can be employed industriously in all sciences. He introduced his sermon "The Usurpation of Reason" by stating:

> I propose now to make some remarks upon the place which Reason holds in relation to Religion, the light in which we should view it, and certain encroachments of which it is sometimes guilty; and I think that, without a distinct definition of the word, which would carry us too far from our subject, I can make it plain what I take it to mean. Sometimes, indeed, it stands for all in which man differs from the brutes, and so includes in its signification the faculty of distinguishing between right and wrong, and the directing principle in conduct. In this sense I certainly do not here use it, but in that narrower signification, which it usually bears, as representing or synonymous with the intellectual powers, and as opposed as such to the moral qualities, and to Faith. This opposition between Faith and Reason takes place in two ways, when either of the two encroaches upon the province of the other.[69]

In addition to denouncing the magnification of reason and its treading upon moral sense, Newman also criticized its constraint to one explicit mode of reasoning that privileged the mechanical application of logic to the point of excluding other habits of the mind. Newman never denied, however, that the mind must be guided by the laws of logic; what he rejected was the notion that logic should completely dominate its operations. Newman upheld the freedom and creativity of the person who is capable of going beyond explicit modes of reasoning and argued that "all men have a reason, but not all men can give a reason."[70]

68. *Ess*, i 31.
69. *US*, 58–59 (1831).
70. *US*, 259 (1840).

Newman also challenged the rationalist principle brought forth by the scientific revolution that dictates that certainty can only be achieved when every possibility of doubt is excluded. This principle sought to equate the study of philosophy and theology to mathematics and the physical sciences. Newman argued, however, that each science had its own methodology and that certitude could also be attained through the accumulation of probabilities and the Illative Sense. In this context, Newman made a clear distinction between reason as a critical power and reason as a creative power, explaining that although reason cannot originate certain truths, such as religious truths, it can test and verify them.[71]

A third aspect of rationalism that Newman challenged was the exaltation of the individual as the arbiter of truth: "the Rationalist makes himself his own centre [...]. Our private judgment is made everything to us, is contemplated, recognized, and consulted as the arbiter of all questions, and as independent of everything external to us. Nothing is considered to have an existence except so far forth as our minds discern it."[72] He spoke of the exaltation of reason as blindness, since it prevents the intellect from making full use of its resources and abilities. Newman understood the subject who knows as a person in relation, not as a disembodied reasoning power. Further, he believed that growth in knowledge and the attainment of truth are not individualistic endeavors but collective ones. In his sermon on the usurpation of reason, he included a footnote in which he listed the following terms to better make his point: "officious reason," "captious reason," "usurping reason," and "rebellious reason."[73]

Throughout his writings, Newman detailed the problems caused by this misconception of reason, especially for apologetics and education. With the rise of rationalism, Christian clerics often turned to evidential apologetics to defend the faith, reducing the entire body of Christian revelation, dogma, and tradition to a system of reasoned evidence, thus falling into the same rationalism by which they were being attacked. While Newman believed that "reason rightly exercised, leads the mind to the Catholic faith," he maintained that the evidentialist approach damaged the faith, since reason is too blunt an

---

71.   See *US*, 134 (1832). Newman's developments in this line are coherent with an understanding of faith as a reasonable act, not a rational one.

72.   *Ess*, I 33–34.

73.   See *US*, 62 (1831).

instrument to encompass the totality of Christian revelation and convey the efficacy of its saving message.[74]

It was not only clerics who attempted to introduce rationalism in their craft. Many educators also followed this path, believing that if men were to think scientifically and logically, then all truths would inevitably become clear to them. Robert Peel (1788–1850) promoted reason as the great principle of social cohesion and moral stability for the country. For his part, Newman understood that the liberal quest to create equality among people through reason alone was an illusion because it ignored the fact that thinking is essentially a personal activity, and no two individuals reason in the exact same manner.

Although Newman was highly critical of the overreach of reason, he was also an avid defender of its rights and capabilities. He offered a subtle analysis of how reason works, not only in relation to religion, but in relation to all sciences. Identifying the shortcomings of fideism and rationalism, Newman presented an alternative understanding of the complementarity between faith and reason, since he believed that the human intellect can go far beyond the mere application of logical rules:

> The intellect of man [...] energizes as well as his eye or ear, and perceives in sights and sounds something beyond them. It seizes and unites what the senses present to it; it grasps and forms what need not have been seen or heard except in its constituent parts. It discerns in lines and colours, or in tones, what is beautiful and what is not. It gives them a meaning, and invests them with an idea. It gathers up a succession of notes into the expression of a whole, and calls it a melody; it has a keen sensibility towards angles and curves, lights and shadows, tints and contours. It distinguishes between rule and exception, between accident and design. It assigns phenomena to a general law, qualities to a subject, acts to a principle, and effects to a cause. In a word, it philosophizes.[75]

Making recourse to the Illative Sense, Newman broadened the rationalist understanding of reason and argued that "probabilities which did not reach

---

74. *Idea*, 181. In *Tract* 73 Newman distinguishes the act of *rationalizing* in matters of revelation from the ways in which the *use of reason* in religious matters is not only acceptable, but commendable. See *Ess*, I 31–32.

75. *Idea*, 74–75.

to logical certainty, might suffice for a mental certitude [and] that the certi-tude thus brought about might equal in measure and strength the certitude which was created by the strictest scientific demonstration."[76] Instead of the rationalism of his time, Newman proposed a novel philosophy based on his conception of the self as a person, a being more complex than reason alone. In saying that "it is the mind that reasons, and that controls its own reason-ings, not any technical apparatus of words and propositions,"[77] Newman referred to the person as a free subject for whom formal inferences are only one aspect of the reasoning process; "after all, man is not a reasoning animal; he is a seeing, feeling, contemplating, acting animal. He is influenced by what is direct and precise."[78]

In reference to his conversion, Newman explained in the *Grammar*: "We have arrived at these conclusions—not *ex opere operato*, by a scientific necessity independent of ourselves, but by the action of our own minds, by our own individual perception of the truth in question, under a sense of duty to those conclusions and with an intellectual conscientiousness."[79] Since the person, not impersonal reason, is the subject of knowledge and of belief-formation, Newman argued that different individuals can reach different conclusions in moral matters.[80] Newman's theory of personal reason and his rejection of the claim that faith ought to be exempt from rational analysis are the grounds on which some contemporary philosophers call him a soft rationalist.[81] In short,

76.   Garnett, "Joseph Butler," 140.

77.   *GA*, 353.

78.   John Henry Newman, *Discussions and Arguments on Various Subjects* (London: Long-mans, Green and Co., 1907), 294 (hereafter, *DA*).

79.   *GA*, 318. See also *Apo*, 109.

80. See *GA*, 375. Newman also remained open to mysteries that go beyond reason:

We experience Newman's breasth [*sic*] of mind in a particularly convincing way in those cases in which we realize that Newman himself does not understand how two truths can be consistent with each other, though he adheres firmly to both of them [...] he ends by letting the mystery stand, which he recognizes to be beyond him. He knows nothing of that rationalistic impatience which is quick to posit contradictions, and which likes to get rid of mysteries by affirming the one term of a supposed contradiction and denying the other. (John Crosby, "The 'Coincidentia Oppositorum' in the Thought and in the Spirituality of John Henry Newman," *Anthropotes* 6, no. 2 [1990]: 196)

81.   See William Abraham, "Revelation," in *The Oxford Handbook of John Henry Newman* (Oxford: Oxford University Press, 2018), 311. Mitchell writes that Newman "is, undoubt-

Newman did not attempt to separate faith from reason; instead he broadened the understanding of reason, so it could embrace the truths of faith.

Newman's position on liberalism has been widely studied, with some authors speaking of him as the most formidable agent of Catholic liberalism in England, and others presenting him as the champion of the nineteenth century's anti-liberal movement.[82] Newman's writings, particularly a few often quoted but decontextualized phrases from the *Apologia* and his "Biglietto Speech," seem to support claims of his staunch anti-liberalism; however, his position is quite nuanced, for two reasons. First, there is no unequivocal understanding of liberalism; the term has virtually no explicit meaning today, and even in the nineteenth century, it meant a wide variety of things. The common thread of its multiple definitions is the recognition of liberty as an inalienable right, the fundamental bounty of all humanity.[83] Second, although Newman's thought shows ample coherence and consistency, it matured over six decades of intense intellectual and pastoral work. Newman's mind is complex, nuanced, and profound; he was so deeply concerned with a great range of issues over such a long period that it is unreasonable to interpret his thought in closed terms such as liberal or anti-liberal.[84]

Newman's intellectual stance at once embodies and contradicts the spirit of his age, which is why modernists, liberals, and conservatives can all find

---

edly, a rationalist of some kind, albeit one who is sensitive to the many different ways in which rationality can be manifested." Mitchell, "Newman as a Philosopher," 240. Aquino introduces his account of Newman's epistemology by stating that "though reason plays an important role in evaluating the process of belief-formation, it does not follow that faith springs from a formal account of Christian belief, nor does it follow that reason is reducible to an explicit kind of reasoning and that faith is dependent upon this kind of reasoning." Frederick Aquino, "Epistemology," in *The Oxford Handbook of John Henry Newman* (Oxford: Oxford University Press, 2018), 378.

82.   See Denis Gwynn, *A Hundred Years of Catholic Emancipation (1829–1929)* (London: Longmans, Green and Co., 1929), 170; Cyril O'Regan, "Newman's Anti-Liberalism," *Sacred Heart University Review* 12, no. 1 (1992): 83–108; Robert Carballo, "Newman and the Transition to Modern Liberalism," *Humanitas* 7, no. 2 (1994): 19–41.

83.   See Guido de Ruggiero, *The History of European Liberalism* (London: Oxford University Press, 1927), 357–58.

84.   See Adrian Hastings, "Newman as Liberal and Anti-Liberal," in *The Theology of a Protestant Catholic* (London: SCM Press, 1990), 118. Jost points out that "few words are more ambiguous than 'liberalism', and when we speak of it in connection with an extraordinarily complex man [...] we seem to invite confusion." Edward Jost, "Newman and Liberalism: The Later Phase," *The Victorian Newsletter* 24 (1963): 1.

excerpts in his writings to support their position.[85] When Leo XIII recounted Newman's elevation to the cardinalate, he exclaimed, "It was not easy; no, it was not easy. They said he was too liberal; but I was determined to honor the Church by honoring Newman. I have always felt a deep veneration for him. I am proud that it has been given me to honor such a man."[86] However, in his acceptance speech for this honor, Newman himself exclaimed, "For thirty, forty, fifty years I have resisted to the best of my powers the spirit of liberalism in religion."[87]

Newman was concerned with religious matters throughout his life. When he wrote about liberalism, he often stated explicitly that what he opposed was liberalism in religion. At the same time, he recognized that the growing political and cultural liberalism of his time was good and true. Moreover, his *Idea of a University* is a defense of the liberal elements in education. In 1864 Newman wrote that "the Liberalism which gives a colour to society now, is very different from that character of thought which bore the name thirty or forty years ago."[88] By this time, almost four decades after he delivered the first sermon in which he engaged with this topic, Newman had come to recognize that liberalism was not only an ecclesiastical and theological matter but also a social and cultural phenomenon. He understood that the Church needed to learn to live in this emerging reality and that liberalism can prove beneficial to her mission if correctly embraced.[89]

---

85.   Norman explains, "The independence and isolation of Newman's mind did not mean that others avoided seeking to claim his authority for their own party positions. Within the Catholic Church most of the opponents of ultramontanism, whether Old Catholic or liberal, sought to identify him as a supporter. But as an Anglican he had tried to keep clear of parties and as a Catholic he certainly did so." Edward Norman, *Roman Catholicism in England* (Oxford: Oxford University Press, 1985), 98. Jaki adds, "Just as in Arian times, when both orthodox and unorthodox parties tried to secure the vote of Anthony, *the* saint of the day, so today both parties try to claim Newman to themselves." Stanley Jaki, "Newman's Assent to Reality, Natural and Supernatural," in *Newman Today* (San Francisco: Ignatius Press, 1989), 226.

86.   Quoted in Paul Thureau-Dangin, *The English Catholic Revival in the Nineteenth Century* (London: Simpkin & Co., 1914), 362. The citation is accompanied by the following footnote: "This account is taken from a letter written on January 26, 1888, immediately after the interview [between Leo XIII and Sir Roundell Palmer, Lord Selborne (1812–1895)] and has been communicated to me by Lord Selborne's daughter."

87.   *AR*, 64.

88.   *Apo*, 261.

89.   It is worth noting that, using the political sense of the word, Newman wrote an essay in 1854 in which he commends the popes for the times they upheld liberalism in their

The years Newman spent traveling to Ireland to establish the Catholic University provided him with a personal experience of the dangers of ultramontanism and the resistance to cultural pluralism. This led him to reflect on the potential benefits of political liberalism.[90] Through the discourses compiled in his *Idea*, one can appreciate his growing awareness that liberalism was a consequence of accepting social pluralism, which did not imply a renunciation of truth but of the right to impose it by coercion. As a social movement in the nineteenth century, liberalism advocated for the diffusion of knowledge, social reform, and economic progress; in this regard, Newman characterized his time as one of "superabundant temporal advantages" and recognized "that there is much in the liberalistic theory which is good and true; for example, not to say more, the precepts of justice, truthfulness, sobriety, self-command, benevolence."[91] Moreover, Newman was one of the few Christian intellectuals who did not identify the cause of the Church with that of political reactionaries who condemned the rise of democratic sentiments.

What Newman meant when he spoke of liberalism in religion was the proclamation of the absolute power of reason to achieve all knowledge, which reduces revealed religion to a private sentiment. Three elements can be identified in Newman's discussion of liberalism in religion: the overreaching of the intellect, the reduction of knowledge to what can be empirically proven, and the consequent understanding of religion as a personal sentiment or opinion. Regarding the aggrandizement of the intellect, liberalism is built on the erroneous assumption that makes human reason the measure

---

actions: "And, thus independent of times and places, the Popes have never found any difficulty, when the proper moment came, of following out a new and daring line of policy [...] of leaving the old world to shift for itself and to disappear from the scene in its due season, and of fastening on and establishing themselves in the new." John Henry Newman, *Historical Sketches* (London: Longmans, Green and Co., 1909), iii 134 (hereafter, *HS*). He added:

> A Conservative, in the political sense of the word [...] means a man who upholds government and society and the existing state of things [...] not because it is good and desirable [...] but rather because he himself is well off in consequence of it [...] It means a man who defends religion, not for religion's sake, but for the sake of its accidents and externals; and in this sense Conservative a Pope can never be, without a simple betrayal of the dispensation committed to him. (*HS*, iii 131–32. See also Terrence Merrigan, "Newman and Theological Liberalism," *Theological Studies* 66, no. 3 [2005]: 608)

90. See Jost, "Newman and Liberalism," 2; Merrigan, "Newman and Theological Liberalism," 613.

91. *AR*, 68.

of what is real and submits to personal judgment those revealed doctrines that are, by their nature, beyond reason and independent of it. Newman explained, "By Liberalism I mean false liberty of thought, or the exercise of thought upon matters, in which, from the constitution of the human mind, thought cannot be brought to any successful issue, and therefore is out of place. Among such matters are first principles of whatever kind; and of these the most sacred and momentous are especially to be reckoned the truths of Revelation."[92]

In this text, Newman refers to liberalism as the philosophical theory that maintains that there is no legitimate way of attaining knowledge of the truth except by formal argumentation or empirical demonstration. This understanding leads to the eventual replacement of religion by humanism: precisely what Newman opposed during his years at Oxford. Since he dedicated most of his efforts to the exercise of thought upon religious matters, it must be understood that this is not what he indiscriminately condemned. In his own words, Newman did not object to liberty of thought but rather to *false* liberty of thought. He did not suggest that the exercise of thought should be restrained in all cases but insisted that the natural limitations of our reasoning faculties should not be ignored. By exalting the dogmatic principle over liberalism in religion, Newman did not mean to encourage a passive acceptance of religious truths or discourage religious inquiry. Although he defended the rigorous exercise of thought on religious matters, he was profoundly aware of the fact that religion could not be reduced to an intellectual endeavor.

Newman's attitude towards liberalism underwent a steady evolution as his personal life and ministry developed through distinct phases that mirrored the world in which he was immersed. When he wrote his *Apologia* as the history of his religious beliefs in 1864, he was compelled to include a lengthy explanatory note regarding his stance on liberalism. This is his most systematic text on the matter, and it is significant that he wrote it twenty years after his reception into the Catholic Church. Short excerpts are often quoted; however, a more extended passage reveals Newman's thought much more clearly:

I have been asked to explain more fully what it is I mean by "Liberalism," because merely to call it the Anti-dogmatic Principle is to tell very little about it. An explanation is the more necessary, because such good Catholics and distinguished writers as Count Montalem-

---

92. *Apo*, 288.

bert and Father Lacordaire use the word in a favorable sense, and claim to be Liberals themselves. [...] I do not believe that it is possible for me to differ in any important matter from two men whom I so highly admire. In their general line of thought and conduct I enthusiastically concur, and consider them to be before their age. [...] If I hesitate to adopt their language about Liberalism, I impute the necessity of such hesitation to some differences between us in the use of words or in the circumstances of country; and thus I reconcile myself to remaining faithful to my own conception of it, though I cannot have their voices to give force to mine. Speaking then in my own way, I proceed to explain what I meant as a Protestant by Liberalism, and to do so in connexion with the circumstances under which that system of opinion came before me at Oxford.[93]

Two elements in this text are often overlooked. First, Newman recognized that Catholic men he admired have embraced liberalism and expressed his concurrence with them at the level of ideas, although not at the level of their expression. Second, he prefaced the remainder of his text, in which he listed eighteen tenets of liberalism, by stating that he is explaining what he meant when as a Protestant in Oxford he led the Tractarian Movement. Further, Newman asserted that the degree to which the Liberal Movement of the 1830s subscribed to these tenets and the sense in which he opposes them at that moment would be a topic for another extended essay. By stating this, he admitted that he does not hold without qualification what he wrote then regarding liberalism and its pitfalls.

After his conversion, Newman progressively aligned himself with scholars who called themselves liberal Catholics, and although he never accepted the label of liberal, he regarded favorably some of its main premises outside the realm of religion. In *An Essay on Development* (1845) he talked about the necessity of recognizing change; *The Idea of a University* (1852) is, among other things, a defense of a liberal education; in *On Consulting the Faithful* (1859) he expounded upon the need for private judgment while recognizing its limits; *The Grammar of Assent* (1870) is a book about reason and its operations; and the *Letter to the Duke of Norfolk* (1875) included a strong defense of conscience and civil freedom.

In 1879, upon receiving notice that the pope wanted to make him a

93. *Apo*, 285–86.

cardinal, he wrote to his dear friend Dean Church (1815–1890), "All the stories which have gone about of my being a half Catholic, a liberal Catholic, under a cloud, not to be trusted, are now at an end."[94] During his acceptance speech, he stated, "For thirty, forty, fifty years I have resisted to the best of my powers the spirit of liberalism in religion. [...] Liberalism in religion is the doctrine that there is no positive truth in religion. [...] It teaches that all are to be tolerated, for all are matters of opinion. Revealed religion is not a truth, but a sentiment and a taste."[95] The liberalism to which Newman referred in this well-known discourse is "quite other from the liberalism he was suspected of advancing and yet the two were not wholly unrelated either in the minds of his adversaries or his own mind or indeed in the objectivity of things."[96]

Perhaps a more relevant question than the general query of Newman's blanket acceptance or rejection of liberalism is what he did about it. He realized before most that the rationalistic philosophy that permeated the nineteenth century would burn itself out, leaving a profound intellectual desolation. Reflecting upon his mission, in 1863 he wrote in his journal, "From first to last education, in this large sense of the word has been my line."[97] His response to the intellectual desolation brought about by the overreach of reason was to propose a genuinely liberal education, whose objective he defined with these words: "To open the mind, to correct it, to refine it, to enable it to know, and to digest, master, rule, and use its knowledge, to give it power over its own faculties, application, flexibility, method, critical exactness, sagacity, resource, address, eloquent expression."[98] In *The Idea of a University* "liberal" stands for greatly desired virtues: freedom, equitableness, moderation, wisdom, and courtesy. Further, Newman placed liberalism, thus understood, within the foundations of the educated person and right social relationships.

Newman focused his efforts on educating the laity in order to provide them with the intellectual tools needed for a real assent of their beliefs. He realized that faith and morals could no longer be adequately sustained by the culture and worked tirelessly to form a laity "who know their religion, who

94.   *LD*, xxix 72 (1879).
95.   *AR*, 64.
96.   Hastings, "Newman as Liberal and Anti-Liberal," 129.
97.   *AW*, 259 (1863).
98.   *Idea*, 122.

enter into it, who know just where they stand, who know what they hold, and what they do not, who know their creed so well, that they can give an account of it, who know so much of history that they can defend it [...] an intelligent, well-instructed laity."[99] In 1875 Newman concluded his *Letter to the Duke of Norfolk* with a hopeful tone: "In centuries to come, there may be found out some way of uniting what is free in the new structure of society with what is authoritative in the old."[100] The breadth and coherence of Newman's proposal make him a valuable conversation partner for contemporary philosophers. Scholars with diverse theological and philosophical positions eagerly claim him to their side and can do so with sufficient evidence. But to profit from his thought in its totality, Newman should be read on his own terms. His works composed over six decades of continuous growth provide a helpful resource for this endeavor. The truth behind his thought is more clearly revealed in his ability to bring together seemingly opposed tendencies.

In his fight against religious liberalism, Newman sought to avoid two apparently opposed philosophical positions: skepticism and fundamentalism. Both are expressions of an incorrect understanding of reason—an understanding that leads individuals to exercise it in areas where it cannot properly operate, and to disregard it completely when they experience the limitations of its outcomes. Although skepticism may seem to indicate confidence in reason, it is often a product of disenchantment with its capabilities; it is very similar to fundamentalism in that both positions are sustained by the mistrust of reason.

As has been argued, Newman believed that the search for truth is a strenuous task: "It is the very law of the human mind in its inquiry after and acquisition of truth to make its advances by a process which consists of many stages, and is circuitous."[101] However, he never despaired of the potential of reason to attain truth. Unlike many of his contemporaries who argued that there was "a moral obligation to doubt and not to extend the

---

99. *Prepos*, 390. In this respect Walgrave writes, "Newman has always defended the apologetic principle along with the dogmatic principle: faith is to be justified by reason. Newman's originality does not consist in affirming this principle but in his fuller concept of reason." Jan Walgrave, "Faith and Dogma in Newman's Theology," trans. Edward Miller, *Newman Studies Journal* 15, no. 1 (2018): 51.

100. *Diff*, ii 268.

101. *Idea*, 474.

limits of their knowledge through either approximation or pride,"[102] Newman maintained that error always has some measure of truth in it, but truth has a reality that error does not, and therefore with honesty and fair talent, truth could emerge.

Newman integrated into his theory of knowledge the limitations of human thought and the unavoidable shortcomings of language. This recognition, paired with his awareness of the individual's natural orientation towards truth, allowed him to find a clear pathway between rationalism on one end and skepticism and fundamentalism on the other and to present a fruitful integration of faith and reason. Although he steered clear of both skepticism and fundamentalism and explicitly refuted them in his writings, Newman was criticized as a skeptic and as a fideist during his lifetime, and early scholarship often held these opinions as well.

As has been discussed, Newman derived the underlying principles of a significant portion of his beliefs from Butler's *Analogy*. Butler's understanding of probability as the guide of life was the basis for Newman's development of the Illative Sense, which stood in sharp contrast with the absolute certainty sought by most rationalists. Newman explained that his adherence to Butler's principle of probability "led to a charge against me both of fancifulness and of scepticism."[103] Newman described the reason for this change as his adherence to dogma, which caused many to discredit his thought.[104]

The fiercest exponent of the view that Newman was a skeptic who did not care for truth was Charles Kingsley, whose essay in *MacMillan's Magazine* led Newman to write the *Apologia* as a defense of his intellectual honesty. Kingsley began this controversy by stating, "Truth, for its own sake, had never been a virtue with the Roman clergy. Father Newman informs us that it need not, and on the whole ought not to be."[105] At that moment in his life,

102. Leggett, "Froude, Newman and Scientific Practice," 577.

103. *Apo*, 114.

104. See John Griffin, "Cardinal Newman and the Origins of Victorian Skepticism," *Heythrop Journal* 49, no. 6 (2008): 980. Dulles explains Newman's position: "[He] gave no quarter to dogmatic relativism. He argued vigorously for the irreversibility of dogmas, not necessarily in their wording, but in their meaning. His balanced position represents a middle course between a fluid historicism and a rigid dogmatism." Avery Dulles, *John Henry Newman* (London: Continuum, 2009), 79.

105. Charles Kingsley, "Review of Froude's *History of England*, Vols. VII and VIII," *MacMillan's Magazine* 9 (1864): 217.

twenty years after his conversion, Newman had already encountered much contradiction and disapproval; however, it was the charge of untruthfulness that prompted his thorough reply. Although the publication of his *Apologia* restored Newman's reputation among Protestants, Anglicans, and Catholics and marked a new beginning in his public life, in some circles it was received as evidence of his rationalistic and skeptical mind.[106]

Seventeen years later in *The Grammar of Assent*, Newman pursued a twofold objective: to show that one can believe what one cannot understand, and that one can believe what one cannot absolutely prove. His appeal to feeling, experience, and the personal dimension of assent made some suspect that he was falling into the liberal Protestantism that had attracted him in his youth. These lines from Thomas Harper's (1821–1893) review of the *Grammar* exemplify this suspicion: "Either my inference is formally valid, or it is not. If it be formally valid, it is *ipso facto* moulded by logical law; if it is not, it is no inference at all. For a similar reason, I cannot see my way to admit of an illative sense in any way distinct from the *logos* or reason."[107]

Contemporary scholarship is much more understanding of Newman's intentions. In her exposition of how Newman built on Butler's principle of probability, Garnett explains that

> Newman sought out the problematic elements in the world which threatened to operate powerfully and disruptively on people's imaginations, and drew on Butler to create a dynamic idea of development and of faith which could stand firm, on the one hand, against rationalism and the privileging of certain forms of "paper logic" and, on the other, against fideism.[108]

106. See George Denison, "Review of Newman's *Apologia pro Vita Sua*," *Church and State Review* 27, no. 5 (1864): 56. Another reviewer accused Newman of "reckless skepticism taking the form of the wildest superstition." James Stephen, "Dr. Newman's *Apologia*," *Fraser's Magazine* 70, no. 417 (1864): 285. A vast exposition of similar reviews to these can be found in Jan Klaver, "The Apologia," in *The Oxford Handbook of John Henry Newman* (Oxford: Oxford University Press, 2018), 462–64.

107. Thomas Harper, "Dr. Newman's *Essay in Aid of a Grammar of Assent*," *The Month* 12, no. 6 (1870): 688. Another reviewer stated that with the introduction of the Illative Sense, "any attempt at a common measure of truth as an 'objective test' is explicitly pronounced impossible." Leslie Stephen, "Dr. Newman's Theory of Belief II," *The Fortnightly Review* 22, no. 132 (1877): 808.

108. Garnett, "Joseph Butler," 141.

Newman sought to prove that knowledge that is not logically or scientifically warranted, whether in religious or secular matters, can be reasonable. As he labored, he had two groups of people in mind: educated Victorian rationalists, such as his friend William Froude, who were taught to regard the acceptance of more than was demonstrated as an offense to truth; and the uneducated masses who did not have the time or intellectual resources to ground their beliefs in scientific or logical explanations. Newman's philosophical appeal comes from his ability to expand both groups' intellectual horizons and offer new and constructive possibilities.

In his *Apologia,* Newman denounced "the all-corroding, all-dissolving scepticism of the intellect," and in his *Theological Papers* he defined skepticism as "the system which holds that no certainty is attainable, as not in other things so not in questions of religious truth and error."[109] The general difficulty for religious belief in Newman's time, in which skepticism was rapidly growing, was not helped by the fundamentalism with which some clerics responded. For his part, Newman attempted to counter skepticism by appealing to "the natural"—to how the person is constituted. Instead of pondering how men *ought to think*, he described how in fact *they do think*. He realized that the epistemological requirements that many of his contemporaries sought were unrealistic and accused "Locke and others of judging of human nature, not from facts, but from a self-created vision of optimism by the rule of 'what they think it ought to be'. This is arguing, not from experience, but from pure imagination."[110] Newman proposed a different route, one that was better grounded in reality and considered the nature of reasoning in the context of ordinary human experience and practice.

In his theory of knowledge, Newman captured the interweaving of the personal and interpersonal, the formal and informal elements that make up the process of reasoning. His main argument built upon the validity of the individual's natural ability to reach correct conclusions through "the cumulation of probabilities, independent of each other, arising out of the nature and circumstances of the particular case which is under review; probabilities too fine to avail separately, too subtle and circuitous to be convertible into syllogisms."[111] He named this faculty the Illative Sense and used it to sanction the individual's right to believe beyond logical or scientific demonstration.

109. *Apo*, 243; *TP*, i 150.
110. *LD*, xxv 115 (1870).
111. *GA*, 288.

Because Newman understood human nature, he was aware that philosophical skepticism leads to authoritarianism: When the possibility of discovering truth by using reason is discredited, other means of achieving certitude are required. Through his introduction of the Illative Sense, Newman evaded skepticism without yielding to a system of authoritarian dogmatic assertion. He found the proper balance by recognizing the limits of human reason while upholding its ability to know and freely assent to reality. In this way, his theory of knowledge avoided the trap of fundamentalism. Newman maintained that formulas and dogmas are but symbols, expressions of a much deeper truth, which by its very nature cannot be contained by any one specific proposition. For Newman, a real idea is timeless and eternal; however, the formulations in which it is understood and communicated are relative to time and context.[112]

Context is also essential for understanding the full scope of Newman's achievement. Speaking about his understanding of reason and its operations, Anselm Ramelow provides an insightful framework for Newman's work that serves as a fitting transition for the discussion of Newman and fundamentalism:

> The modern quest for certainty would never have arisen, had the certainty of faith never been experienced. Without this experience, modern man would not despair over the apparent inability of natural reason to find certainty. This is not the diagnosis of J. H. Newman, but it might provide the proper context for his explorations of the problem of certainty. *His response is not a simple and fideistic return to the certainty of faith, but the analysis and restoration of the normal workings of natural reason.* Natural reason has its own certitude, but it is different from the certainty at which modern thought aims.[113]

In the *Grammar*, Newman claimed that the scope and range of reason covers much more territory than formal logic and scientific demonstration and argued that non-syllogistic mental processes are reasonable despite being informal. When he faced the limits of reason, instead of abdicating from it, Newman expanded the prevailing view of rationality to include that which

112. See *US*, 331–32 (1843); *Dev*, 40.

113. Anselm Ramelow, "Knowledge and Normality: Bl. John Henry Newman's *Grammar of Assent* and Contemporary Skepticism," *Nova et Vetera* 11, no. 4 (2013): 1082 (emphasis added).

is practical, concretely lived, and not strictly scientific. Reason is enlarged by Newman's theory, not diminished. When talking about the abdication or constraint of reason in the context of Newman's writings, one could speak of fideism, dogmatism, or fundamentalism. Although these terms have different connotations depending on the context in which they are used, I use them univocally in this chapter and give preference to the term *fundamentalism*.[114]

Even though Newman encouraged others to grow in their understanding of the world through study and inquiry, he maintained that intellectual reasons are not enough to uphold one's beliefs. He wrote in the *Grammar*:

> Why am I to begin with taking up a position not my own, and unclothing my mind of that large outfit of existing thoughts, principles, likings, desires, and hopes, which make me what I am? If I am asked to use Paley's argument for my own conversion, I say plainly I do not want to be converted by a smart syllogism; if I am asked to convert others by it, I say plainly I do not care to overcome their reason without touching their hearts. I wish to deal, not with controversialists, but with inquirers.[115]

While intellectual grounding is important for belief, it is not sufficient. Newman wrote to Robert Ornsby (1820–1889), a professor at the Catholic University of Dublin, about how the latter should proceed with the education of the young men under his care: "Cut and dried answers out of a dogmatic treatise are no weapons with which the Catholic Reason can hope to vanquish the infidels of the day. [...] Truth is wrought out by many minds working together freely."[116] In this letter, Newman strongly encouraged inquiry and the free and fair play of the intellect as the best means not only for intellectual development but for moral growth as well. He concluded by expressing his discontent when free inquiry is not allowed.

114. Even though Newman frequently spoke about dogma (development of dogma, defense of dogma, etc.), in the few instances in which he used the term "dogmatism," he did so with a different meaning than it has today. In an *Essay on Development*, he referred to the centuries-long process of the development of the faith as dogmatism, and in "The Tamworth Reading Room" he used it to denote the contents of the faith. See *Dev*, 360; *DA*, 277.

115. *GA*, 424–25. William Paley (1743–1805), known for his work *Natural Theology or Evidences of the Existence and Attributes of the Deity* (1802), is considered one of the first Christian evidentialists.

116. *LD*, xx 425–26 (1863).

Newman also argued that when new problems arise, conserving known formulas does not necessarily mean preserving right doctrine. Regarding the foundation and governance of the Oratory, which at his time had a history of two centuries, Newman asked himself, "Did loyalty to the past mean development or revival? Did fidelity to the tradition imply growth or imitation? It was one of [his] deepest convictions that to cling to the literal letter of the past was to lose its essential spirit, and therefore to betray it."[117] One of the fundamental principles in his *Essay on Development* is that "if a great idea is duly to be understood [...] its vital element needs disengaging from what is foreign and temporary [...]. In time it enters upon strange territory [...] and old principles reappear under new forms. *It changes with them in order to remain the same.*"[118] Alongside this principle of discernment and adaptation, Newman upheld freedom of thought. He believed that a person should be "kept from scepticism, not by any external prohibition, but by admiration, trust, and love."[119]

Newman's theory of knowledge provides a nuanced understanding of the potential and the limitations of reason. The way he overcame rationalism and religious liberalism and steered clear of skepticism and dogmatism shows the individual how to tolerate a certain ambiguity in doctrinal formulations and understand that the formula's limits do not imply an impoverishment, but can even enrich its comprehension. In Newman's life, we see how human reason flourishes within this balance and allows the individual to strengthen his commitment to truth.

Newman's Reception in the Twentieth and Twenty-First Centuries

Contemporary philosophers continue to engage with Newman, finding a rich source of inspiration in his writings. There is much resonance between Newman's insights and current issues. While he cannot be expected to provide ready-made answers to today's questions, his writings provide a framework of meaning and a method for contemporary investigation. Newman offered an original and coherent response to the idealism and rationalism that permeated much of nineteenth-century philosophy: a response that was, naturally, conditioned by its time. Nevertheless, it has borne fruit in

---

117. Ker, *Biography*, 441.

118. *Dev*, 40 (emphasis added).

119. *LD*, xx 430 (1863).

different philosophical traditions, and some thinkers who subscribe to these traditions have claimed Newman as their own. Since Newman did not enter the philosophical discourse of his day but chose to remain on its periphery, his thought remains open to diverse—and sometimes contradictory—interpretations and adscriptions.

Regarding the interpretation of his works, Newman himself wrote in his *Philosophical Notebook*: "If there be a subject, in which one is removed from the temptation of writing for popularity etc., it is this, for if there is any thing at once new and good, years must elapse, the writer must be long dead, before it is acknowledged and received."[120] Pragmatism, phenomenology, and personalism have been identified as three currents of Newman's philosophical reception. Broadly speaking, at least in their origins, these traditions are grounded in realism and share a rejection of rationalism and the skepticism that results from it. They also have in common a vast fecundity that has generated several avenues of thought and several methods of investigation.[121]

William James, following Giovanni Papini (1881–1956), qualified pragmatism as a great corridor-theory, "a collection of attitudes and methods [...] like a corridor in a hotel, from which a hundred doors open into a hundred chambers."[122] Phenomenology is widely accepted as a method or style of thought, not as a philosophical school. One of its prominent historians, Herbert Spielberg (1904–1990), maintained that "it would go too far to say that there are as many phenomenologies as there are phenomenologists. But it is certainly true that, on closer inspection, the varieties exceed common features."[123] Regarding personalism, Jacques Maritain (1882–1973) stated that "there are, at least, a dozen personalist doctrines, which, at times, have

---

120. *PN*, 86.

121. Hochschild explains that "scholars have attempted to classify Newman's philosophy in relation to various familiar categories and figures in the history of philosophy. Classification is complicated by the fact that most of his writings are occasional and theological, rather than systematic and philosophical [...]. While Newman's thought is marked by both originality and eclecticism, it also displays a remarkable coherence, and a consistency over the course of his long life." Joshua Hochschild, "The Re-Imagined Aristotelianism of John Henry Newman," *Modern Age* 45, no. 4 (2003): 334.

122. William James, "G. Papini and the Pragmatist Movement in Italy," *Journal of Philosophy, Psychology and Scientific Methods* 3, no. 13 (1906): 339.

123. Herbert Spiegelberg, *The Phenomenological Movement, a Historical Introduction* (The Hague: Martinus Nijhoff, 1965), 1:xxvii.

nothing more in common that the term 'person.' "[124] Within the framework of this broad understanding, I will now discuss Newman's reception by these three philosophical currents.[125]

In a 1914 lecture devoted to Newman's philosophy, Wilfrid Ward (his first biographer) developed what he perceived to be Newman's connection with pragmatism. He said that Newman "traced lines afterwards included, though with some differences, in another modern theory—which has become known as pragmatism—a theory which estimates the significance of thought by its bearing on what is practical."[126] In this lecture, he quoted a letter from the Oxford pragmatist Ferdinand Schiller (1864–1937) in which Schiller wrote: "I recognise [...] that Newman was one of the forerunners and anticipators of pragmatism, and that he discovered in a quite original and independent manner the great discrepancy there is between the actual course of human reasoning and the description of it in the logical text-books."[127]

Ward proceeded to explain two confluences between Newman and pragmatism: the fact that Newman gave precedence to real assent over notional assent and the fact that he identified the ideas that relate to concrete realities and inform our actions as those that matter most: "We shall never have done beginning, if we determine to begin with proof. We shall ever be laying our foundations [...]. Life is for action. If we insist on proofs for every thing, we

124. Jacques Maritain, *The Person and the Common Good*, trans. John Fitzgerald (New York: Charles Scribner's Sons, 1947), 2–3.

125. This sketch compiles Newman's philosophical profile based on the work of others. In the genre of dissertations, Cyprus Mitchell wrote "Pragmatism in J. H. Cardinal Newman" (University of Missouri, 1913), and Reed Frey wrote "*Cor ad Cor Loquitur:* The Philosophical Personalism of J. H. Newman" (University of Pittsburg, 2015). Both John Cronin in his thesis "Cardinal Newman: His Theory of Knowledge" (The Catholic University of America, 1935) and Daniel Morris-Chapman in "Scepticism, Truth and Religious Belief in the Thought of J. H. Newman" (University of Bristol, 2014) analyzed Newman's reception by philosophical systems of the twentieth and twenty-first centuries. Finally, Laurence Richardson published his dissertation as *Newman's Approach to Knowledge* (2007) and linked Newman to phenomenology.

126. Ward, "Newman's Philosophy," 74.

127. Ward, "Newman's Philosophy," 86–87. Although Schiller was one of the main promoters of pragmatism in Europe in his time, his approach was substantially different from Peirce's realistic pragmatism. Nubiola maintains that some of the hostility towards pragmatism in Europe was caused by Schiller's arrogance and disdain for others. See Jaime Nubiola, "Pragmatism in the European Scene: The Heidelberg International Congress of Philosophy, 1908," *Rivista di Storia della Filosofia* 72, no. 3 (2017): 397.

shall never come to action: to act you must assume."[128] Ward also recognized some differences in their understanding; the main one being that, unlike James, Newman held that even if we do not fully comprehend a truth, it may have practical significance.

As Ward was preparing this lecture, Cyprus Mitchell was defending a thesis on the same topic at the University of Missouri. Although I do not share his interpretation of Newman's achievements, Mitchell's work is worth mentioning because he found in textual references sufficient basis for attempting a thesis on Newman's pragmatism. Twenty years later, in his doctoral thesis on Newman's theory of knowledge, James Cronin wrote that the resemblance between certain principles of Newman's philosophy and the central tenets of pragmatism has long been acknowledged. Although this might be an overstatement, he did show several connections.[129] Throughout his thesis, Cronin argued that all that is true in pragmatism can be found in Newman. To support this view, he quoted Walker's book *Theories of Knowledge*, published in 1911, where Walker asserted that there is scarcely a single doctrine upheld by pragmatists that is not found in *The Grammar of Assent*.[130]

The convergence between Newman and pragmatism that Mitchell and Cronin identify can be summarized in four points: the antagonism to individualistic epistemological systems, the dismissal of absolute claims made by logic, the centrality of the person in the reasoning process, and the emphasis on real ideas that lead to action. After acknowledging that many of the pragmatists' claims are found in the *Grammar*, Walker also identified that the value of truth is not its pragmatic value and that the method by which truth is attained does not signify its validity. He concluded by stating that Newman is not a pragmatist because his standpoint is psychological and human rather than philosophical.

There are very few twentieth-century studies that relate Newman and pragmatism; one is Nicola Abbagagnano's *Storia della Filosofia*, in which he

128. *GA*, 95.

129. Mitchell presents Newman as a rigid logician who despite his best efforts became the historical and logical father of the Modernists. See Cyprus Mitchell, "The Pragmatism of John Henry Cardinal Newman" (master's thesis, University of Missouri, 1913), 1; Cronin, "Newman's Theory of Knowledge," 115.

130. See Leslie Walker, *Theories of Knowledge* (London: Longmans, Green and Co., 1911), 648.

identifies Newman as the initiator of the philosophy of action, also known as pragmatism.[131] A plausible explanation for the lack of other studies is that the First World War revolutionized the European intellectual world, making pragmatism and idealism a thing of the past. Academic interest in the connection between Newman and pragmatism has, however, resurfaced in the last three decades.[132]

In a 1993 article devoted to Peirce's realism, Edward Oakes made a passing reference to the former's insistence that good morals and good reasoning go hand in hand: a thesis also maintained by Newman. Joan Fontrodona expounded on this connection a couple of years later. In 1995 Brian Cosgrove published a paper that seeks to present a viable alternative to postmodern skepticism based on the dissimilar, yet compatible, approaches of Newman and James. In 2012 Jaime Nubiola presented a paper on this topic. He explained how Whately's *Elements of Logic* was a foundational work for Newman and Peirce and examined the references that Peirce made to Newman. Nubiola concluded that Newman's and Peirce's views are quite similar because neither grounded his confidence in the self-sufficiency of the individual's reason and because both opposed the rationalistic individualism typical of modernity.[133]

Perhaps the most comprehensive recent study conducted on the parallels between Newman and pragmatism (specifically between Newman and Peirce) is that of Matthew Moore, who enumerated the points both philosophers have in common:

131. See Nicola Abbagnano, *Historia de la filosofía*, trans. Juan Estelrich and J. Pérez Ballestar (Barcelona: Hora, 1994), 3:374; Gabriel Alonso García, "J. H. Newman como autor filosófico," *Revista Española de Teología* 61, no. 4 (2001): 506.

132. Jay Newman mentioned three other authors who make this connection. After examining their texts, however, the resemblance seems remarkably loose. Jay Newman, *The Mental Philosophy of John Henry Newman* (Waterloo, Ont.: Wilfrid Laurier University Press, 1986), 28. In his thesis, Morris-Chapman mentioned thirteen authors who have discussed Newman's writings in relation to pragmatism. The relevant references are noted here. See Daniel Morris-Chapman, "Scepticism, Truth and Religious Belief in the Thought of John Henry Newman: A Contribution to Contemporary Debate" (PhD diss., University of Bristol, 2014), 34–35.

133. See Edward Oakes, "Discovering the American Aristotle," *First Things* 38, no. 12 (1993): 27; Joan Fontrodona, *Ciencia y práctica en la acción directiva* (Madrid: Rialp, 1999), 198–99; Brian Cosgrove, " 'We Cannot Do without a View' John Henry Newman, William James and the Case Against Scepticism," *Irish Theological Quarterly* 61, no. 1 (1995): 32–43; Nubiola, "Newman y Peirce."

They both write to oppose positivism; they both break away from modern philosophy and out of the critical problem; they both affirm philosophic realism; they both re-embody the intellect philosophically after its Cartesian philosophical disembodiment; [...] they both have theories of continuity/development that were articulated in response to evolution theories of the time; [...] both go beyond traditional logic by asserting some logical method of reasoning about singular facts and the concrete world; both develop theories of practical decision making by the personal, not subjective, interpretation of signs; both claim that the signs from which man reasons are in themselves only probable, not definitive, indicators, that require an interpretant.[134]

Newman's connection with pragmatism is the central theme of this project, and I will delve into it in the following chapter. These introductory remarks show that although Newman was framed as a forerunner of the pragmatic tradition soon after his death, study of this topic was short-lived and has only been revived in the past three decades. With the rise of the phenomenological method in the twentieth century, more philosophers have linked Newman to that current of thought.

The editor of Newman's *Philosophical Notebook* places him within the philosophical tradition of phenomenology, stating that he can be considered a forerunner of contemporary phenomenologists. The first person to connect Newman with phenomenology was likely Matthias Laos (1882–1965), the leading figure of Newman's reception in Germany in the first decade of the twentieth century. Jan Walgrave (1911–1986) stated in 1939 that Newman might have called his main work "The Phenomenology of Assent." Likewise, in his lengthy treatise on Newman's epistemology published in 1955, Adrian Boekraad maintained that although Newman lived long before phenomenology was developed, his method resembles phenomenology quite naturally.[135]

134. Matthew Moore, "Newman and Peirce on Practical Religious Certainty," in *Semiotics Yearbook* (New York: Semiotic Society of America, 2008), 48.

135. See Sillem, *Philosophical Notebook*, 127–28, 135; Jan Walgrave, *Newman the Theologian: The Nature of Belief and Doctrine as Exemplified in His Life and Works* (New York: Sheed & Ward, 1960), 73; Adrian Boekraad, *The Personal Conquest of Truth According to J. H. Newman* (Louvain: Nauwelaerts, 1955), 139. Boekraad's opinion is especially significant, because he concluded the edition of Newman's *Philosophical Notebook* after Sillem passed away.

In the introduction to the *Philosophical Readings in Cardinal Newman*, James Collins expounded upon the elements that Husserl's and Newman's methods have in common, and Edward Sillem did the same eight years later in his introduction to Newman's *Philosophical Notebook*. For his part Ian Ker wrote in the introduction to the *Grammar* that fruitful parallels can be drawn between his thought and phenomenology. Some contemporary scholars continue to study Newman in relation to phenomenology. Ono Ekeh wrote that an aspect of Newman's originality that has not been fully explored is his philosophical phenomenology, and Richardson's dissertation expounded on the similarities between Newman and phenomenology. Richardson concluded his study by stating that Newman's methodology can be identified as descriptive phenomenology. The editor's essay in the 2019 special issue of the *American Catholic Philosophical Quarterly* (which was dedicated to Newman's philosophy) noted that he can be considered a proto-phenomenologist.[136]

The connections between Newman and phenomenology are commonly accepted and have stood the test of time. However, their specifics vary depending on each author's understanding of phenomenology. Regarding the connection between Newman and particular phenomenologists, Morris-Chapman made a case for Newman's influence on Franz Brentano (1838–1937), who is widely accepted as a forerunner of phenomenology. In 1872 Brentano visited Newman at the Oratory and later described the *Grammar* as an interesting work.[137] The connection with Edmund Husserl (1859–1938) does not seem to be so direct, although Richardson recognizes a similarity in their philosophical development, and Jay Newman points out that there is a striking resemblance between their texts.[138]

136. See Collins, "Newman and Philosophy," 30–31; Sillem, *Philosophical Notebook*, 129; Ian Ker, introduction to *An Essay in Aid of a Grammar of Assent*, by John Henry Newman, ed. Ian Ker (Oxford: Clarendon Press, 1985), lv; Ono Ekeh, "The Phenomenological Context and Transcendentalism of John Henry Newman and Edmund Husserl," *Newman Studies Journal* 5, no. 1 (2008): 35; Richardson, *Newman's Approach to Knowledge*, 170; Crosby, "Newman and Philosophers Today," 14.

137. See Franz Brentano, *The Origin of the Knowledge of Right and Wrong*, trans. Cecil Hague (Westminster: Archival Constable & Co., 1889), 53. The first translation of the *Grammar* into German was done in 1921 by Theodor Haecker (1879–1945); as a result, Haecker converted to Catholicism.

138. See Richardson, *Newman's Approach to Knowledge*, 161; Jay Newman, *The Philosophy of Newman*, 24.

The resemblance between Newman's epistemology and phenomenology can be identified in four points. First, in opposition to empiricist theories, both Newman and the phenomenologists argue that knowledge is not limited to sense data. Second, both give a central place to the knowledge of concrete reality: Newman through his notion of real assent, and the phenomenologists through their motto, "to the things themselves." In the words of Newman: "I would confine myself to the truth of things, and to the mind's certitude of that truth."[139] The third similarity is their insistence that one must be willing to engage with and learn from reality. Newman considered things in their relation to our awareness of them and inferred that the perception of moral conscience implies the existence of a corresponding external object. Fourth, and finally, there is a close affinity between Newman's detailed description of mental acts and their objects, and the method of descriptive phenomenology.

Along with these similarities, some points of divergence must also be noted. Having begun his career in the realist camp, Husserl eventually fell into idealism. If Newman's method is to be considered phenomenological, then a firm grounding in reality must be guaranteed. In this regard, Newman did not accept Husserl's limitation to the intentional or formal object, nor did he accept the exclusion of the real material object as existent. However, like Husserl, Newman explored the correlation of the subjective and objective elements in the person's way of knowing, and his method was likewise subject to misrepresentation as psychologism.

Within the discussion of Newman's phenomenological method, Sillem gave a perceptive description of his philosophical project:

> Newman's method was designed to show that the life work of a philosopher is a persistent development and deepening of the personal knowledge he has of the things and people in the world around him. It was designed to bring his whole self into an ever closer touch with real things, so that he could enquire into their structure and mutual relations, and to do this he had to keep his mind clear from all forms of subjective "clouding." [...] Newman designed his method to enable him to apprehend and think of things for himself.[140]

---

139. *GA*, 344.
140. Sillem, *Philosophical Notebook*, 134.

For Newman, knowledge was more than reasoning; it was an actual possession of the known objects. This approach is known today as phenomenology, or perhaps more precisely, as Christian personalism. In a similar way, Crosby maintains that "Newman's personalism as it is found in the *Grammar*, in his teaching on conscience and on doctrinal development make me call him a proto-phenomenologist."[141] These lines serve as a fitting transition to the discussion of Newman's reception by the personalist tradition. More specific in focus, some expressions of personalism can be considered an offspring of the phenomenological method. Pointedly, Sillem argued that Newman's phenomenology led him to personalism and concluded the study of his philosophy by stating that Newman is the pioneer of a new philosophy of the person.[142]

Newman was connected to personalism as early as 1922. In *The Personalist* Edgar Brightman (1884–1953) commented that "personalism is an empirical method, aiming at practical certainty; Cardinal Newman's *Grammar of Assent* illustrates it."[143] Around that time, William Inge (1860–1954) wrote an essay for the *Edinburgh Review* in which he speaks of Newman's personalism. The French philosopher Emmanuel Mounier (1905–1950) also mentioned Newman among the pioneers of the personalist movement in England, and Jan Walgrave, a Dutch scholar, wrote that Newman's method resembled contemporary personalism.[144] These early studies not only show a similar understanding of Newman's philosophy but also its worldwide relevance.

Several contemporary scholars also consider Newman's personalism as a core characteristic of his philosophy. Mary K. Tillman develops it at length, and Avery Dulles speaks of Newman as the outstanding master of personalism in theological epistemology. In his discussion of Newman's philosophical relevance,

---

141. John Crosby, "The Philosophical Legacy of John Henry Newman," *American Catholic Philosophical Quarterly* 94, no. 1 (2019): 1.

142. See Sillem, *Philosophical Notebook*, 250.

143. Edgar Brightman, "The Use of the Word Personalism," *The Personalist* 3, no. 4 (1922): 257. The connection Brightman draws between personalism and pragmatism highlights the personal element in pragmatism: "In its logical use, the word 'personalism' is equivalent to the humanistic form of pragmatism for which not reason alone, but the whole personal life with all its needs, is the guide to truth. It is a reaction against the rigor and vigor of absolutism as well as against the vague excesses of mysticism." Brightman, "Personalism," 257.

144. See William Inge, "Cardinal Newman," in *Outspoken Essays* (London: Longmans, Green and Co., 1926), 204; Emmanuel Mounier, *Personalism* (London: Routledge, 1950), xx; Jan Walgrave, "The Rediscovery of Newman," *New Blackfriars* 49, no. 578 (1968): 519.

Michele Marchetto comments on the three qualities of the person developed by Romano Guardini (1885–1968) and anticipated by Newman: incommunicability, unrepeatability, and singularity. Most recently, John Crosby published a study titled *The Personalism of John Henry Newman* in which he calls Newman a grandfather of Christian personalism. Reed Frey concludes his thesis by stating that Newman is relevant to contemporary philosophy precisely because of his personalism.[145]

One of Newman's central theses in the *Grammar* is that "instead of saying, as logicians say, that [...] two men differ only in number, we ought, I repeat, rather to say [*sic*] that they differ from each other in all that they are, in identity, in incommunicability, in personality."[146] He expounds on this principle regarding each person's individuality:

> To be rational, to have speech, to pass through successive changes of mind and body from infancy to death, belong to man's nature; to have a particular history, to be married or single, to have children or to be childless, to live a given number of years, to have a certain constitution, moral temperament, intellectual outfit, mental formation, these and the like, taken altogether, are the accidents which make up our notion of a man's person, and are the ground-work or condition of his particular experiences.[147]

Newman's personalism is a natural reaction to rationalism, through which he sought to replace impersonal reason with the personal mind. He decried the fact that, cut off from its lifegiving roots in the individual, reason has come to represent the intellectual powers in their totality. For him, knowledge can only belong to the person; consequently, he developed a person-centered epistemology. His teaching on notional and real apprehension and the distinction he made between formal and informal inferences

---

145. See Mary K. Tillman, "The Personalist Epistemology of John Henry Newman," *Proceedings of the American Catholic Philosophical Association* 60 (1986): 236; Dulles, *John Henry Newman*, 45; Marchetto, "Philosophical Relevance of Newman," 325–26; John Crosby, *The Personalism of John Henry Newman* (Washington, D.C.: The Catholic University of America Press, 2014); Crosby, "Newman and Philosophers Today," 6; Reed Frey, "*Cor ad Cor Loquitur.* The Philosophical Personalism of John Henry Newman" (master's thesis, University of Pittsburgh, 2015), 66.

146. *GA*, 282.

147. *GA*, 240.

show his appreciation for the way the person actually reasons. These postulates, along with his understanding of conscience as a profoundly personal avenue to God, are characteristics of his personalist thought. In his 1839 sermon "The Individuality of the Soul," Newman expressed that

> every being in that great concourse is his own centre [...]. He has his own hopes and fears, desires, judgments, and aims; he is everything to himself, and no one else is really any thing. No one outside of him can really touch him, can touch his soul, his immortality; he must live with himself for ever. He has a depth within him unfathomable, an infinite abyss of existence; and the scene in which he bears part for the moment is but like a gleam of sunshine upon its surface.[148]

Well-grounded in realism, Newman's personalism did not lead him into subjectivism; he maintained that the individual's search for truth should be carried out within his intersubjectivity. Further, he gave personal relationships a privileged place in the apprehension and communication of truth. Regarding the apprehension of truth, he wrote, "Instead of devising, what cannot be, some sufficient science of reasoning which may compel certitude in concrete conclusions, [we ought] to confess that there is no ultimate test of truth besides the testimony born to truth by the mind itself."[149] Regarding its communication, he recognized that strong arguments and temporal powers are insufficient to uphold truth, but not personal influence.[150] As a corollary, the choice of his cardinal's motto towards the end of his life, *Cor ad Cor Loquitur*, is an eloquent expression of his personalist vein.

One of the first scholars who studied Newman's philosophy wrote in 1935 that "his philosophy was strange, not because it was false, but because it was truth seen in a new light."[151] The drama of Newman's thought lies in the fruitful tension between the objective and dogmatic and the subjective and personal. In Newman's own words, "One aspect of Revelation must not be allowed to exclude or to obscure another; and Christianity is dogmatical, devotional, practical all at once; it is esoteric and exoteric; it is indulgent and strict; it is light and dark; it is love, and it is fear."[152] What Newman says

148. *PS*, iv 82–83 (1839).
149. *GA*, 350.
150. See *US*, 91–92 (1832).
151. Cronin, "Newman's Theory of Knowledge," 142.
152. *Dev*, 36.

about Christianity can be well applied to his philosophy and its reception; his thought is so rich that it has informed diverse traditions, including pragmatism, phenomenology, and personalism.

The scope and originality of his work have led some to underestimate Newman's philosophical depth. He aimed to explore new grounds and to provide those that came after him not with definitive answers but with novel and challenging perspectives. In 1840 he confided to Mary Holmes (1815–1878):

> Be assured that I have my doubts and difficulties as other people. Perhaps the more we examine and investigate, the more we have to perplex us. It is the lot of man: the human mind in its present state is unequal to its own powers of apprehension; it embraces more than it can master. I think we ought all to set out on our inquiries, I am sure we shall end them, with this conviction.[153]

Newman understood that his analysis of how the individual reasons and comes to the truth was not absolute or infallible. His only intention was to move the conversation forward and aid particular individuals in their quest for the truth. This understanding gives us the key to his philosophy, anticipating to some degree contemporary philosophical doctrines. The introduction to the *Oxford Handbook of John Henry Newman* expresses that the research it contains "does not intend to protect [Newman's] legacy, but to examine his life, writings, thought and significance."[154] This is also the intention of the present investigation, for the specific theme of the affinities between Newman and the pragmatist tradition. My aim is to provide a plausible entry point to study and develop Newman's theory of knowledge, as well as a nuanced understanding of pragmatism as a tool for dialogue in today's world.

153. *LD*, vii 407 (1840).
154. Aquino and King, introduction to *The Oxford Handbook of John Henry Newman*, 1.

Chapter 3

Affinities between Newman and Pragmatism

Considering an account of pragmatism characterized by realism, anti-skepticism, fallibilism, and a commitment to keeping inquiry connected to real-life experience, I have shown that Newman's philosophy shares the three central claims pragmatists tend to uphold. This has opened the way to studying his thought in relation to this tradition and possibly establishing him as one of its forerunners. To continue developing Newman's philosophical principles and to show their relevance, this chapter will explore five further affinities between his claims and pragmatism.

It must be emphasized that to speak broadly of "pragmatism" or "pragmatist philosophers" could be an idle undertaking because from its beginnings through the present day, there has been no clear set of doctrines that unites all pragmatists. Pragmatism can, however, be described as a tradition of thought in which common themes reoccur and are explored using similar approaches. As I explained in the first chapter, an important presupposition for my research is the understanding that

> the centre of pragmatism's contribution to philosophy [lies] in the resources it finds in and develops from our social practices. Pragmatism challenges the often implicit assumption that our practices are necessarily inadequate and require backup from some standard or principle which lies beyond them. It does so while avoiding the kind of relativism or conservatism which holds that those practices are

beyond reform and improvement. For pragmatists, suggestions for improvements are themselves worked up from elements contained within those practices. In other words, pragmatism takes our lives, in all their richness as well as their deficiencies, seriously, and theorizes from that basis.[1]

In the discussion that follows, I will place some claims from pragmatist philosophers in dialogue with Newman and identify the affinities in their understandings. First, I will explain how Newman and the classical pragmatists are well acquainted with the methods of inquiry in the natural sciences, how they subscribe to a realist epistemology, and how they reconnect to the Aristotelian tradition—all of which helps them overcome a reductive conception of reason and open fresh avenues for the understanding of human knowledge. Second, I will discuss Newman's and Peirce's understanding of the unity of knowledge and explain that both place the human subjects who possess knowledge as the axis of their considerations.

Third, I will study the search for truth as a collective pursuit through time as yet another affinity between Newman and pragmatism: Newman placed great emphasis on the efficacy of individuals working together, balancing each other's views, and contributing to a common pursuit; for his part, Peirce held that truth can only be sought within a community of inquirers. Fourth, I will show how Newman and some pragmatist philosophers recognize the crucial role that doubt and error play in the pursuit of truth and how they see these as building blocks in the edifice of knowledge. In this regard, Newman maintained that truth can only be discovered through a laborious process of inquiry—a thesis that finds ample resonance in pragmatism.

Fifth, I will show the clear affinity between Newman's Illative Sense and Peirce's Abductive Reasoning. Both thinkers presented this faculty as innate to the individual, but that nevertheless requires training; they also acknowledged that both the Illative Sense and Abductive Reasoning show that the person's mind is naturally attuned to the truth. When Newman described the process of reasoning in his *University Sermons*, he explained that "one fact may suffice for a whole theory; one principle may create and sustain a system; one minute token is a clue to a large discovery."[2] This "minute token" Newman recognized can easily be identified with the spark that catalyzes

---

1.   Bacon, *Pragmatism*, 1.
2.   *US*, 256–57 (1840).

Peirce's Abduction by providing a plausible hypothesis for a surprising observation. Although the proposed hypothesis is often right, Newman and Peirce acknowledge that certitude does not follow from these modes of inference and their conclusions but must be tested by the wider community and framed within the unity of knowledge.

My objective in discussing these affinities is not to make a detailed analysis of the pragmatists who hold each of these claims and those who do not, but to use these claims as a foil to illustrate Newman's philosophical outlook. This will enrich the understanding of the philosophical resources that can be found in both pragmatism and in Newman's philosophy.

Grounding in the Aristotelian Tradition

Newman and pragmatist philosophers subscribe to a realist epistemology (although they do so with different nuances) and have a strong appreciation for the method of inquiry in the natural sciences.[3] In similar ways, both of them overcome modern rationalism and its accompanying skepticism, and open fresh avenues for knowledge, belief, justification, inquiry, and truth by reconnecting with the Aristotelian tradition.

Peirce's realism has been the subject of much debate. While some speak of his battle for realism and maintain that he was a realist throughout his life, a more balanced approach sees his intellectual trajectory as a process of maturing towards realism, since it is seldom questioned that his later writings are developed within a realist framework. His realism was characterized by a markedly anti-Cartesian understanding of knowledge, science, and reality. He believed that knowledge must begin in experience: experience understood as that which individuals gather when confronted with reality. Peirce built his pragmatism

---

3.   In this context, realism is understood as a direction: "To assert that something is somehow mind-independent is to move in the realist direction; to deny it is to move in the opposite direction." Timothy Williamson, "Realism and Anti-Realism," in *The Oxford Companion to Philosophy*, ed. Ted Honderich (Oxford: Oxford University Press, 2005), 1808. For a detailed description of Peirce's realism, see Sara Barrena and Jaime Nubiola, "Una Introducción a Charles S. Peirce," in *Charles S. Peirce (1839–1914): Un pensador para el siglo XXI* (Pamplona: EUNSA, 2013), 31–32; Fred Michael, "Two Forms of Scholastic Realism in Peirce's Philosophy," *Transactions of the Charles S. Peirce Society* 24, no. 3 (1988): 317; Jaime Nubiola, "Peirce on Complexity," in *Sign Processes in Complex Systems* (Dresden: Thelem, 2001), 12; Michael Raposa, *Peirce's Philosophy of Religion* (Bloomington: Indiana University Press, 1989), 16.

around the practice of inquiry; his pragmatic maxim has a distinctive realist character, as it turns to the effects of a concept to ascertain its meaning: "To develop [a thought's] meaning, we have simply to determine what habits it produces, for what a thing means is simply what habits it involves."[4]

In his search for a method to discern truth, Peirce recognized four approaches to investigation: tenacity, authority, a priori beliefs, and science. He argued that when confronted with doubt, the only method that yields satisfactory results and can withstand the test of ongoing experience is that of science. By upholding the scientific method, Peirce elucidated the commitments regarding what constitutes proper inquiry and set its boundaries, being careful not to overextend the reach of science and its application.

Peircean inquiry is framed as a response to a genuine doubt, and thus it is connected to all previous knowledge. Its fundamental premise is its relation to reality, which Peirce understood as follows:

> There are Real things, whose characters are entirely independent of our opinions about them; those Reals affect our senses according to regular laws, and, though our sensations are as different as our relations to the objects, yet, by taking advantage of the laws of perception, we can ascertain by reasoning how things really and truly are; and any man, if he have sufficient experience and he reason enough about it, will be led to the one True conclusion.[5]

As can be seen, Peirce not only manifested a realist orientation but explicitly upheld it. In one of his later papers, "Issues of Pragmaticism," he named the doctrines of critical common-sensism and scholastic realism as two essential consequences of pragmatism.

James also upheld realism as a characteristic of pragmatism. Putnam described him as "the first philosopher to present a completely worked out version of direct realism in the entire history of modern philosophy."[6] Although James' philosophical insights are often considered in contraposition to realism, towards the end of his life he explicitly stated that he was a natural realist and complained of being misread.[7] Further, James believed

4.   Peirce, *Collected Papers*, 5.400 (1878).

5.   Peirce, *Collected Papers*, 5.384 (1877).

6.   Hilary Putnam, "Pragmatism and Realism," *Cardozo Law Review* 18, no. 1 (1996): 153.

7.   See William James, *The Letters of William James*, ed. Henry James (London: Longmans, Green and Co., 1920), 2:241.

that the ordinary ways of thinking and talking about our perceptions should be taken seriously in philosophy. He rejected the subject-object split proper to Cartesian metaphysics, understood the world to be experienceable, and connected the possibility of authentic knowledge with the need for action: a connection that Newman made half a century earlier. Putnam argued that James, perhaps unaware that he was doing so, thought of perception in an Aristotelian way because he answered skeptical doubts by appealing to tests that in fact work in everyday experience. Putnam noted that this is common among pragmatist philosophers.

Once again, the connection of pragmatism to real-life experience is evidenced as a way to justify its validity. Putnam acknowledged that James led him to appreciate the fundamental importance of realism, which became a central concept in his philosophical career. At first, Putnam upheld a metaphysical realism, then he embraced an internal realism, and finally he described his position as natural or common-sense realism. Through these developments, his rejection of cultural relativism remained constant. Although he did not study Newman's work at length, Putnam recognized him as a careful and responsible thinker and held him up as an example of an intellectually virtuous man.[8]

It is widely accepted that Aristotle played a significant role in the development of Newman's philosophy. Although Newman acknowledged that his mind was formed and disciplined by the study of Aristotle's works, the extent of this influence is up for debate. While Copleston states that nobody would call Newman an Aristotelian, Sillem identifies Aristotle as the most significant influence in Newman's thought.

Newman's admiration for Aristotle spanned his whole life. Thomas Short (1789–1879) started Newman's education in 1817 with lectures on Aristotle's *Rhetoric*. In 1820, Newman shared with his aunt Elizabeth that his principal amusement was the study of Aristotle: "The truth is that of late months, I have been so exclusively ranging the paths of philosophy that I find it very difficulty [*sic*] to descend into the ways of common conversation."[9] The paths of philosophy he was ranging were Aristotle's *Logic*, *Rhetoric,* and *Ethics.*

Once a Fellow at Oriel, Newman was fully engaged in the revival of Aristotelian philosophy, seeking to restore its centrality in university studies.

---

8.   See Hilary Putnam, *Reason, Truth and History* (Cambridge: Cambridge University Press, 1981), 163.

9.   *LD,* i 98 (1820).

His first publications included an essay on Aristotle's *Poetics* and a few articles on Aristotle's philosophy for Whately's *Elements of Logic*. As a tutor, Newman expressed concern that Aristotle may be excluded from the curriculum if the college's government changed. Later in life, he would use Aristotle as a compass for his work. The *Oxford University Sermons, The Idea of a University,* and *The Grammar of Assent* include eloquent tributes to Aristotle.[10] However, Aristotle's influence on Newman is better assessed, not through the consideration of his praises, but through a study of the Aristotelian concepts further developed by Newman; those he overcame should also be considered.

What Newman acquired from Aristotle was a frame of mind or a method. This frame of mind is manifested primarily in Newman's firm grounding in philosophical realism. Like Aristotle, Newman considered our experience of reality as the source from which all knowledge is derived. In the twelfth of his *University Sermons,* he invited his listeners to "take things as we find them: let us not attempt to distort them into what they are not. True philosophy deals with facts. We cannot make facts. All our wishing cannot change them. We must use them."[11] Moreover, Newman considered reality not only as the starting point for knowledge, but also as its goal or objective.

In 1840 Newman credited Aristotle with having provided "the boldest, simplest, and most comprehensive theory which has been invented for the analysis of the reasoning process."[12] Newman, like Aristotle, considered knowledge to be the perfection of man. In the same vein, he explained the exercise of philosophy as

> a thinking of things in and through personal experience which makes them live as they ought to live in the very depths of the mind; [...] an intellectual living with realities, which ought to penetrate beneath the surface of the mind, and, as personal possessions, become the sources and principles of our thinking, while remaining the objects we experience as independent realities.[13]

In this text, Newman acknowledged the existence of reality as independent of the mind and the possibility of the intellect to know reality.

10. The *Grammar* can be cited as an example: "As to the intellectual position from which I have contemplated the subject, Aristotle has been my master." *GA,* 430.

11. *US,* 231 (1839).

12. *US,* 258 (1840).

13. Sillem, *Philosophical Notebook,* 11–12.

A central characteristic of Newman's philosophical outlook, which brings him close to pragmatism, is its connection with action, that is, with "conceivable effects." He repeatedly insisted on the need to realize what we think, write, or say and declared, "We shall never have done beginning, if we determine to begin with proof [...] Life is for action."[14] With these nuances, Newman presented knowledge as a personal possession that transforms the knower. Being a pragmatic man, he believed that ideas must have practical consequences. His journey from the Anglican Church to the Catholic Church provides testimony for this.

Another characteristic of Newman's philosophy is his epistemological realism. In his sermon "On the Nature of Faith in Relation to Reason" he developed this realism as follows:

> We are surrounded by beings which exist quite independently of us, exist whether we exist, or cease to exist, whether we have cognizance of them or no. [...] Of the material [beings] we have direct knowledge through the senses; we are sensible of the existence of persons and things, of their properties and modes, of their relations towards each other, and the courses of action which they carry on. [...] The senses, then, are the only instruments which we know to be granted to us for direct and immediate acquaintance with things external to us. Moreover, it is obvious that even our senses convey us but a little way out of ourselves, and introduce us to the external world only under circumstances, under conditions of time and place, and of certain media through which they act. [...] Now, Reason is that faculty of the mind by which this deficiency is supplied; by which knowledge of things external to us, of beings, facts, and events, is attained beyond the range of sense.[15]

Although Newman is grounded in an Aristotelian frame of mind characterized by realism, he did not develop a philosophy of being as the scholastics

---

14. *DA*, 295; *GA*, 95. When Newman spoke of "realizing" he was referring to the assimilation and fruition of ideas in concrete realities. He understood the person "primarily as a being that realizes itself through conscientious moral action within the framework of a history that is inevitably—even necessarily—ambiguous." Terrence Merrigan, "Conscience and Selfhood: Thomas More, John Henry Newman, and the Crisis of the Postmodern Subject," *Theological Studies* 73, no. 4 (2012): 841–42.

15. *US*, 205–6 (1839).

did, but a philosophy of mind understood as the power of knowing existent beings.[16] His attention to the operations of the mind, his understanding of the mind as personal reason, and his preference for real over notional assent has led some scholars to describe him as a nominalist. However, many others have disproved these claims, and the most common designation ascribed to him is that of a moderate realist. In contemporary categories, Newman's epistemological position could be labeled as a nuanced critical common-sensism because he understood that concepts provide knowledge that is poor and notional and should be complemented with knowledge of the concrete and singular for real assent to be possible.[17]

Had Newman known of Peirce's insights into the method of science, he would likely have offered his approval, as he believed that science yields true, relevant, and necessary knowledge. In the first of his *University Sermons*, he urged his listeners not "to feel jealous and appear timid, on witnessing the enlargement of scientific knowledge."[18] In the University of Dublin, he promoted the advancement of all the sciences, insisting they should follow their proper methodologies. Moreover, he believed that what enables assent to be real is personal experience.

The view that "knowledge is capable of being its own end,"[19] a central thesis in Newman's discourses on university education, is reminiscent of Aristotle's *Metaphysics* where he speaks of understanding and knowledge pursued for their own sake. Further, Newman relied heavily on Aristotle as he envisioned the unity and universality of knowledge for the curriculum of the University of Dublin. Specifically, his explanation of how different sciences require their proper methodology and shape the human mind in their particular way is based on Aristotle's principles. Newman also applied to knowledge Aristotle's distinction between useful and liberal possessions and made it the core of his conception of a liberal education.

Further, Newman built upon Aristotle's thought through the importance he gave to allowing oneself to be guided by others' experience in their fields of

16.   When Newman was asked about the compatibility between his doctrine in the *Grammar* and scholasticism, he replied, "All I can say is I have no suspicion, and do not anticipate, that I shall be found in substance to disagree with St. Thomas." *LD*, xxviii 431 (1878).

17.   See Sillem, *Philosophical Notebook*, 108; Ker, "Newman's Standing as a Philosopher," 72; Charles Dessain, "Cardinal Newman on the Theory and Practice of Knowledge," *The Downside Review* 75, no. 239 (1957): 8–18.

18.   *US*, 4 (1826).

19.   *Idea*, 103.

knowledge. After citing what Aristotle said in this regard, Newman affirmed that "instead of trusting logical science, we must trust persons, namely, those who by long acquaintance with their subject have a right to judge. And if we wish ourselves to share in their convictions and the grounds of them, we must follow their history, and learn as they have learned."[20] Both Aristotle and Newman upheld social transmission and tested experience as central elements in their theories of knowledge. They also shared a nuanced skepticism of the individual assumptions that provide the foundation to reasoning.

These principles are unified by Newman in one of his most original contributions: the Illative Sense. To function correctly, the Illative Sense needs to bring forth implicit knowledge from diverse disciplines and to be adjusted within a community of educated individuals. When introducing these characteristics of the Illative Sense, Newman referred to Aristotle's *phronesis*, explaining that as *phronesis* guides the mind in matters of conduct, the Illative Sense guides it in matters of reason.[21]

As it can be seen through this set of topics, there is much evidence to believe that Aristotle gave Newman the basic themes and direction for many of his works. In a text where Newman discussed these topics, he concluded categorically:

> While the world lasts, will Aristotle's doctrine on these matters last, for he is the oracle of nature and of truth. While we are men, we cannot help, to a great extent, being Aristotelians, for the great Master does but analyze the thoughts, feelings, views, and opinions of human kind. He has told us the meaning of our own words and ideas, before we were born. In many subject-matters, to think correctly, is to think like Aristotle; and we are his disciples whether we will or no, though we may not know it.[22]

20. *GA*, 341–42.

21. The analogy between Newman's Illative Sense and Aristotle's *phronesis* has been widely studied. See Frederick Aquino, "Cultivating Personal Judgement," in *Communities of Informed Judgment: Newman's Illative Sense and Accounts of Rationality* (Washington, D.C.: The Catholic University of America Press, 2004), 48–94; Andrew Meszaros, "The Influence of Aristotelian Rhetoric on J. H. Newman's Epistemology," *Journal for the History of Modern Theology* 20, no. 2 (2013): 192–225; Laurence Richardson, "The Illative Sense," in *Newman's Approach to Knowledge*, 121–26; Gerard Verbeke, "Aristotelian Roots of Newman's Illative Sense," in *Newman and Gladstone Centennial Essays*, ed. James Bastable (Dublin: Veritas Publications, 1978), 177–95.

22. *Idea*, 109–10.

Newman not only built upon Aristotle's philosophy; he left it behind when he considered it too narrow for his purposes. Two aspects can be identified in Newman's dissatisfaction with Aristotle. In the context of his study of the Arian heresies, desiring to uphold his sacramental view of the world, Newman rejected the view that individuals have no intellectual knowledge of particular material things. In his book *The Arians of the Fourth Century* he wrote, "That philosopher's [Aristotle's] logical system confessedly is to baffle an adversary, or at most to detect error, rather than to establish truth."[23] Moreover, in his most mature work on knowledge, *The Grammar of Assent*, he criticized Aristotle for what he considered to be his rather narrow view on reasoning, writing that "in spite of Aristotle, I will not allow that genuine reasoning is an instrumental art."[24] He acknowledged that the reasoning process is not as simple as following a logical rule. This is the context in which he introduced the Illative Sense.[25]

A second subject on which Newman diverted from Aristotle is the importance he ascribed to metaphysics. In the philosophical climate of the University of Oxford of his day, metaphysics had negative notoriety, being unduly associated with Kantian idealism and considered entirely unverifiable. This conception led Newman to write in 1885, "My turn of mind has never led me towards metaphysics; rather it has been logical, ethical, practical."[26] Moreover, after a few years, he abandoned his project of writing a book he had titled *Discursive Enquiries on Metaphysical Subject*, leaving some notes behind, but not his complete thought. Rather than concluding that Newman disagreed with Aristotle in his metaphysical principles, it would be more accurate to say that he did not give them the attention they deserved.

After this exploration of the grounding of Newman and pragmatism in the philosophy of Aristotle, Newman's description of what it means to be "a

23.   John Henry Newman, *The Arians of the Fourth Century* (London: Longmans, Green and Co., 1908), 29.

24.   *GA*, 338.

25.   In his entry on Aristotle, Copleston expresses that it is unjustifiable to claim that his analysis of the reasoning process is complete. To illustrate his point he refers to Newman, saying that "for instance, [Aristotle] did not consider that other form of inference discussed by Cardinal Newman in his *Grammar of Assent*, when the mind derives conclusions, not from certain propositions but from certain concrete facts." Copleston, *A History of Philosophy*, 1:284.

26.   John Henry Newman, *Stray Essays on Controversial Points* (printed by the author, 1890), 94.

learned Aristotelian" provides a suitable conclusion: "A learned Aristotelian, is one who can answer any whatever [*sic*] philosophical questions in the way that Aristotle would have answered them. If they are questions which could not occur in Aristotle's age, he still answers them; and by two means, by the instinct which a thorough Aristotelic intellect, the habit set up in his mind, possesses; next, by never-swerving processes of ratiocination."[27] With this definition as a frame of reference, one can safely assert that both Peirce and Newman were learned Aristotelians.

Interest in the Unity of Knowledge

A second affinity between Newman and pragmatism is their recognition that individuals desire a reasonable integration of the different aspects of reality. They also hold a similar understanding of the unity of knowledge. When dealing with the notion of unity, Newman often spoke of knowledge, while Peirce and Dewey referred to science. However, the analysis of their texts shows a shared understanding and similar approaches. Further, they considered as the axis of their understanding the human subjects who possess knowledge or advance science, and from this perspective, they spoke of the unity of knowledge as something possible and desirable while respecting the inherent characteristics of each science.

James, for his part, wrote that "what our intellect really aims at is neither variety nor unity taken singly, but totality."[28] This is reminiscent of Newman, who believed that knowledge entails a synthesis. He wrote, "In knowledge, we begin with wholes, not with parts. We see the landscape, or the mountain, or the sky. [...] Then we take to pieces, or take aspects of, this general & vague object, which is before us. The idea of unity is prior to the idea of wholeness or totality. The idea of wholeness to the idea of partness."[29]

When speaking of the unity of science, Newman and the classical pragmatists saw it as a dynamic reality that emerges within each individual as he grows in knowledge, especially when he does so within a community. They maintained that the synthesis of the sciences is only adequately achieved through free discussion among experts. In this context, the foundational

27. John Henry Newman, *Theological Papers of John Henry Newman on Biblical Inspiration and on Infallibility*, ed. Derek Holmes (Oxford: Oxford University Press, 1979), 156–57.

28. James, *Pragmatism*, 130.

29. *PN*, 8. A similar description can be found in *Idea*, 331.

principle shared by Newman and Peirce entails an empirical approach to the world based on the methods of the natural sciences and an emphasis on the continuity between human nature and physical nature. Peirce's formal education in chemistry and his thirty years of research in mathematics and astronomy inspired him to find the connections between the various kinds of scientific inquiry. He rigorously observed and recorded physical phenomena; however, he held that these observations in themselves do not constitute science. He thought that something else was needed for science to develop: the knowledge of the relations among isolated facts, which reveals the unity among them. He described a scientist as someone "who has become deeply impressed with the efficacy of minute and thorough observations [...]. Science then may be defined as the business whose ultimate aim is to educe the truth by means of close observation."[30]

With a similar argumentation to Newman's, Peirce recognized the intellect's tendency towards unity and wrote that "reasonableness consists in association, assimilation, generalization, the bringing of items together into an organic whole."[31] The thousands of observations he recorded during his investigations only acquired meaning as parts of a whole, which was not limited to one specific branch of science or area of study. This is why Peirce maintained that a scientist "needs to be more than a mere specialist; he needs such a general training of his mind, and such knowledge as shall show him how to make his powers most effective in a new direction."[32] This understanding led him to develop the notion of Abductive Reasoning.

As a means for a general training of the mind, Peirce made several attempts to develop a classification of the sciences. He wanted to elicit a system that reflected an organic whole in which sciences fit together, and he built it upon Auguste Comte's (1798–1857) work. Like Comte, Peirce understood each science as a historical development. He sought an alternative to Comte's "ladder system," in which each science obtained its

<hr>

30.   Charles S. Peirce, *Historical Perspectives on Peirce's Logic of Science: A History of Science*, ed. Carolyn Eisele (Berlin: Mouton, 1985), 2:1123 (1898).

31.   Charles S. Peirce, "Review of Clark University, 1889–1899. Decennial Celebration," *Science* 11, no. 277 (1900): 621. In the *Idea* Newman states, "We know, not by a direct and simple vision, not at a glance, but, as it were, by piecemeal and accumulation, by a mental process, by going round an object, by the comparison, the combination, the mutual correction, the continual adaptation, of many partial notions, by the employment, concentration, and joint action of many faculties and exercises of mind." *Idea*, 151.

32.   Peirce, *Historical Perspectives*, 2:942–43 (1882).

principles from the discoveries of the more abstract sciences located in the higher rungs while all press upwards and strive to become more abstract. He opted for a tree-like scheme of dependence among the sciences, in which they relate to one another as branches, and thus express their mutual bearings:

> In order to make it useful I wished it to be a natural classification, that is, I wished it to embody the chief facts of relationship between the sciences so far as they present themselves to scientific and observational study. [...] My notion is that what we call "natural classification" is, from the nature of things limited to natural objects. [...] What is a science, as a natural object? It is the actual living occupation of an actual group of living men. It is in that sense only that I presume to attempt any classification of the sciences.[33]

One of the elements Peirce chose to distinguish each science from the others is its means of observation or, more broadly stated, its method of research, as he believed that a natural classification of the sciences must exhibit the living relations between the different branches of the tree of knowledge. This shows that Peirce saw the classification of the sciences as a means to further their connections and harmony, not as a way of driving them in different directions. Moreover, Peirce gave significant recognition to the community of inquirers as the determining factor that holds a science together. He understood that what unites a group of scientists, and ultimately compounds a science, is the familiarity of the researchers with a common methodology and their capacity to communicate with one another. He explained that scientists

> spend their lives in finding out similar kinds of truth about similar things [and] understand what one another are about better than outsiders do. They are all familiar with words which others do not know the exact meaning of, they appreciate each other's difficulties and consult one another about them. They love the same sort of things. They consort together and consider one another as brethren. They are said to pursue the same *branch* of science.[34]

33. Peirce, "Adirondack Summer School Lectures" (MS 1334, 1905), pp. 9–11, The Charles S. Peirce Papers.

34. Peirce, *Historical Perspectives*, 2:804–5 (1904).

Therefore, in Peirce's understanding, a branch of science is not determined by the relationships among topics of study but by the relationships among researchers and their views.

The association of scientists is of central importance for Peirce because he understood science as a cross-disciplinary process in which new knowledge is produced by communication. As Peirce envisioned it, communication involves the effort to share one's discoveries in a language that is accessible to nonspecialized inquirers and to place oneself outside one's realm of expertise, with willingness to be enriched by individuals with diverse backgrounds. However, Peirce did not advocate for a unified line of research. Rather, he argued that when researchers have a variety of interests, a well-rounded understanding of the relationship between the sciences proves to be very useful because it helps them understand that

> their studies must be so closely allied that any one of them could take up the problem of any other after some months of special preparation and [...] each should understand pretty minutely what it is that each one of the other's work consists in; [...] any two of them meeting together shall be thoroughly conversant with each other's ideas and the language [each one] talks and should feel each other to be brethren.[35]

It is through this exchange of discoveries that the different branches of science develop and strengthen one another. Their exchange of findings and quandaries does not lead to their assimilation into one another but is meant to have the opposite effect: their individual strengthening. The aim of collaboration is not the unity of the sciences in themselves but the unity of the scientists as inquirers into the truth. Jaime Nubiola comments that Peirce's view on the unity of science is quite relevant to the contemporary understanding of its nature because it "shifts the emphasis of the discussion from the view of sciences as objects to be classified towards the lives of real men and women involved in scientific research. Indeed, in Peirce's view, the sciences of discovery are to be identified with the lives of their practitioners."[36]

---

35. Peirce, "Adirondack Summer School Lectures," 1905 (MS 1334, 1905), pp. 13–14, The Charles S. Peirce Papers.

36. Jaime Nubiola, "The Classification of the Sciences and Cross-Disciplinarity," *Transactions of the Charles S. Peirce Society* 41, no. 2 (2005): 276.

James also paid attention to these themes. He dedicated his fourth lecture on pragmatism to the topic of unity. As has been quoted, in its introductory lines he noted that "what our intellect really aims at is neither variety nor unity taken singly, but *totality*. In this, acquaintance with reality's diversities is as important as understanding their connexion."[37] James' insight on the diversifying elements among the sciences being as important as their connections is central to Newman's arguments in this topic. He further analyzed different aspects of unity and recognized that it is only possible when "manyness" or diversity is presupposed and accounted for, arguing that unity does not lead to uniformity but to pluralism. He stated that in pragmatism, a "hypothesis of a world imperfectly unified still, and perhaps always to remain so, must be sincerely entertained. This [...] hypothesis is pluralism's doctrine."[38]

These themes were developed by Newman in a similar way. The unity of knowledge and the relations among the sciences are topics that run through his discourses on university education; he also deals with these topics in the *University Sermons* and the *Grammar*, identifying the quest for comprehensiveness as a central need of the person: "General love of order, congruity, and symmetry [...] that very desire of arranging and adjusting [...] must, in its essence, be considered, if anything is considered, [as] an original principle of human nature."[39] Time and again he circled back to the principle of organic development and wrote that only "by piecemeal and accumulation, by a mental process, by going round an object, by the comparison, the combination, the mutual correction, the continual adaptation of many partial notions" can reality be apprehended.[40]

Newman shared the assumptions of the British naturalists who maintained the existence of a connection among all existing things and of general laws that guide them. This unity of law and existence implies that knowledge of one aspect of reality is a legitimate means for knowledge of other aspects. Newman explained that "if we may justly regard the universe, according to the meaning of the word, as one whole, we may also believe justly that to know one part of it is necessarily to know much more than that one part."[41] He upheld the notions of unity and wholeness as conditions for the enlargement

37.   James, *Pragmatism*, 130.
38.   James, *Pragmatism*, 161.
39.   *US*, 108 (1832).
40.   *Idea*, 38.
41.   *GA*, 260.

of the mind, arguing that without them, the result achieved through gathering new information would be shallowness, not enlargement and criticized those who ignore a unified vision of reality:

> They conceive that they profess just the truth which makes all things easy. They have their one idea or their favourite notion, which occurs to them on every occasion. They have their one or two topics, which they are continually obtruding, with a sort of pedantry, being unable to discuss, in a natural unconstrained way [...]. Perhaps they have discovered, as they think, the leading idea, or simple view [...] and they insist upon this or that isolated tenet, selected by themselves or by others not better qualified.[42]

Like Peirce, who based his research on minute observations aware that they would lead him to the truth, Newman understood the value of each particular observation, piece of data, or fact, and explained how all of them ought to be fit together in the individual's quest for truth. For Newman, truth was necessarily an organic affair in which different aspects of reality could not be apprehended apart from their relationship to one another:

> Truth means facts and their relations [...]. All that exists, as contemplated by the human mind, forms one large system or complex fact, and this of course resolves itself into an indefinite number of particular facts, which, as being portions of a whole, have countless relations of every kind, one towards another. Knowledge is the apprehension of these facts, whether in themselves, or in their mutual positions and bearings.[43]

In a similar way to Peirce, who understood reasonableness to be the operation that brings together several items into an organic whole, Newman believed that the quest for a comprehensive view of reality is not only natural but necessary, and as such, an end in itself. Then, for Newman, comprehensiveness was not an accidental aspect of knowledge; rather, it was essential and required intentionality and training. In this process, one must make a special effort to understand how a newly discovered truth coheres with

---

42.   *US*, 306 (1841). See also *Idea*, 142.
43.   *Idea*, 45.

previously held truths, as there is a strong tendency to assert the former at the expense of tradition, thus hindering the advancement of knowledge. In this regard, Newman described a genuinely great intellect as "one which takes a connected view of old and new, past and present, far and near, and which has an insight into the influence of all these one on another; without which there is no whole, and no centre. It possesses the knowledge, not only of things, but also of their mutual and true relations."[44]

According to Newman, sciences can only develop within this web of relations because they are nothing other than partial and incomplete perspectives of the one whole. From this angle, the centrality that he gave to the relational aspect among the different branches of science is duly understood. He sought a comprehensive view of all branches of truth, of the relations and mutual bearings between the different sciences, and of their proper values as an indispensable condition for the person to grow in her knowledge of reality. Since reality is multifaceted, a plurality of sciences is necessary to properly engage with it, because no science can adequately deal with the whole array of perspectives from which an object should be studied. These considerations provide an adequate context for Newman's definition of science: "These various partial views or abstractions, by means of which the mind looks out upon its object, are called sciences, and embrace respectively larger or smaller portions of the field of knowledge [...]. Now these views or sciences [...] *have far more to do with the relations of things than with things themselves.* They tell us what things are, only or principally by telling us their relations."[45]

Since sciences are partial views, and therefore incomplete in themselves, they need external assistance from one another. The connected view of the whole is precisely what affords sciences their truth and efficacy; this is why in his *Idea* Newman vigorously advocated for sciences to be presented as a whole in their relation to one another. If one science is omitted, "you cannot keep its place vacant for it; that science is forgotten; the other sciences close up, or, in other words, they exceed their proper bounds, and intrude where they have no right."[46] Newman was deeply persuaded that "a science which exceeds its limits falls into error," since "almost every statement [it pronounces] is perverted and made false, because it is not the

44. *Idea*, 134.
45. *Idea*, 46 (emphasis added).
46. *Idea*, 73.

whole truth."[47] As Peirce chose and developed the classical metaphor of the tree of knowledge, Newman spoke of a circle of universal science to imply interdependence—not subordination—among the sciences.

In his lecture "Christianity and Scientific Investigation," Newman argued that knowledge is gained from a synthesis of the sciences. He advocated for free discussion as a suitable means for progress in knowledge and stated that the investigator should be free, independent, and unshackled in his movements. Only in the free interchange among scholars of different disciplines does "a breadth and spaciousness of thought [come forth], in which lines, seemingly parallel may converge at leisure and principles, recognized as incommensurable, may be safely antagonistic."[48] For Newman, the ideal of knowledge entailed a comprehensiveness of view that sees the universal in each particular and holds in tensile unity the whole body of sometimes conflicting views about those particulars.

The best setting for achieving this is the university, where different disciplines are taught and explored by professors and students united by a common desire for truth. Peirce's and Newman's understandings of the unity of knowledge, or the unity of the sciences, depicts one more point of affinity between Newman and pragmatism and provides a common ground for the development of their theories of knowledge.

The Search for Truth as a Collective Pursuit through Time

Pragmatists hold that intellectual achievement is not an individualist endeavor but the result of complex conversations within a community of the living and the dead; this was also Newman's conception of intellectual development. He engaged in this conversation from the beginning of his career at Trinity College. A few years later, he found excellent interlocutors in the Fathers of the Church, who preceded him by a millennium, and in his contemporaries, remaining an active participant in this conversation until the end of his life. Although Newman believed that knowledge is a personal possession, he saw an assemblage of learned scholars as the best setting for its achievement. This is yet another way Newman and pragmatists attempt to overcome modern rationalism, which is characterized by isolation and a lack of continuity.

47. *Idea,* 74, 200.
48. *Idea,* 460.

Descartes identified certainty as residing within the individual conscious-ness and made the criteria for its attainment private rather than collective. He enthroned the individual as the final judge of truth and opposed any reliance on tradition and authority. From the beginning of his career, Peirce chal-lenged the individualistic spirit of Cartesianism and established the notion of community as a central element in his pragmatic proposal. He saw the cogni-tive community as a way out of the false dilemma that there are two mutually exclusive epistemic alternatives: dogmatism and skepticism.

Peirce did not forsake the possibility of truth; rather, he detailed the conditions for its attainment. He approached it as a community enterprise open to revision and maintained through time. He understood that "truth and reality, though independent of any individual, are defined in terms of the long-run agreement of the whole community of inquirers."[49] Peirce did not bind truth to a particular inquirer; thus, neither did he unbind it from inquiry itself, but firmly grounded it in collective inquiry.

In a 1982 paper, Susan Haack makes a succinct and helpful comparison between Descartes' and Peirce's epistemologies, which is worth reproducing with some modifications to highlight my line of argumentation.[50]

DESCARTES	*PEIRCE*
1. Method of radical doubt	Method of radical doubt is impossible: doubt is not voluntary; it requires specific reasons and must be grounded in current beliefs
2. Individualistic	Community-oriented
Rejection of tradition and authority	Truth is discovered through intersubjective agreement
Certainty of self-consciousness	Self-consciousness is gauged through interactions with others
3. Dogmatism and quest for certainty	Fallibilism: no infallible intuition or indubitable first principles
Understands knowledge as a chain of inference	Understands knowledge as a cable made up of many arguments

49.   Haack, "Descartes, Peirce and the Cognitive Community," 158.
50.   See Haack, "Descartes, Peirce and the Cognitive Community," 158.

In contrast to Cartesianism, which holds that only intuitions acquired within one's self-consciousness are certain, pragmatism aims to acquire certainty through the method of science, which Peirce understood as a collective activity of discovery. For him, the notions of reality and community were intrinsically united: "The real, then, is that which, sooner or later, information and reasoning would finally result in, and which is therefore independent of the vagaries of me and you. Thus, the very origin of the conception of reality shows that this conception essentially involves the notion of a COMMUNITY, without definite limits, and capable of an indefinite increase of knowledge."[51]

Along with the pragmatic maxim, Peirce's definition of truth and its relationship to inquiry are the pillars upon which he built his philosophical system. He wrote that "the opinion which is fated to be ultimately agreed to by all who investigate is what we mean by the truth."[52] He claimed that genuine inquiry, carried out through the rigorous testing of hypothesis and with openness to revising these however many times it is necessary as new evidence emerges, would unequivocally result in truth. Consequently, truth is not what the community chooses to agree upon, but the conclusion that inquiry brings forth, as long as the inquirers operate within the boundaries of real things, whose nature is entirely independent of one's opinions about them.[53]

In his search for the means to ascertain truth, Peirce determined that only the method of science puts our doubts at ease in a satisfactory way. This method is intrinsically social and fallibilist; it is distinguished from the other methods of inquiry by its cooperative and public character, and by the fact that it is subject to constant revision and improvement: "[Science] conceives of evidence as an objective factor inviting universal examination and compelling ultimate unanimity; it conceives of its results as essentially provisional or corrigible; and for these reasons it ensures measurable progress."[54] One

51.   Charles S. Peirce, *Writings of Charles S. Peirce: A Chronological Edition*, ed. Max Fisch (Bloomington: Indiana University Press, 1982–2009), 2:239.

52.   Peirce, *Collected Papers*, 5.407 (1878).

53.   Misak summarized Peirce's outlook as follows: "Inquirers, at any given stage of investigation, do not determine or create the truth; truth is not a matter of what inquirers happen to think. The objective truth of the matter is that which inquiry would determine." Cheryl Misak, *Truth and the End of Inquiry: A Peircean Account of Truth* (Oxford: Clarendon Press, 2004), 135.

54.   Justus Buchler, introduction to *Philosophical Writings of Peirce*, by Charles S. Peirce, ed. Justus Buchler (New York: Dover Publications, 1955), x.

of Peirce's crucial epistemological proposals entailed a shift from the individual consciousness to the cognitive community. He wrote that "to make single individuals absolute judges of truth is most pernicious. [...] We individually cannot reasonably hope to attain the ultimate philosophy which we pursue; we can only seek it, therefore, for the community of philosophers. Hence, if disciplined and candid minds carefully examine a theory and refuse to accept it, this ought to create doubts in the mind of the author of the theory himself."[55]

Peirce conceived the philosopher, or scientific inquirer, as a contributor to a vast enterprise that extends in and across generations. Aware that ideas mature in a lively and intersubjective process of questioning, wondering, answering, and arguing, he invited scientists to make their work available to other specialists so they can reaffirm their conceptions or propose a new direction. Peirce explained that

> different minds may set out with the most antagonistic views, but the progress of investigation carries them by a force outside of themselves to one and the same conclusion. This activity of thought by which we are carried, not where we wish, but to a foreordained goal, is like the operation of destiny. No modification of the point of view taken, no selection of other facts for study, no natural bent of mind even, can enable a man to escape the predestinate opinion. This great law is embodied in the conception of truth and reality.[56]

Peirce's confidence that inquiry will lead to truth rests on two premises: the idea that evolutionary adaptation has provided human beings with an instinct to guess what is right and the belief that induction tends to be self-corrective. This understanding is accepted by those who have followed Peirce; however, there is some disagreement about whether inquiry can ever be said to have concluded or if its results are intrinsically provisional. In this regard, Jaime Nubiola commented that "truth with a small 't' has not been discovered once and for all, but rather is a living body that grows and

---

55. Peirce, *Collected Papers*, 5.265 (1868).

56. Peirce, *Collected Papers*, 5.407 (1878). In the same vein, Newman said that men would realize that their opinions are not that dissimilar if they only continued their conversation long enough to understand each other: "When men understand what each other mean, they see, for the most part that controversy is either superfluous or hopeless." *US*, 201 (1839).

remains open to everyone's contribution."[57] Those who understand science in this way, as "a living and growing body of truth" or as a method "which seeks cooperation in the hope that the truth may be found see themselves as inquirers necessarily bound to their interactions with others."[58] Therefore, they express their achievements in a public language and hold the maintained agreements of the community as the criteria of truth.

A community of inquiry is not defined by time or space; instead, the connection among the inquirers is forged by a common question, problem, or interest. The careful examination of the historical standards and practices that have been distilled in the course of inquiry is essential to progress. In this sense, inquiry does not begin from scratch but at the point where previous inquiry arrived. Genuine inquiry assumes all inquirers' cumulative work gathered in a centuries-long history of trials, errors, amends, and successes.

The historical character of truth should not, however, become a ballast that prevents inquiry from moving forward. Central to the scientific method is the ability to suspend belief and consider new evidence and ideas. Attentive listening and good communication are thus essential for scientific progress. Jane Addams (1860–1935) developed and applied many of the principles of pragmatism in a concrete social setting and collaborated with Dewey, providing him with practical insights. Her settlement was her community of inquiry, of which she said:

> The only thing to be dreaded in the Settlement is that it lose its flexibility, its power of quick adaptation, its readiness to change its methods as its environment may demand. It must be open to conviction and must have a deep and abiding sense of tolerance. It must be hospitable and ready for experiment. It should demand from its residents a scientific patience in the accumulation of facts and the steady holding of their sympathies as one of the best instruments for that accumulation. It must be grounded in a philosophy whose foundation is on the solidarity of the human race.[59]

57.   Jaime Nubiola, "La búsqueda de la verdad en la tradición pragmatista," *Tópicos*, no. 8–9 (2001): 186 (translation mine).

58.   Peirce, *Collected Papers*, 6.428 (1893), 7.54 (ca. 1902).

59.   Jane Addams, *Twenty Years at Hull-House* (New York: Macmillan, 1912), 126. Jane Addams cofounded Chicago's Hull House, a settlement house, and became the first American woman to be awarded the Nobel Peace Prize for her social work serving immigrants. As a philosopher, she made important contributions to the pragmatist tradition, since she "viewed

The notions of convergence, consensus, and community were central to Dewey's pragmatism, which focuses on developing its political consequences. Dewey believed that inquirers should handle the input they receive as members of a social practice ruled by shared norms, the most important of which is to justify one's assertions in dialogue with others: "No scientific inquirer can keep what he finds to himself or turn it to merely private account without losing his scientific standing. Everything discovered belongs to the community of workers. Every new idea and theory has to be submitted to this community for confirmation and test."[60] Dewey did not understand the community as an embodiment of a timeless order but as an experiment in cooperation and adaptation. Therefore, he thought it should be open to specialist and amateur members alike.

As Dewey emphasized the notions of community and practice in his development of pragmatism, Putnam developed (among other traits) its historical contingency. He explained that his pragmatist enlightenment was the realization that the contextual resolution of ethical conflicts can be warranted without being absolute and that the solutions to problems do not need to be free from a contingent historical perspective to be valid. He understood that history provides not only context but also grounding to resolutions. In this sense, Putnam argued that to separate doing philosophy from studying its history (or in other words, to separate an idea from its development) is impoverishing.

In relation to the notion of community, Putnam stated that the two errors of Cartesian rationalism that pragmatism overcame are the claims that there are truths that can be known a priori and that these truths are accessible to individuals, independently from society. He followed Dewey's lead and argued that the results of inquiry would be more advanced if all members of a community expressed their views and evaluated alternative solutions to a problem. For her part, Misak tightly bound the notions of truth, inquiry, and community by stating that "trying to give up the concept of truth is not something we can do, for it would require too radical a change in our practices of communication and engagement with others. We do assert, we do

---

her settlement work as a grand epistemological endeavor but in the process she also never forgot the humanity of her neighbors. [She] was indeed a public philosopher—one who was not afraid to get her hands dirty." Maurice Hamington, "Jane Addams," in *The Stanford Encyclopedia of Philosophy*, ed. Edward Zalta, updated May 23, 2018, https://plato.stanford.edu/entries/addams-jane/.

60.   Dewey, *Later Works*, 5:115.

believe, we do engage with others, we do take disagreement to matter. These practices are central to who we are."[61] As will be shown, Newman whole-heartedly agreed with these statements and enriched them with a particular nuance, namely, the personal nature of truth and knowledge.

In his discourses on university education, Newman succinctly stated that "all greater matters are carried on and perfected by a succession of individual minds."[62] Although he asserted time and again that truth is a personal possession, he argued with the same resolution that it is not an individualistic endeavor, but a pursuit to be carried on with others, in a community of learning: "The development then of an idea [...] is carried on through and by means of communities of men and their leaders."[63] For Newman, a community was not a convenient add-on, but an essential aspect of inquiry; he even claimed that to ensure learning in a university setting, the community was more critical than assignments or examinations.

Newman, like Peirce, held the natural sciences in high esteem. After stating that the characteristics of each science must be respected, he described the method of inquiry as follows:

> It is the very law of the human mind in its inquiry after and acquisition of truth to make its advances by a process which consists of many stages, and is circuitous. There are no short cuts to knowledge; nor does the road to it always lie in the direction in which it terminates, nor are we able to see the end on starting. [...] Moreover, it is not often the fortune of any one man to live through an investigation; the process is one of not only many stages, but of many minds. What one begins another finishes; and a true conclusion is at length worked out by the cooperation of independent schools and the perseverance of successive generations. This being the case, we are obliged, under circumstances, to bear for a while with what we feel to be error, in consideration of the truth in which it is eventually to issue.[64]

The circumspection of the process Newman envisioned, the importance he ascribed to the cooperation of many minds during a lengthy period, and

61.   Cheryl Misak, "Making Disagreement Matter: Pragmatism and Deliberative Democracy," *Journal of Speculative Philosophy* 18, no. 1 (2004): 19.

62.   *Idea*, 312.

63.   *Dev*, 38.

64.   *Idea*, 474–75.

his certainty that truth would eventually come to light, are akin to Peirce's conditions for genuine inquiry. Furthermore, like Peirce, Newman believed that Cartesian rationalism is sterile because of the isolation in which it left the human mind. Newman wrote that the attempt to devise a science of reasoning to reach certitude is a futile project, since progress towards truth "is a living growth, not a mechanism; and its instruments are mental acts, not the formulas and contrivances of language."[65] He understood truth as an inward endowment transmitted from person to person and effective only when incarnated in daily life.

Reflecting on Newman's approach to philosophy, Sillem wrote that in his understanding "a philosopher [...] is not a thinking machine, but a living person, and persons think about existing realities together as necessarily as they live and work together. A philosopher therefore philosophizes well, if he is a normal man, not alone with his thoughts, systems or books, but in a lived union of mind with other persons, by collating his thoughts with, and measuring them against, those of other people."[66] Throughout his life, Newman constantly measured his thoughts against those of others, first at Oxford and St. Mary's, then at the Oratory and the Catholic University. This is also evidenced through his copious correspondence and his vast array of publications, most of which have several editions. Newman considered his colleagues' opinions to be a great incentive for his growth and often made corrections to his work.

Newman's esteem for the Fathers of the Church is further evidence of his belief that knowledge and truth cannot be constrained to a system. He commented on their fruitfulness, stating that "St. Athanasius [and] St. Augustine had a life, which a system of theology has not."[67] His deep appreciation for the Fathers resulted from his conviction that a person holds the truth in a way no argument, abstract system, or reasoning process can. He believed that personal inquiry and reflection were more fruitful when carried out in communion with others, in a heart-to-heart conversation with others who were grappling with similar issues to those calling one's own attention. He maintained that truth results from many minds exploring the implications of living ideas under the impact of foreign and even hostile ideas. Only by such

---

65. *GA*, 350.

66. Sillem, *Philosophical Notebook*, 76.

67. John Henry Newman, *Lectures on the Doctrine of Justification* (London: Longmans, Green and Co., 1908), 31.

collisions can a true idea grow and become known in all its aspects and rich consequences.[68]

As Newman led the Oxford Movement to strengthen the Catholicity of the Church of England, he chose to rely on personal reflection within a community, not on an institutional or systematic approach. The *Tracts for the Times*, the Movement's most notorious vehicle of action, "were not intended as symbols è cathedrâ, but as the expression of individual minds [since] no great work was done by a system; whereas systems rise out of individual exertions."[69] Newman was convinced that great philosophical systems were futile if separated from the individuals who think in similar ways through each successive century.

The arguments provided so far portray Newman's understanding of truth as a personal possession, which could suggest that he did not value community as strongly as Peirce did. But this is far from the truth. Like Peirce, Newman dismissed abstraction, which he called "paper logic." In one of the best-known passages of his *Idea*, Newman detailed the fruitfulness of the interaction between living minds:

> If I had to choose between a so-called University, which [...] gave its degrees to any person who passed an examination in a wide range of subjects, and a University which [...] merely brought a number of young men together for three or four years, and then sent them away [...] I have no hesitation in giving the preference to that University which did nothing [...]. How is this to be explained? I suppose as follows: When a multitude of young men [...] come together and freely mix with each other, they are sure to learn one from another [...] the conversation of all is a series of lectures to each, and they gain for themselves new ideas and views, fresh matter of thought, and distinct principles for judging and acting, day by day.[70]

68.   Newman's motto, *Cor ad Cor Loquitur*, sheds light on these reflections and shows the centrality of relationships and community in his understanding of life, learning, and the pursuit of truth. See Blehl, "The Intellectual and Spiritual Influence of Newman," 251. Newman believed that "truth was many-sided and only likely to emerge out of an atmosphere of free discussion." Christopher Hollis, "Newman the Man: Freedom and Love," *Wiseman Review*, no. 492 (Summer 1962): 182–90, quoted in Merrigan, "Newman and Theological Liberalism," 615.

69.   *Apo*, 144.

70.   *Idea*, 145–46.

Newman knew that great acts take time and identified two outcomes of a collegial and patient approach to the search for truth. On the one hand, he realized that ideas become purer or rather, more precise, since the input of different persons through time trims and balances beliefs so they can reach their full potential, which is never actually settled. On the other hand, he believed that ideas are strengthened through time and cooperation, and their power of attraction grows as the one-sidedness of the single living mind, however penetrating, is corrected by coordinating his perceptions with those of other inquirers. In 1863 Newman pondered the conditions for intellectual flourishing. He wrote to Robert Ornsby (1820–1889): "Why was it that the Medieval Schools were so vigorous? Because they were allowed free and fair play—because the disputants [...] could move their limbs freely and expatiate at will. [...] Truth is wrought out by many minds, working together freely."[71] This insight on truth will be fundamental for the notion of the Illative Sense, which he developed in *The Grammar of Assent*.

Not only did Newman uphold the notion of community, but he enriched it with a nuanced understanding of tradition, stating that communities are maintained through traditions that guarantee cohesion and continuity over time. Although most of what he wrote about tradition refers to the Catholic Church, it can be understood as having a broader scope, since he approached tradition as an ongoing development that reveals how the past and present become progressively intelligible and mutually illuminating. This is how truth develops not only in ecclesiastical venues but in secular communities as well.

In his work *The Via Media,* first published in 1837, Newman described tradition in the following enigmatic yet precise way:

It is latent, but it lives. It is silent, like the rapids of a river, before the rocks intercept it. It is [an] unconscious habit of opinion and sentiment; which [humanity] reflects upon, masters, and expresses, according to the emergency. We see then the mistake of asking for a complete collection of [...] traditions; as well might we ask for a full catalogue of a man's tastes and thoughts on a given subject. Tradition in its fulness is necessarily unwritten; it is the mode in which a society has felt or acted during a certain period, and it cannot be

71. *LD,* xx 426 (1863).

circumscribed any more than a man's countenance and manner can be conveyed to strangers in any set of propositions.[72]

Newman likened tradition to an atmosphere and clarified that it cannot be embodied, constrained, or fully systematized within a treatise; but rather, it is maintained and passed on through the life of a community. While recognizing that tradition is rooted in history, Newman argued that tradition is not stifled by it. Writing about a group of scholars who demanded an explicit historical framework for a novel proposal, Newman exclaimed: "I think them utterly wrong in what they have done and are doing; and, moreover, I agree as little in their view of history as in their acts. Extensive as may be their historical knowledge [...] they seem to me to expect from History more than History can furnish."[73] In Newman's view, history can provide facts, but these need to be developed. In another instance, he talked about the systematic treatment of a doctrine as a swaddling band wrapped so tightly around an infant (he referred to an infant to represent a budding truth) that it prevents him from growing.[74]

While Newman held the conventional understanding of tradition, he argued for development as a trait that must be incorporated in the understanding of truth. Chadwick writes that

> the idea of development was the most important single idea which Newman contributed to the thought of the Christian Church. This was not because the idea of development did not exist already. But it was a very restricted idea, so restricted that it posed insuperable problems for anyone who studied history with open eyes. Newman made it wider and vaguer, and thereby far more fertile in conception, and more useful to anyone who cared about intellectual honesty.[75]

72.   John Henry Newman, *The Via Media of the Anglican Church* (London: Longmans, Green and Co., 1901), i 32.

73.   *Diff,* ii 311–12.

74.   See *LD*, xxiv 316 (1869). Newman's imagery is so rich that the sentence is worth quoting in full: "Our theological philosophers are like the old nurses who wrap the unhappy infant in swaddling bands or boards—put a lot of blankets over him—and shut the windows that not a breath of fresh air may come to his skin as if he were not healthy enough to bear wind and water in due measure."

75.   Owen Chadwick, *Newman: A Short Introduction* (Oxford: Oxford University Press, 2010), 48.

Through his understanding of the development of ideas, Newman broadened the sense of community, enabling it not only to harbor diverse coetaneous individuals but also to acquire a wider reach amidst successive generations. He invited his contemporaries to be deep *in* history, that is, to place themselves not at the endpoint of history but amidst its making—amidst the reflection and transgenerational transmission of knowledge and truth. Newman understood that truth unfolds as individuals "compare, contrast, abstract, generalize, connect, adjust, classify" distinct ideas and argued that a true development "is an addition which illustrates, not obscures, corroborates, not corrects, the body of thought from which it proceeds."[76]

The notion of time is as important as the notions of community and tradition in Newman's theory of knowledge. He deeply revered the rhythm of growth and flourishment and knew that things that are in themselves good may not be possible at just any time. The way he upheld the historicity of truths is quite remarkable considering the historical period in which he lived. He introduced his famous *Essay on Development* as follows:

It is indeed sometimes said that the stream is clearest near the spring. Whatever use may fairly be made of this image, it does not apply to the history of a philosophy or belief, which on the contrary is more equable, and purer, and stronger, when its bed has become deep, and broad, and full. It necessarily rises out of an existing state of things, and, for a time, savours of the soil. Its vital element needs disengaging from what is foreign and temporary, and is employed in efforts after freedom which become more vigorous and hopeful as its years increase. Its beginnings are no measure of its capabilities, nor of its scope. At first no one knows what it is, or what it is worth. It remains perhaps for a time quiescent; it tries, as it were, its limbs, and proves the ground under it, and feels its way. From time to time it makes essays which fail, and are in consequence abandoned. It seems in suspense which way to go; it wavers, and at length strikes out in one definite direction. In time it enters upon strange territory; points of controversy alter their bearing; parties rise and fall around it; dangers and hopes appear in new relations; and old principles

---

76. *Dev*, 33, 200.

reappear under new forms. It changes with them in order to remain the same. In a higher world it is otherwise, but here below to live is to change, and to be perfect is to have changed often.[77]

The vivid imagery in these lines is an apt illustration for Peirce's method of inquiry, which maintained that truth is clarified over time. In fact, Newman mentioned several times in his correspondence the adage that "truth is the daughter of time."[78]

In the fifth of his *University Sermons,* Newman argued that truth "has been upheld in the world not as a system, not by books, not by argument, nor by temporal power, but by the personal influence of such [...] who are at once the teachers and the patterns of it."[79] Both Newman and Peirce are good exemplars of such teachers and patterns. Not only in their writings but also in their lives, Newman and Peirce (along with many pragmatist philosophers) upheld the notion of truth as a collective pursuit through time.

Recognition of the Role of Difficulties
in the Pursuit of Knowledge

A fourth affinity between Newman and pragmatism is their regard for the role that difficulties, doubt, and error play in the growth of knowledge and the attainment of truth. Acknowledging that the pragmatist view of truth entails a fallibilist epistemology, pragmatists do not see doubts and errors as obstacles in the process of inquiry; rather, they welcome them as essential building blocks for this endeavor. Peirce talked about doubt as what gives purpose to inquiry. For his part, Newman saw it as a positive state because it is contrary to inactivity; he invited his listeners to opt "not [for] formal doubt, but [for] a state of mind which recognizes the possibility of doubting."[80]

Peirce held a nuanced understanding of fallibilism and doubt, which acknowledged the limitations of his own capacity to advance truth. His personal fallibility did not make him question the possibility of acquiring truth or knowledge; rather, it made him seek a community of inquirers to balance,

77.   *Dev,* 40.

78.   See *LD,* x 375 (1844), xvi 106 (1854), xxiii 16 (1867), xxv 279 (1871), xxix 337 (1881).

79.   *US,* 91–92 (1832).

80.   *US,* 215 (1839). See also *GA,* 77; Peirce, *Collected Papers,* 5.376 (1903).

contrast, correct, and advance his reflection. While he maintained that any specific claim could be overturned in the course of inquiry, he upheld his beliefs with enough confidence until a reason to question them arose.

Thus, Peirce's position offers an attractive compromise between the individual's cognitive limitations and aspirations, and it acknowledges the individual's cognitive dependence on others and his susceptibility to error while preserving the prospect of attaining genuine knowledge. Recognizing the limitations of reason, Peirce offered fallibilism as an epistemological thesis and recommendation: a thesis because it describes the person's propensity to hold false beliefs and a recommendation because it advises that one should always be open to revising her beliefs in light of new available evidence. In a manuscript from 1897, he described fallibilism as follows:

> For years in the course of this ripening process, I used for myself to collect my ideas under the designation *fallibilism*; and indeed the first step toward *finding out* is to acknowledge you do not satisfactorily know already; so that no blight can so surely arrest all intellectual growth as the blight of cocksureness [...]. Indeed, out of a contrite fallibilism, combined with a high faith in the reality of knowledge, and an intense desire to find things out, all my philosophy has always seemed to me to grow.[81]

Even though the remark "contrite fallibilism" appears only once in Peirce's writings, it is one of his best-known terms. Peirce chose the adjective *contrite* because he held that progress can only be made within a community of dedicated investigators, that it will be characterized by setbacks along the way, and that the part each individual plays will be small. Following Peirce's thought, in the context of this discussion, fallibilism is understood as a doctrine regarding the person as a cognitive agent, not as a doctrine regarding truth and knowledge as objective realities.

Peircean pragmatists see inquiry as a process that removes incoherent claims from one's expectations and beliefs. In other words, inquiry leads to a belief that is coherent with one's experience, and thus is able to guide one's actions without engendering doubts. This method is intrinsically self-correcting, which means that even though the appeal to particular arguments may change over time, the rationality of the process is not called into question.

81. Peirce, *Collected Papers*, 1.13–14 (ca. 1897).

When inquiry is viewed in this way and carried out responsibly as an attempt to discover truth, it involves several tasks: "Evidence has to be collected, experiments have to be devised and carried out, dialogues must be engaged in with fellow inquirers, decisions must be made about when we have scrutinized our opinions enough to trust our results."[82] If and when this point is ever reached is a matter of discussion among pragmatists. Peirce believed that it is never actually reached, as he held that inquiry "is not standing upon the bedrock of fact. It is walking upon a bog, and can only say, this ground seems to hold for the present. Here I will stay *till it begins to give way*."[83]

As has been seen, Peirce developed his notion of inquiry, not as a certain destination, but as the road that goes from doubt to belief: "The irritation of doubt causes a struggle to attain a state of belief. I shall term this struggle *Inquiry*."[84] However, it cannot be said without qualification that the starting point for inquiry is generalized doubt, as Peirce explicitly stated that "we cannot begin with complete doubt. We must begin with all the prejudices which we have when we enter upon the study of philosophy. These prejudices are not to be dispelled by a maxim."[85] For Peirce, the starting point for inquiry was a surprising experience that disappointed an expectation. This surprising experience does not take place in a void but within a settled body of beliefs, which serves as the context for developing a specific doubt, described by Peirce as a real and living doubt. Then, the individual's body of background beliefs is only susceptible to doubt on a *piecemeal* basis, which implies that it must be regarded as true, until a surprising experience causes a disruption. Once this disruption takes place, it must be dealt with methodically. Peirce explained that a philosopher is distinguished "by the great value he attaches to doubt, provided only that it be the weighty and noble metal itself, and no counterfeit nor paper substitute. He is not content to ask himself whether he does doubt, but he invents a plan for attaining to doubt, elaborates it in detail, and then puts it into practice."[86]

---

82.   Christopher Hookway, *Truth, Rationality, and Pragmatism: Themes from Peirce* (Oxford: Clarendon Press, 2002), 246.

83.   Peirce, *Collected Papers*, 5.589 (1898) (emphasis added). In an earlier writing, Peirce explained, "The desire to learn forbids him [the inquirer] to be perfectly cocksure that he knows already." Peirce, *Collected Papers*, 1.55 (ca. 1896).

84.   Peirce, *Collected Papers*, 5.374 (1877).

85.   Peirce, *Collected Papers*, 5.265 (1868).

86.   Peirce, *Collected Papers*, 5.451 (1905).

In a later essay, Peirce contrasted what he calls "paper doubts" with genuine doubts and argued that the latter should be attained through a deliberate plan. A genuine or specific doubt arises in the context of a settled body of beliefs and is ignited by a surprising experience. This characterization of doubt as a specific reality versus the generalized Cartesian method of doubt is a significant claim of pragmatist philosophers—one that resembles the understanding of doubt that Newman supported.

In his paper "The Fixation of Belief" Peirce defined doubt as "an uneasy and dissatisfied state from which we struggle to free ourselves and pass into the state of belief" and argued that doubt is the opposite state to belief.[87] When a person examines the belief she holds against a new recalcitrant experience or an unexpected occurrence, a doubt arises and sets a new process into motion: inquiry. Since doubt entails the interruption of a belief by a novel experience, inquiry must start in a determined context; one must have had an earlier belief, the interruption of which throws one into doubt.

For Peirce, a genuine doubt was relative to belief and dependent upon it. He argued that a person needs a reason to doubt what she initially believed. This is another instance where Peirce upheld his claim that inquiry does not begin with a blank slate but with held beliefs. Understanding doubt as the detonator for inquiry in the context of held beliefs, Peirce saw it as a valuable asset in the quest for truth: "Thus, both doubt and belief have positive effects upon us, though very different ones. Belief does not make us act at once, but puts us into such a condition that we shall behave in a certain way, when the occasion arises. Doubt has not the least such active effect, but stimulates us to inquiry until it is destroyed."[88]

In Peirce's eyes, the capital offense in philosophical investigation was to block the way of inquiry. Genuine or specific doubts achieve the opposite effect. They keep inquiry open and inform it with an objective, since "when doubt ceases, mental action on the subject comes to an end; and if it did go on, it would be without a purpose."[89] Doubt is not considered a liability or a problem, but rather an asset and an art. Along with his recognition of the value of doubts, Peirce also acknowledged the value of errors within the process of inquiry. Peircean inquiry does not entail the systematic development of truth from one single premise. Instead, this systematic development

87.   Peirce, *Collected Papers*, 5.372 (1877).
88.   Peirce, *Collected Papers*, 5.373 (1877).
89.   Peirce, *Collected Papers*, 5.376 (1903).

results from weaving together diverse findings, where even failures become "one of the carcasses over which future generations of inquirers climb as they finally storm the fortress of knowledge."[90] Both favorable and unfavorable outcomes are threads in the cable of reasoning, "a cable whose fibres may be ever so slender, provided they are sufficiently numerous and intimately connected."[91]

Because of his understanding of fallibilism, Peirce maintained that any—but not all—of our beliefs can be mistaken. Therefore, he placed fallibilism as an intermediate epistemological position between Cartesian dogmatism and outright skepticism. Peirce's account of knowledge is fallibilist, meaning that the individual could always be wrong, but committal, meaning that he acts upon his hypothetical beliefs. These two characteristics of Peirce's account of knowledge—fallibilism and commitment, along with a recognition of the crucial role that doubt and error play in the pursuit of knowledge—are clearly discernable in Newman's life and works.

While Newman described a method of inquiry similar to that of Peirce, he was more concerned with the attainment of truth than with the avoidance of error in the development of his theory of knowledge; his aim was to help his contemporaries realize the truths they were already professing.[92] Traces of pragmatism can be discerned in his emphasis on the realization of truth. He explained this in his *Idea* as a capacity of the human intellect, which

> discerns in lines and colours, or in tones, what is beautiful and what is not. It gives them a meaning, and invests them with an idea. It gathers up a succession of notes into the expression of a whole, and calls it a melody; it has a keen sensibility towards angles and curves, lights and shadows, tints and contours. It distinguishes between rule

---

90. Susan Haack, "Pragmatism," in *The Blackwell Companion to Philosophy* (Malden: Blackwell, 2003), 778. The metaphor of carcasses brings to mind Ratzinger's description of the history of dogma as a "graveyard of heresies." Joseph Ratzinger, *Introduction to Christianity* (San Francisco: Ignatius Press, 2004), 172.

91. Peirce, *Collected Papers*, 5.265 (1868). Peirce chose the image of a cable rather than that of a chain, which is no stronger than its weakest link. Newman also described knowledge as a cable woven from numerous cords. See *LD*, xxi 146 (1864).

92. See Crosby, *The Personalism of Newman*, 34. Newman's emphasis on the realization of truth is also seen in the priority he gives to real assent over merely notional assent. See also *Dev*, 37–38; *Idea*, 473–78.

and exception, between accident and design. It assigns phenomena to a general law, qualities to a subject, acts to a principle, and effects to a cause.[93]

This description of the path that the human mind follows in the process of inquiry is reminiscent of Peirce's call to consider practical effects in the discernment of truth.

Although he expressed himself in different terms, Newman understood the necessity and the benefits of inquiry and considered doubt as a positive step in the attainment of truth: "If we are intended for great ends, we are called to great hazards; and, whereas *we are given absolute certainty in nothing*, we must in all things choose between doubt and inactivity."[94] As Peirce and other pragmatists would do a few decades later, Newman accepted the lack of absolute certainty as an inherent characteristic of the human condition and preferred doubt over inactivity, or in Peirce's words, preferred grappling with doubt over blocking the way of inquiry.

Newman understood the pursuit of truth—the method of inquiry—as a living process of continuous development in which different pieces of evidence are examined and found to strengthen, interpret, or adjust each other, and thus approximate an idea to its perfect expression. He held that antagonist principles correct each other and concluded his description of inquiry by stating that this process of continuous correction is the only way to learn a new science.[95] When commenting upon a particular historical situation, he referred to the definition of a doctrine in two different moments at which diverse statements on the same subject were considered true and skillfully integrated both of them by concluding that the second moment "trimmed the balance of doctrine by completing it."[96] Newman offered this example to illustrate that the understanding of knowledge and truth is cumulative. This notion is widely present in his works: "We are aware, while we do so, that they [words] are inadequate, but we have the alternative of doing so, or nothing at all. We can only remedy their insufficiency by confessing it. [...] We can only set right one error of expression by another."[97]

93.   *Idea*, 74–75.

94.   *US*, 215 (1839) (emphasis added).

95.   See *LG*, 170.

96.   *Diff*, ii 307.

97.   *TP*, i 102. See also *Dev*, 37; *Idea*, 474–76; *GA*, 192–93.

Although Newman dealt with the topics of inquiry, investigation, difficulty, doubt, and error primarily in an *Essay on the Development of Doctrine* and in *The Idea of a University*, he spoke of doubt in several of his works. He ascribed various meanings to it, among which we can identify three. The first meaning is the understanding of doubt in relation to doctrinal statements; the two statements that Newman gave as examples for this meaning are God's existence and Christ's divinity. Understanding doubt in this particular context, Newman stated that "the Church does not allow her children to entertain any doubt of her teaching [because] faith is incompatible with doubt."[98] This is not the context for the present discussion.

A second meaning that Newman ascribed to doubt is that of a complete skepticism or suspension of all belief. In this regard, he said, "There are writers who seem to have gone far beyond [...] reasonable scepticism, laying down as a general proposition that we have no right in philosophy to make any assumption whatever, and that we ought to begin with a universal doubt. [...] I would rather have to maintain that we ought to begin with believing everything that is offered to our acceptance, than that it is our duty to doubt of everything."[99] As has been shown, Peirce shared this criticism of the method of doubt brought forth by Cartesian rationalism.

Newman, like Peirce, maintained that genuine doubt arises within a settled body of beliefs. He wrote in the *Grammar*, "Doubt itself is a positive state, and implies a definite habit of mind, and thereby necessarily involves a system of principles and doctrines all its own."[100] This understanding of doubt as a positive state is the third meaning Newman ascribed to the term, to which he also referred as mere investigation: "mere investigation [...] into the grounds of our [subject] is not to doubt; nor is it doubting to consider the arguments urged against it, when there is good reason for doing so."[101] In the context of this project and in consonance with the pragmatic understanding of doubt that has been developed, it is possible to identify what

98.   John Henry Newman, *Discourses Addressed to Mixed Congregations* (London: Longmans, Green and Co., 1906), 215 (hereafter, *Mix*). Newman's well-known adage is expressed within this context: "Ten thousand difficulties do not make one doubt, as I understand the subject; difficulty and doubt are incommensurate." *Apo*, 239.

99.   *GA*, 377.

100. *GA*, 377.

101. *Mix*, 226–27. This term is qualified by Dahm as Newman's normal use of doubt in his epistemological works. See Dahm, "The Certainty of Faith," 137.

Newman describes in the *Grammar* as a positive state, with Peirce's genuine doubt. Angelo Bottone is of this mind, as he states that "in many sections of the *Grammar* Newman recognises that doubt carries an important value in the investigation," and Ian Ker writes that although "an investigation may lead to a loss of assent [...] the sense of the possibility of this loss is not the same as doubt—nor does assent imply an intention never to change one's mind, but instead the absence of any imagination of ever changing."[102] Aware of the liability of reason, both Newman and Peirce believe that the person can advance towards truth through the method of inquiry.[103]

When Peirce talked about the process of inquiry, he referred to the community of philosophers; similarly, Newman spoke of educated minds:

> In the case of educated minds, investigations into the argumentative proof of the things to which they have given their assent, is an obligation, or rather a necessity. Such a trial of their intellects is a law of their nature, like the growth of childhood into manhood [...]. The intellectual assents, in which they have in like manner been instructed from the first, have to be tested, realized, and developed by the exercise of their mature judgment.[104]

It is telling that Newman talked about inquiry as a trial of the intellect, and Peirce described it as a struggle. Further, as Peirce upheld that "the opinion which is fated to be *ultimately* agreed to by all who investigate is what we mean by the truth," Newman said that "we are obliged, under circumstances, to bear for a while with what we feel to be error, in consideration of the truth in which it is *eventually* to issue."[105]

Newman and Peirce upheld the objectivity of truth, maintaining that it can be discovered through inquiry. Moreover, both acknowledged that many detours would be encountered during this process and did not see them as adverse circumstances. In fact, Newman saw them as a condition for success,

102. Angelo Bottone, "Newman and Wittgenstein after Foundationalism," *New Blackfriars* 86, no. 1001 (2005): 71; Ker, introduction to *The Grammar of Assent*, xvi.

103. As Peirce recognized his contrite fallibilism, Newman wrote in a moment of turmoil, "I had been deceived greatly once; how could I be sure that I was not deceived a second time? I then thought myself right; how was I to be certain that I was right now?" *Apo*, 318.

104. *GA*, 192–93.

105. Peirce, *Collected Papers*, 5.407 (1878); *Idea*, 475 (emphasis added).

stating that there is "no intellectual triumph of any truth [...] which has not been preceded by a full statement of what can be said against it,"[106] and Peirce talked of a whole cartload of beliefs that might need to be discarded. In the final chapter of his *Apologia,* Newman detailed the benefits of this process:

> Many a man has ideas, which he hopes are true, and useful for his day, but he is not confident about them, and wishes to have them discussed. He is willing or rather would be thankful to give them up, if they can be proved to be erroneous or dangerous, and by means of controversy he obtains his end. He is answered, and he yields; or on the contrary he finds that he is considered safe.[107]

One of Newman's most significant works deals with the development or growth of our knowledge of the truth. The following paragraph where he described the process of inquiry is worth quoting almost in its entirety because it brings together many of the elements discussed in this chapter:

> There will be a general agitation of thought, and an action of mind upon mind. There will be a time of confusion, when conceptions and misconceptions are in conflict, and it is uncertain whether anything is to come of the idea at all, or which view of it is to get the start of the others. New lights will be brought to bear upon the original statements of the doctrine put forward; judgments and aspects will accumulate. [...] As time proceeds, one view will be modified or expanded by another, and then combined with a third [...]. It will be surveyed too in its relation to other doctrines or facts, to other natural laws or established customs, to the varying circumstances of times and places, to other religions, polities, philosophies, as the case may be. How it stands affected towards other systems, how it affects them [...] will be gradually wrought out. It will be interrogated and criticized by enemies, and defended by well-wishers. The multitude of opinions formed concerning it in these respects and many others

---

106. *Idea,* 475–76. Newman's own way of dealing with controversy exemplifies this principle: "By entering into the objections, his position does not become more diffuse, but clearer. It gains in breadth, but also in sharpness. [...] He knows that the objections will give him the opportunity to sharpen his convictions, and so he approaches them with sovereign calm." Crosby, "Coincidentia Oppositorum," 199.

107. *Apo,* 358.

will be collected, compared, sorted, sifted, selected, rejected, gradually attached to it, separated from it, in the minds of individuals
and of the community. [...] Thus in time it will have grown [...]
according to its capabilities: And this body of thought, thus labori-
ously gained, will after all be little more than the proper representative of one idea, being in substance what that idea meant from
the first, its complete image as seen in a combination of diversified
aspects, with the suggestions and corrections of many minds, and
the illustration of many experiences.[108]

The pragmatic notion of inquiry values errors as stepping stones on the
way towards the attainment of beliefs. Newman saw error from a similar
perspective, recognizing that "it is the very law of the human mind in its
inquiry after and acquisition of truth to make its advances by a process which
consists of many stages, and is circuitous."[109] He introduced two analogies to
explain this law: that of a person hiking and needing to turn now and again to
find adequate paths and that of a ship that changes course on its way to port.

As he accepted fallibilism as inherent to the human condition, Newman
also believed that truth and error are often found together and that errors are
not an obstacle to truth: "Error having always some portion of truth in it,
and the truth having a reality which error has not, we may expect, that when
there is an honest purpose and fair talents, we shall somehow make our way
forward, the error falling off from the mind, and the truth developing and
occupying it."[110] These claims bring to mind the pragmatist notion of the
self-corrective nature of scientific inquiry. Newman went as far as to say that
"in scientific researches error may be said, without a paradox, to be in some
instances the way to truth, *and the only way.*"[111]

Developing his analogy of a ship at sea, Newman wrote that "the
passenger should not have embarked at all, if he did not reckon on the
chance of a rough sea, of currents, of wind and tide, of rocks and shoals"
and gave a recommendation to those who set out on the path of inquiry:
"We should act more wisely in discountenancing altogether the exercise of
Reason than in being alarmed and impatient under the suspense, delay, and

108. *Dev*, 37–38.
109. *Idea*, 474.
110. *GA*, 377.
111. *Idea*, 474 (emphasis added).

anxiety."[112] As can be seen, for Newman and Peirce, the search for truth was not a straight path, and it was not always luminous; nevertheless, it was ultimately worthwhile.

Newman's Illative Sense and Peirce's Abductive Reasoning

The path and fruitfulness of the search for truth are further expressed in Newman's and Peirce's work through the former's development of the Illative Sense and the latter's development of Abductive Reasoning. A detailed study of these two theories shows affinity and complementarity, not only in their understanding of knowledge but also in the language and images they use to communicate their insights. In 1914 Ward explained that the Illative Sense

> has a close connection with pragmatism, [as Newman] emphasised the fact that all the thought that most matters for us in life relates to the concrete, and bears on our actions. [...] The theory of the Illative Sense is an attempt to include [...] the *maximum* of actually existing and practically influential evidence (explicit and implicit), not to limit it to that portion only which is scientific in form. All this is in accord with Mr. Peirce's and Professor James's principle of pragmatism.[113]

In the introductory paragraphs of the ninth chapter of the *Grammar,* in which Newman developed his theory of the Illative Sense, he argued that the perfection of the individual's reasoning powers "is a living growth, not a mechanism; and its instruments are mental acts, not the formulas and contrivances of language" and qualified this phenomenon as perplexing.[114] Peirce, speaking of the same matter, called it baffling: "For the methods of thinking that are living activities in men are not objects of reflective consciousness. They baffle the student, because they are a part of himself."[115] The religious and scientific environment in which both worked gave undue weight to logic as an overarching science, which both challenged and sought to overcome. In this regard, Newman wrote the following:

112. *Idea,* 475.
113. Ward, "Newman's Philosophy," 90.
114. *GA,* 350.
115. Peirce, *Collected Papers,* 3.404 (1892).

Logic [...] does not really prove; it enables us to join issue with others; it suggests ideas; it opens views; it maps out for us the lines of thought; it verifies negatively; it determines when differences of opinion are hopeless; and when and how far conclusions are probable; but for genuine proof in concrete matter we require an *organon* more delicate, versatile, and elastic than verbal argumentation.[116]

Coincidentally, both Newman and Peirce were well trained in logic through their acquaintance with Richard Whately's work.[117] Although they held logic in high esteem, Newman and Peirce also recognized its limitations and argued that the reasoning capacity entails much more than the direct application of logic's rules and principles. Both studied induction and deduction as modes of inference but could not account for how individuals think with only these two operations of the mind. While deduction draws the necessary and verifiable conclusions that follow if a hypothesis were true and induction verifies a hypothesis in a limited number of cases, a third mode of reasoning is needed to bestow meaning on disparate details and introduce new ideas.

Peirce discussed this topic in his 1878 papers, and in his mature years, he called this third way of reasoning Abduction: not merely a logical operation, but the spontaneous activity of the mind, which makes the strange familiar. Abduction is thus defined as the process by which hypotheses are generated to explain surprising facts. Similarly, after analyzing deduction and induction in chapter 8 of the *Grammar* and calling attention to the fact that "it is the mind that reasons, and [...] controls its own reasonings, not any technical apparatus of words and propositions,"[118] Newman set the stage for the introduction of the Illative Sense to which he alluded thirty years prior

116. *GA*, 271.

117. Newman's relationship with Whately was detailed in chapter 2. Peirce studied Whately's *Elements*, which was Harvard's core text for teaching logic. He narrated:

It must have been in the year 1851, when I should have been 12 years old, that I remember picking up Whately's *Logic* in my elder brother's room, and asking him what logic was. I see myself, after he had told me, stretched on his carpet and poring over the book, and I must have past most of my time so during that week, since subsequent severe tests showed that I had then mastered Whateley's [*sic*] work [...]. From that day to this logic has been my passion. (Charles S. Peirce, "One, Two, Three," [MS 905, 1907], p. 12, The Charles S. Peirce Papers)

118. *GA*, 353.

in his *University Sermons*. Within the modes of inference, the Illative Sense can be considered a perfecting touch in the individual's inferential capacity. After an insightful exposition of Newman's and Peirce's contributions to philosophy, Matthew Moore concluded that "Newman and Peirce [...] identify a new method of reasoning that would allow man to make assertions that are neither induced nor deduced [...]. In Abduction and Illative Sense, Newman and Peirce go beyond the limits of traditional logic to achieve a way of knowing practical and concrete matters. Such profound similarities between two such monumental thinkers requires academic attention."[119]

As operations of the mind, deduction, induction, and abduction are not necessarily independent from one another. Some authors argue that the mature Peirce considered the three of them as stages in a single process of inquiry.[120] Within this process, the role of abduction is to provide the inquirer with a hypothesis to be tested through induction, and if proven false, to provide further hypotheses, until one of them is verified. In Peirce's words: "All that makes knowledge applicable comes to us via Abduction. [...] Not the smallest advance can be made in knowledge beyond the stage of vacant staring, without making an abduction at every step."[121]

Newman explained that the Illative Sense operates in a similar way, having "its function in the beginning, middle, and end of all verbal discussion and inquiry, and in every step of the process [...] and [attending] upon the whole course of thought from antecedents to consequents, with a minute diligence and unwearied presence."[122] Newman's portrayal of the Illative Sense and Peirce's account of Abduction show how individuals in fact reason. Their theory of knowledge is an expression of their lived experience: Newman's as a pastor who was highly engaged in the intellectual debates of his time and Peirce's as an experimental researcher who worked within an international community of scientists.

Newman identified the Illative Sense as that "power of judging and concluding, when in its perfection."[123] A broader definition could be the following: the function of the intellect that enables the person to integrate and evaluate all available evidence, along with the conclusions of her inferences,

---

119. Moore, "Newman and Peirce," 55.

120. See Kuang Fann, *Peirce's Theory of Abduction* (The Hague: Martinus Nijhoff, 1970), 10.

121. Peirce, *Historical Perspectives*, 2:899–900 (1901).

122. *GA*, 361.

123. *GA*, 353.

to ascertain if a particular conclusion is true. Likewise Peirce, having the available evidence as a point of departure and truth as a destination, wrote that "Abduction consists in studying facts and devising a theory to explain them" and understood it to be an instinctive ability: "A primary hypothesis underlying all abduction [is] that the human mind is akin to the truth in the sense that in a finite number of guesses it will light upon the correct hypothesis. [...] For the existence of an instinct for truth is, after all, the sheet-anchor of science."[124]

Peirce's understanding of Abduction as an instinctive ability can be related to Newman's explanation of the Illative Sense as an individual's natural inheritance. To explain that the Illative Sense is present in all persons from their birth, Newman drew a parallel between this faculty and good sense, common sense, and the sense of beauty, which he understood as innate but undeveloped faculties that all persons possess. Newman called the Illative Sense "a living *organon* [...] a personal gift, and not a mere method or calculus" and explained that it exists in varying degrees of perfection in each individual depending on his personal experience and training.[125] Further, he clarified that its development is not a mechanical matter, but that it depends on the individual's effort.

Similarly, Peirce's Abductive Reasoning results from the development of one's natural instincts and of one's rational adaptation to the environment. It can also be called *creativity*, an innate but undeveloped faculty.[126] For his part, Newman stated that it is the individual's gift "to be the creator of his own sufficiency; and to be emphatically self-made. This is the law of his being, which he cannot escape; and whatever is involved in that law he is bound, or rather he is carried on, to fulfil."[127] Through creative inquiry, the person not only perfects herself but enriches the world around her. Peirce held that creativity resides in the individual's intrinsic capacity for growth and learning; thus, he saw creativity not only as a personal talent but as a responsibility.

---

124. Peirce, *Collected Papers*, 5.145 (1903), 7.220 (ca. 1901).

125. *GA*, 316. Ker explains that "the use of the word sense [...] is justified by the need to emphasize the element of the personal in the living intellect for our conclusions in informal reasoning are judgements arrived at [...] by our own individual perception of the truth in question." Ker, introduction to *The Grammar of Assent*, lxvi.

126. See Sara Barrena and Jaime Nubiola, "Abduction: The Logic of Creativity," in *Bloomsbury Companion to Contemporary Peircean Semiotics* (London: Bloomsbury, 2019), 194.

127. *GA*, 349.

In summary, the Illative Sense and Abductive Reasoning are innate faculties that must be intentionally developed if they are to reach their perfection. Their development is, in Newman's words, "necessarily a matter of training," although their exercise is not necessarily a conscious act.[128] Likewise, Peirce argued that "the methods of thinking that are living activities in men are not objects of reflective consciousness."[129] In this regard, Newman devoted particular attention to the operations of the mind of which the individual is unaware. In his 1840 sermon "Implicit and Explicit Reason," Newman made an insightful distinction between the process of reasoning in itself and the person's self-awareness of that process. The former—the process of reasoning in itself or implicit reason—is what Newman identified three decades later as the Illative Sense:

> Here, then, are two processes, distinct from each other, the original process of reasoning, and next, the process of investigating our reasonings. All men reason, for to reason is nothing more than to gain truth from former truth [...] but all men do not reflect upon their own reasonings, much less reflect truly and accurately [...]. In other words, all men have a reason, but not all men can give a reason. We may denote, then, these two exercises [...] as Implicit Reason and Explicit Reason [...] The process of reasoning is complete in itself and independent. The analysis is but an account of it; it does not make the conclusion correct; it does not make the inference rational.[130]

Throughout his writings, Newman used various synonyms to refer to the Illative Sense: he called it a reasoning faculty as exercised by well-prepared minds, an inductive sense, and even philosophy. Similarly, Peirce called Abductive Reasoning a fair guess, a hypothesis, a presumption, or retroduction.[131] Regardless of the term they used, their understanding of a foundational faculty of the mind that is not only in play in professional affairs but is particularly useful for ordinary activities remained constant. Barrena and Nubiola discuss Peirce's Abduction in the context of scientific research and artistic development, while Athié explores four settings Newman gives for

128. *Idea*, 151.

129. Peirce, *Collected Papers*, 3.404 (1892).

130. *US*, 258–59 (1840).

131. See *GA*, 361; *LD*, xxx 148 (1882); *Idea*, 125; Peirce, *Collected Papers*, 2.623 (1878), 2.625 (1878), 6.469 (1908).

the exercise of the Illative Sense: moral problems, professional endeavors, fine arts, and personal ventures.[132]

An excerpt from Newman's *University Sermons* presents a full description of what he understands to be the exercise of reason; as can be seen, it is compatible with Peirce's notion of Abduction:

> Reason, according to the simplest view of it, is the faculty of gaining knowledge without direct perception, or of ascertaining one thing by means of another. In this way it is able, from small beginnings, to create to itself a world of ideas, which do or do not correspond to the things themselves for which they stand, or are true or not, according as it is exercised soundly or otherwise. *One fact may suffice for a whole theory; one principle may create and sustain a system; one minute token is a clue to a large discovery.* The mind ranges to and fro, and spreads out, and advances forward with a quickness which has become a proverb, and a subtlety and versatility which baffle investigation. It passes on from point to point, gaining one by some indication; another on a probability; then availing itself of an association; then falling back on some received law; next seizing on testimony; then committing itself to some popular impression, or some inward instinct, or some obscure memory [...]. And such mainly is the way in which all men, gifted or not gifted, commonly reason—not by rule, but by an inward faculty. Reasoning, then, or the exercise of Reason, is a living spontaneous energy within us, not an art.[133]

"One minute token is a clue to a large discovery." This minute token can be easily identified with the spark that catalyzes Peirce's Abduction.

Two further examples that Newman and Peirce related serve as poignant illustrations of the correspondence of their thought in these topics. Newman alluded to how it is known that Great Britain is an island, arguing that this fact does not rest on logical proof but in an assemblage of data of diverse epistemic value: natural, informal, and formal inferences. These support one another and, through their combination, provide the conditions required for assent:

132. See Barrena and Nubiola, "Abduction: The Logic of Creativity," 194–202; Rosario Athié, *El asentimiento en J. H. Newman,* Cuadernos de Anuario Filosófico 141 (Universidad de Navarra, 2001), 76–77.

133. *US,* 256–57 (1840) (emphasis added).

We are all absolutely certain, beyond the possibility of doubt, that Great Britain is an island. We give to that proposition our deliberate and unconditional adhesion. [...] Our reasons for believing that we are circumnavigable are such as these: first, we have been so taught in our childhood, and it is so in all the maps; next, we have never heard it contradicted or questioned; on the contrary, every one whom we have heard speak on the subject of Great Britain, every book we have read, invariably took it for granted [...]. I am not at all insinuating that we are not rational in our certitude; I only mean that we cannot analyze a proof satisfactorily.[134]

Newman went on to explain that even if one were to obtain logical proof, it would not make one more certain of the fact that Great Britain is an island than one already was by employing the Illative Sense.

Peirce, for his part, illustrated Abductive Reasoning with the following story:

I once landed in a seaport in a Turkish province; and, as I was walking up to the house which I was to visit, I met a man upon horseback, surrounded by four horsemen holding a canopy over his head. As the governor of the province was the only personage I could think of who would be so greatly honored, I inferred this was he. This was a hypothesis.[135]

The hypothesis, or Abduction, that Peirce made in this narrative is not a necessary conclusion but merely a probable one. It is meant to explain an observed phenomenon and suggest a strategy for further inquiry. As these examples suggest, the Illative Sense aids the individual in the formulation of practical knowledge, which brings forth the possibility for theorizing through Abductive Reasoning.[136]

---

134. *GA*, 294–96. Ker explains that "it is rather the cumulation of probabilities, which cannot be reduced to a syllogism, which leads to certainty in the concrete." Ker, introduction to *The Grammar of Assent*, xviii.

135. Peirce, *Collected Papers*, 2.625 (1878).

136. See Jeff Gold, "Scholarly Practice Is HRD Research," in *Handbook of Research Methods on Human Resource Development* (Edward Elgar Publishing, 2015), 56. This is one of the few sources of academic literature in which the author discusses the Illative Sense and Abductive Reasoning side by side.

In his discussion on the existence of the Illative Sense, Newman pointed to the teleological nature of the universe, which evidences order and finality. Through analogy, he explained that the person possesses a faculty that enables her to know truth in concrete realities, as *phronesis* allows her to make concrete decisions: "There is a faculty in the mind which [...] when properly cultivated and used, answers to Aristotle's *phronesis*, its province being, not virtue, but the '*Inquisitio veri*', which decides for us, beyond any technical rules, when, how, etc. to pass from inference to assent."[137]

Newman recognized that although "an ethical system may supply laws, general rules, guiding principles, a number of examples, suggestions, landmarks, limitations, cautions, distinctions, solutions of critical or anxious difficulties," these are not enough to guide decisions in particular matters, and *phronesis* is needed to navigate daily life.[138] Likewise, deductive reasoning is not enough to reveal truth in concrete realities, and the Illative Sense acts as the mind's power of spontaneously reasoning and concluding, which enables the individual to form reliable beliefs, possibly without the awareness of how these are justified. For Peirce, the only justification for Abduction is that if we are to understand things at all, then it must be in that way; that is, reality can only be understood through the study of facts and the formulation of hypotheses to justify them. He believed that without Abductive Reasoning, it would be impossible to explain how knowledge comes to be.[139]

Further, as Newman pointed to the teleological nature of the universe in his justification of the Illative Sense, Peirce pointed to a "natural light," in order to explain the surprising ability to guess the correct answer from a great variety of possibilities. He wrote, "There is a reason, an interpretation, a logic, in the course of scientific advance, and this indisputably proves to him who has perceptions of rational or significant relations, that man's mind must have been attuned to the truth of things to discover what he has discovered; it is the very bedrock of logical truth."[140] For Peirce, the teleological nature of Abduction acts as a guarantor of its truth. Newman, for his part, wrote that the structure of the universe speaks of the Creator

137. *LD*, xxix 115 (1879).

138. *GA*, 354.

139. See Peirce, *Collected Papers*, 5.145 (1903), 2.753 (1883), 5.603 (1903).

140. Peirce, *Collected Papers*, 6.476 (1908). Peirce was mesmerized by the individual's ability to choose correctly between many hypotheses more often than not. See Barrena and Nubiola, "Abduction: The Logic of Creativity," 192–93.

who made it, and therefore inquiry will lead us to material for assent, that is, to truth:

> It is He who teaches us all knowledge; and the way by which we acquire it is His way. He varies that way according to the subject-matter; but whether He has set before us in our particular pursuit the way of observation or of experiment, of speculation or of research, of demonstration or of probability, whether we are inquiring into the system of the universe, or into the elements of matter and of life, or into the history of human society and past times, if we take the way proper to our subject-matter [we] shall find, besides abundant matter for mere opinion, the materials in due measure of proof and assent.[141]

Peirce's notion of Abduction also led him to acknowledge a Creator.[142] Both Newman and Peirce discovered and accepted God's existence not because they had strict rational justification for their beliefs, but because they received the world as it was and allowed themselves to be surprised by the reality it presented in all its detail and beauty.

Following this line of thought, it is helpful to repeat that Peirce understood Abduction as "studying facts and devising a theory to explain them."[143] This resembles Newman's sanction of the Illative Sense, which he introduced with these words: "We are in a world of facts, and we use them; for there is nothing else to use. We do not quarrel with them, but we take them as they are, and avail ourselves of what they can do for us."[144] These facts are the threads or fibers that make up knowledge. To explain the formation of knowledge, both Newman and Peirce use a remarkably similar metaphor; Newman chooses that of a cord and Peirce that of a cable, and both do so for almost identical reasons.

In 1864 Newman explained to John Walker (1800–1873), who had written him inquiring about his thoughts on probability, that the best illustration of his views is

> that of a *cable*, which is made up of a number of separate threads, each feeble, yet together as sufficient as an iron rod. An iron rod

141. *GA*, 351–52.
142. Oakes, "Discovering the American Aristotle," 33.
143. Peirce, *Collected Papers*, 5.145 (1903).
144. *GA*, 346.

represents mathematical or strict demonstration; a cable represents [...] an assemblage of probabilities, separately insufficient for certainty, but, when put together, irrefragable.[145]

Four years later, in 1868, Peirce articulated his metaphor in similar words:

Philosophy ought to imitate the successful sciences in its methods, so far as to proceed only from tangible premises which can be subjected to careful scrutiny, and to trust rather to the multitude and variety of its arguments than to the conclusiveness of any one. Its reasoning should not form a chain which is no stronger than its weakest link, but a cable whose fibers may be ever so slender, provided they are sufficiently numerous and intimately connected.[146]

The cord and cable metaphors, though limited as all metaphors are, serve as fruitful antidotes to the analogies that view knowledge as a chain, which have dominated much of the epistemology since Descartes. These images show that what matters is not the strength of a particular proposition but its connection to others: in the same way that the number and interconnection of fibers is what makes a cable strong, the number and interconnection of beliefs is what gives validity to the reasoning process.[147]

Through their notions of the Illative Sense and Abductive Reasoning, Newman and Peirce gave credibility to the varied sparks, or "minute tokens" in Newman's words and "fair guesses" in Peirce's, that initiate the processes of the discovery and development of knowledge. Further, both explained that certitude does not necessarily result from these modes of inference, but that the conclusions reached must be tested through induction and presented to the broader community. Newman's Illative Sense and Peirce's Abductive Reasoning are different concepts developed by men formed in different traditions across the Atlantic. However, their affinity in this concept and in other areas discussed in this chapter serves as a testimony to the validity of their philosophical heritage and upholds the understanding of Newman as an illustrious forerunner of pragmatism.

145. *LD*, xxi 146 (1864).
146. Peirce, *Collected Papers*, 5.265 (1868).
147. See Paul Thagard and Craig Beam, "Epistemological Metaphors and the Nature of Philosophy," *Metaphilosophy* 35, no. 4 (2004): 507–8.

Chapter 4

Prospects That Emerge from This Comparison

Throughout his life, Newman was deeply aware of the uniqueness of his position and of his capacity to make a contribution and steer the course of rationalistic thought towards a more wholesome understanding of reason. In 1848, soon after his conversion, he wrote in his diary: "God has created me to do Him some definite service; He has committed some work to me which He has not committed to another. I have my mission [...] I have a part in this great work; I am a link in a chain, a bond of connexion between persons. [...] I shall be an angel of peace, a preacher of truth in my own place."[1]

As it has been argued, Newman's commitment to truth was the thread that wove together his reflections, writings, and choices. He did not limit himself to analyzing the progress made in the natural sciences and philosophy and denouncing some of its abuses; rather, he sought to find a way forward from the reductionist views that dominated his intellectual environment, as he believed that "to murmur and rail at the state of things under which we find ourselves, and to prefer a former state, is not merely indecorous, it is absolutely unmeaning."[2] His commitment to truth underpinned his efforts as a preacher, apologist, educator, philosopher, and theologian and gave his missionary undertakings a unified purpose, which consisted in

---

1. John Henry Newman, *Meditations and Devotions of the Late Cardinal Newman*, ed. William Neville (London: Longmans, Green and Co., 1907), 301–2.

2. *US*, 67 (1831).

equipping his contemporaries with the intellectual resources they needed to uphold their beliefs and values.

In his analysis of Newman's philosophical relevance, Michele Marchetto identifies a "third way" that Newman proposes in contrast to ascertaining either irrationality or the supremacy of reason. He identifies the following five elements as the core of Newman's proposal: the assertion of the person as a living system, the enlargement of the idea of reason, the recognition of conscience as its own center, the identification of a tradition that embodies the truth and sustains individuals and communities, and the delineation of one absolute truth in multiple forms of personal existence.[3]

Although each philosopher who has engaged with Newman's work has brought out different nuances, as shown in chapter 2, Newman is often regarded as the pioneer of a new philosophy of the person. It is commonly agreed that one of his main concerns was to enable individuals to justify their assent to truth beyond scientific or logical demonstration, that is, to help people realize the truths they hold by appealing not only to their intellect but to their heart as well. Newman undertook this task by developing the Illative Sense and aiming for real assent, grounding it in the individual's conscience.[4]

In a manner that resembles the Illative Sense, in which the strength of a cable (a proposition) lies in the combination of several separate threads bound together (formal and informal inferences), this final chapter identifies four resources within Newman's vast contributions that help strengthen the individual's commitment to truth. Newman did not identify one unique thread to uphold right belief; rather, he claimed that the consideration of a broad range of notions is what aids the person in her growth in knowledge and attainment of truth.

While not all of these resources are broadly discussed in Newman's works, there is enough evidence to merit their inclusion. First, I will discuss Newman's understanding of a liberal education and its purpose. Afterward, I will show that his understanding of personal influence is an effective means of formation. Then, I will give an account of his understanding of conscience as the core of the individual. In the fourth section, I will bring these elements

3.   See Marchetto, "Philosophical Relevance of Newman," 321.

4.   In his repeated insistence on the need to realize what one thinks, writes, or says, Newman anticipates by half a century some insights held by pragmatist philosophers. There is a clear connection between his orientation towards real assent and the pragmatist notions of practices and conceivable effects.

together and examine them in relation to fallibilism and pluralism and show how these philosophical positions support the whole edifice of Newman's philosophy and how they sustain a life committed to truth.

Liberal Education

In 1863 Newman wrote in his diary, "From first to last education, in this large sense of the word, has been my line."[5] This "large sense of the word," refers to intellectual excellence: the object he consistently pursued in the nine discourses that comprise his *Idea of a University*. Newman understood the goal of education as "nothing more or less than intellectual excellence."[6] Moreover, he set liberal studies as an essential element in its attainment. He saw the liberal arts as the best instruments for the cultivation of the mind, since he believed that "knowledge is not a mere extrinsic or accidental advantage, which is ours today and another's tomorrow, which may be got up from a book, and easily forgotten again, which we can command or communicate at our pleasure, which we can borrow for the occasion, carry about in our hand, and take into the market; it is an acquired illumination, it is a habit, a personal possession, and an inward endowment."[7]

Newman believed that the best way to acquire this inward endowment is a liberal education understood as a training process, in contraposition to a passive acquisition of knowledge. He followed the views of the provost at Oriel College, Edward Copleston (1776–1849), who maintained that the business of education was to exercise the mind of the student, not to pour facts into it.[8] In a similar way, Newman understood the intellect's training as a dialectical process that involves giving and receiving insights, principles, and methodology.

In addition to developing the habits of reason and opening unknown horizons through new content, a liberal education transforms the knower. Newman was convinced that intellectual labor bears its fruit in virtuous behavior, clear judgment, articulate expression, and lively imagination. Thus, he proposed a liberal education as the most effective means to form good citizens.

5.   *AW*, 259 (1863).

6.   *Idea*, 121.

7.   *Idea*, 113.

8.   See William Copleston, *Memoir of Edward Copleston, Bishop of Llandaff* (London: John Parker, 1851), 38.

Framed within the whole of his philosophical project, Newman asked two cardinal questions about education: "How best to strengthen, refine, and enrich the intellectual powers? [...] What subjects beget the genuine habit of mental cultivation?"[9] He envisioned education as a continual process of improvement of human nature, which is achieved "not by undoing it, but by adding to it what is more than nature, and directing it towards aims higher than its own."[10] This process, which constitutes Newman's educational ideal, rests on three pillars: the unity, universality, and utility of knowledge. One of Newman's core educational theses is that knowledge can be its own end, and consequently should not be subjugated to any other objective, which at first sight may appear to be more useful or beneficial. Newman began his seventh discourse on university education with this rhetorical question:

> On the supposition that the article called "a Liberal Education" does not teach us definitely how to advance our manufactures, or to improve our lands, or to better our civil economy; or again, if it does not at once make this man a lawyer, that an engineer, and that a surgeon; or at least if it does not lead to discoveries in chemistry, astronomy, geology, magnetism, and science of every kind, what is its real worth in the market?[11]

Newman was aware that many objected to his *Idea* because they saw a liberal education as useless. However, he held that utility is an important end of education and presented knowledge as the most useful of goods to be sought. To explain this matter, he drew a parallel between knowledge and bodily health and argued that health is a good in itself: even though we cannot identify any concrete product it effects, it is worth seeking and caring for. Despising health because it does not enable one to perform a particular task would be absurd, because it empowers us to perform any task. Newman applied this principle to knowledge as a good to be sought for its own sake, since it empowers the individual to perform any task more easily and with better results.

9.   Edward Miller, "Newman's *Idea of a University*: Is It Viable Today?," *Current Issues in Catholic Higher Education* 12, no. 1 (1991): 8.

10.   *Idea*, 123. Aquinas' maxim comes to mind: "Grace does not destroy nature but perfects it." Thomas Aquinas, *Summa Theologica*, trans. Fathers of the English Dominican Province (New York: Christian Classics, 1981), I, q. 1, a. 8.

11.   *Idea*, 153.

Nevertheless, Newman maintained that the utility of education is found in itself, not in what it enables the individual to achieve. He affirmed that the useful is not limited to what is immediately good, but also encompasses what tends towards the good or is instrumental for it. Arguing from the very foundations of the discussion, Newman presented his conception of utility and its relationship to knowledge: "Though the useful is not always good, the good is always useful."[12] To illustrate his views, he wrote:

> *Looking always to real utility as our guide*, we should see, with equal pleasure, a studious and inquisitive mind arranging the productions of nature, investigating the qualities of bodies, or mastering the difficulties of the learned languages. We should not care whether he was chemist, naturalist, or scholar, because we know it to be as *necessary* that matter should be studied and subdued *to the use of man*, as that taste should be gratified, and imagination inflamed.[13]

Although Newman wanted his students to acquire marketable skills, he believed that the real utility of knowledge lay in the fact that it directs the person to better understand her identity. He incorporated a school of engineering and a school of medicine at the Catholic University of Dublin and made liberal education the foundation of both, as he knew that a greater dominion over the world was useless if the individual was unaware of the finality of such dominion. Newman observed that individuals were rapidly growing in their technical capacities but did not know what they needed to do, and much less for what purpose. Since these answers are provided by a liberal education, not by professionalization, Newman advocated for the former as a basis for the latter.

He also denounced the depersonalization of education that had begun to take hold in universities at his time. He noted that "there is to be nothing individual in [a utilitarian education]. What the steam engine does with matter, the printing press is to do with mind; it is to act mechanically, and the population is to be passively, almost unconsciously enlightened."[14] In contrast to this view, Newman promoted a personalized education, which recognizes and intertwines objective meaning and subjective perception.

---

12. *Idea*, 164.
13. *Idea*, 161.
14. *Idea*, 142–43.

In Newman's mind, education was conducted through lively inquiry within a community setting; he argued that only "when we are free from necessary duties and cares, [...] we are in a condition for desiring to see, to hear, and to learn."[15] He understood the freedom of students to inquire and to build relationships as a necessary means to achieve intellectual excellence and thus, humanize knowledge. In this regard, Newman observed that an excess of information may prove detrimental for education. He affirmed that "training is a matter of rule; it is not mere application, however exemplary, which introduces the mind to truth, nor the reading many books, nor the getting up many subjects, nor the witnessing many experiments, nor the attending many lectures."[16] Since he believed that a liberal education entailed interpreting specific information within a broad horizon of knowledge, he saw the acquisition of intellectual excellence as an eminently active process in which the student is the leading actor in his growth.

Regarding the broad but superficial exposure to multiple subjects, Newman commented that the proliferation of scientific and literary works would only be a benefit for the general public if people first receive a liberal education that enables them to understand what they read and properly value it within the circle of knowledge. He feared that the attempt to remedy the lack of education by the reading of many books would lead to narrow-mindedness, and even to the tyrannizing of the mind: "Such readers are only possessed by their knowledge, not possessed of it; nay, in matter of fact they are often even carried away by it, without any volition of their own. Recollect, the Memory can tyrannize, as well as the Imagination."[17]

Newman's understanding of liberal education did not consist of a set of subjects, and rather than being related to content, it was related to method. He considered liberal education in opposition to illiberal or technical education, which enabled a person to practice a profession. Illiberal education is oriented towards production, and as such, it is eminently utilitarian. In contrast, liberal education seeks to form the free man, the citizen, who is not bound by any particular task but is free for contemplation, hence the adjective *liberal*. In short, liberal education is the one that liberates the mind from the preoccupations and occupations that impede its flourishing. It is not necessarily equated with mental pursuits, as illiberal education is not necessarily

15. *Idea*, 104.
16. *Idea*, 151–52.
17. *Idea*, 140–41.

equated with bodily tasks. Newman held that some bodily pursuits are liberal while some pursuits of the mind are not; for example, he used gymnastics as an example of a bodily, yet liberal, art. He described liberal knowledge as that "which stands on its own pretensions, which is independent of sequel, expects no complement, and refuses to be *informed* (as it is called) by any end, or absorbed into any art."[18] Newman upheld freedom for inquiry as another means to intellectual excellence. He considered an educated person as one who inquires about the truth of things and believed students must be given sufficient time and space to freely explore reality, since this exploration is an essential requirement for the development of thought. A person's creativity is sparked when thought is not constrained by the boundaries of time. Newman saw it as a grave problem in education—perhaps the gravest—that students "have too much on their hands to indulge themselves in thinking or investigation."[19] He observed that they have so much work to *do* that they do not have time to *think*. After speaking about "the drudgery so ignoble" to which students are exposed when they are taught a vast array of subjects, he exclaims, "How much more profitable for the independent mind, after the mere rudiments of education, to range through a library at random, taking down books as they meet him, and pursuing the trains of thought which his mother wit suggests! How much healthier to wander into the fields, and there with the exiled Prince to find 'tongues in the trees, books in the running brooks!' "[20]

18.   *Idea*, 108.

19.   *Idea*, 149. The relationship between creativity and timelessness has been widely studied: "Scholars and poets have suggested over the years that the timeless intensity of the present moment is a gateway to creativity and joy. Creativity in particular is associated with highly intrinsically motivated states, loss of self-consciousness and the sense of time." Charalampos Mainemelis, "When the Muse Takes It All: A Model for the Experience of Timelessness in Organizations," *The Academy of Management Review* 26, no. 4 (2001): 548.

20. *Idea*, 149–50. Newman quotes Shakespeare's play *As You Like It*, act 2, scene 1, which puts these words in the mouth of Duke Senior:

> Sweet are the uses of adversity
> Which, like the toad, ugly and venomous,
> Wears yet a precious jewel in his head;
> And this our life, exempt from public haunt,
> Finds tongues in trees, books in the running brooks,
> Sermons in stones, and good in everything.
> I would not change it.

Jorge Luis Borges's counsel fits well in this context: "Seek for the pleasure in seeking, not in finding."[21] This is what Newman would describe as elbow room for inquiry. He was well aware that the intellect does not possess a preconceived route for knowledge; rather, it searches, explores, finds dead ends, and starts all over again. To exemplify this principle, Newman spoke of a mountain hike and said that nó one can go up on a straight path; one instead needs to roam a bit, or a lot, to find sure support and clear pathways for one's ascent.[22]

While giving students enough time and space for inquiry was a central priority for Newman, he argued that inquiry is only profitable when informed by the right attitude, which he called a philosophical approach to reality. This approach involves pursuing answers to those questions posed by ordinary people, not only by professional philosophers. Whatever their level of culture, individuals desire to know and to understand. Newman spoke of the necessary conditions for a person to acquire a philosophical habit of mind. He found in leisure an efficient means to counteract the superficiality, thoughtlessness, and celerity by which the life of his contemporaries is permeated, and to prepare them to be transformed by the knowledge they acquired. Aware that leisure and enlargement of the mind go hand-in-hand, Newman understood leisure not as an occasion for mental dispersion but as the tranquility and openness of soul necessary for intellectual growth. He advocated for liberal studies, because they free the intellect and, in doing so, enable its growth.

Having a philosophical attitude towards reality also means that questions are more important than answers, and even though answers may be found, philosophy is kept alive through the continual examination of questions. Throughout history, philosophers have transmitted to their disciples this art of asking questions rather than particular answers. This is what Newman called a philosophical approach to reality, which does not mean that scholars are to move in endless circles or that advances cannot be made. The attainment of truth advances in spirals, dealing over and over with the same themes and, if done honestly, allowing for a more precise understanding.[23] In this

---

21.   Jorge Luis Borges, *Poesía completa*, ed. Sara Luis del Carril (Barcelona: Ediciones Destino, 2009), 332 (translation mine).

22.   See *Idea*, 474–75.

23. One may note pragmatist themes in these assertions: the understanding that there are better and worse ways to conduct inquiry and that these are always perfectible. In particular, Dewey's admonition follows Newman's understanding of philosophy:

respect, Alasdair MacIntyre comments that good philosophers understood their writing "as contributing to an ongoing philosophical conversation, a conversation that had had a long history before they became a part of it and that would continue after they had fallen silent. This self-understanding enabled them to treat their readers [...] as likewise contributing to that same conversation."[24]

Newman believed that this philosophical conversation must not be circumscribed to a particular branch of knowledge but should take place between the different sciences and especially between the humanities and the natural sciences. To have a philosophical approach to reality means to be willing to engage, both as a listener and as a speaker, in this ongoing conversation that touches upon the most fundamental questions of every branch of knowledge.

In Newman's understanding, a liberal education is a necessary first step to prepare the person for any and every professional path. It "is the indispensable condition of expansion of mind, and the instrument of attaining to it; this cannot be denied, it is ever to be insisted on; I begin with it as a first principle."[25] Among the qualities of education he considers a first principle, Newman lists force, steadiness, comprehensiveness, versatility, command of the intellect over its own powers, the capacity to view and express relationships, the ability to estimate things as they pass before us, and competence to contrast conclusions and principles.[26] Newman maintained that an enlarged mind sees more, compares more, and judges relations with greater insight; thus a liberal education prepares one for positions that require leadership and vision. The knowledge acquired through a liberal education that pursues intellectual excellence

---

Philosophy recovers itself when it ceases to be a device for dealing with the problems of philosophers and becomes a method, cultivated by philosophers, for dealing with the problems of men. Emphasis must vary with the stress and special impact of the troubles which perplex men. Each age knows its own ills, and seeks its own remedies. One does not have to forecast a particular program to note that the central need of any program at the present day is an adequate conception of the nature of intelligence and its place in action. (Dewey, "The Need for a Recovery of Philosophy," 65–66)

24. Alasdair MacIntyre, *The Tasks of Philosophy: Selected Essays* (Cambridge: Cambridge University Press, 2006), 130–31.

25. *Idea*, 129.

26. See *Idea*, xvi.

expands and enlarges the mind, excites its faculties, and calls those limbs and muscles into freer exercise which, by too constant use in one direction, not only acquire an illiberal air, but are apt also to lose somewhat of their native play and energy. And thus, without directly qualifying a man for any of the employments of life, it enriches and ennobles all. Without teaching him the peculiar business of any one office or calling, it enables him to act his part in each of them with better grace and more elevated carriage; and, if happily planned and conducted, is a main ingredient in that complete and generous education which fits a man to perform justly, skillfully, and magnanimously, all the offices, both private and public, of peace and war.[27]

In short, when Newman spoke of the knowledge acquired through a liberal education, he referred to it as a personal possession, saying that "it *is* a something, and it *does* a something" to its proprietor, allowing him to have a better grasp of truth.[28]

Personal Influence

In addition to having a strong commitment to community, Newman dedicated much time and effort to personal relationships. In 1829 he wrote to his sister Jemima, "It requires one to be intimate with a person, to have a chance of doing him good."[29] Newman's philosophy of personal influence unifies his theory of knowledge and his writings on education. It is also a constant theme in the *Apologia*, where he shared his life's witness, and in his letters, where personal influence was not only the stimulus but a central part of the advice he gave to others.[30] Understanding Newman's doctrine of personal influence is essential for comprehending his rich legacy.

Newman dedicated the fifth of his *University Sermons* to the topic of personal influence. He introduced it by asking the following:

27.   *Idea*, 169.

28.   *Idea*, 148.

29.   *LD*, ii 119 (1829). Three years later he explained in a sermon, "We could scarcely in any situation be direct instruments of good to any besides those who personally know us, who ever must form a small circle." *US*, 98 (1832).

30.   Newman's marked preference for personal influence as the best possible means of education is coherent with the pragmatist notion of a cognitive community as the best possible setting for the advancement of truth.

What is that hidden attribute of the Truth, and how does it act, prevailing, as it does, single-handed, over the many and multiform errors, by which it is simultaneously and incessantly attacked? [...] It is proposed to consider, whether the influence of Truth in the world at large does not arise from *the personal influence*, direct and indirect, of those who are commissioned to teach it. [Truth] has been upheld in the world not as a system, not by books, not by argument, nor by temporal power, but by the personal influence of such men [...] who are at once the teachers and the patterns of it.[31]

Early in his life, Newman's religious sense was shaped by his aunt, Elizabeth Newman, and by his grandmother, Elizabeth Good, who taught him how to read the Bible and pray: "I was instructed in religious knowledge by kind and pious friends, who told me who my Maker was, what great things he had done for me, how much I owed to Him, and how I was to serve Him. All this I learned from them, and I rejoice that they taught it to me."[32] He attributed his first conversion to the testimony of Thomas Scott, and in Oriel College his relationship with Richard Whately became foundational for his adult life. Although they eventually parted ways over theological disagreements, Newman always treasured what he learned from him. His mind and spirit were mostly shaped by encounters that bore fruit because of the generosity and personal witness of his interlocutors, not because of their keen arguments.

After obtaining his fellowship, Newman insisted on making his relationship with his pupils at Oriel College a pastoral one and having direct influence over their moral and intellectual development. However, the provost, Edward Hawkins, thought his role should be limited to imparting lectures, since it was more cost effective for the college. Since Newman would not yield, Hawkins decided not to assign him any more students, which brought his short career as a tutor to an abrupt end in 1829. Mark Pattison (1810–1884), a fellow with Newman at Oriel, explained that personal influence was the point that Newman refused to give up, and over which he resigned, or rather was let go.[33]

The Catholic University of Dublin was intended to be a humanizing enterprise in which the search for truth transformed not only the students

31.   *US*, 76, 79–80, 91–92 (1832).
32.   *PS*, viii 110 (1825).
33.   Pattison, *Memoirs*, 87.

but the professors as well. Newman described it as "an *Alma Mater*, knowing her children one by one, not a foundry, or a mint, or a treadmill."[34] Although most of his writings on education refer to the university, Newman's formal engagement in one was relatively brief compared to the rest of his endeavors. Therefore, in the context of this discussion on personal influence, education can be understood not exclusively as the university's business but in a broad sense, as a relationship that leads to the growth of the parties involved.

Newman's emphasis on personal influence was also the deciding factor for ending his career as Rector of the University. In that period, his most considerable hardship was dividing his time between the university in Dublin and the oratory in Birmingham, since both institutions, and their members, required his constant attention. In a letter in which he explained the motives behind his resignation, Newman stated that he "had ever acted, not *by formal authority and rule, but by* influence, and this power cannot be well exerted when absent."[35] Besides valuing the effects his personal influence had on those under his care, Newman regarded it as a core element in his personal quest for perfection.[36] It was such an essential aspect in his life and mission that he immortalized it in his motto as a cardinal: "*Cor ad Cor Loquitur.*"

Through his writings, Newman identified personal influence as the great instrument for propagating truth. He believed that only a living person can infuse an abstract subject with vitality and bring others to real assent: "A man finds himself in a definite place; he grows up in it and into it; he draws persons around him; they know him, he knows them; thus it is that ideas are born which are to live, that works begin which are to last."[37] For this reason, he credited the success of the Oxford Movement to the Tractarians' personal influence over their circle of friends and acquaintances: "Individuals who are seen and heard, who act and suffer, are the instruments of Providence in all great successes."[38]

Time and again, Newman ascertained that only when an individual is convinced of what he holds to be true is he in a position to engage, delight, and absorb the interest of another person through natural sympathy.[39] In his

34.   *Idea*, 144–45.

35.   *LD*, xviii 217 (1857).

36.   Peter Nockles, "Oriel and the Making of John Henry Newman: His Mission as College Tutor," *British Catholic History* 29, no. 3 (2009): 421.

37.   *Prepos*, 381.

38.   *LD*, iv 68 (1833).

39.   See *HS*, iii 186.

argumentation to uphold this principle, Newman explains that he is following one of Aristotle's maxims: "We are bound to give heed to the undemonstrated sayings and opinions of the experienced and aged, not less than to demonstrations; because, from their having the eye of experience, they behold the principles of things."[40] Within his explanation of natural inferences, Newman commented on these words of Aristotle in a penetrating way:

> Instead of trusting logical science, we must trust persons, namely, those who by long acquaintance with their subject have a right to judge. And if we wish ourselves to share in their convictions and the grounds of them, we must follow their history, and learn as they have learned. We must take up their particular subject as they took it up, beginning at the beginning, give ourselves to it, depend on practice and experience more than on reasoning, and thus gain that mental insight into truth, whatever its subject-matter may be, which our masters have gained before us. By following this course, we may make ourselves of their number, and then we rightly lean upon ourselves, directing ourselves by our own moral or intellectual judgment, not by our skill in argumentation.[41]

Newman recognized that the alternative to personal influence was authoritarianism, which he opposed because he saw it as limited in reach and prone to degradation into persecution. For matters of belief, he compared the inefficacy of sheer argument to that of torture, and in the university setting, he opposed excessive regulation since "the minute labor of a discretionary rule is too fatiguing to be exercised on a large number."[42] After being criticized for setting very few rules to govern St. Mary's College (the house directly under his care in the Catholic University), Newman explained the reasoning behind his formative style in a report to Archbishop Cullen:

> In proposing rules on this subject, I shall begin with laying down, first, as a guiding principle, what I believe to be the truth, that the young for the most part cannot be driven, but, on the other hand, are open to persuasion, and to the influence of kindness and personal

40. Aristotle, *Nicomachean Ethics*, VI.11, trans. John Henry Newman, in *GA*, 341.

41. *GA*, 341–42. See also *HS*, iii 8–9.

42. John Henry Newman, *My Campaign in Ireland*, ed. William Neville (Aberdeen: A. King & Co., 1896), 39 (hereafter, *Camp*). See also *US*, 63 (1831).

attachment; and that, in consequence, they are to be kept straight by indirect contrivances rather than by authoritative enactments and naked prohibitions.[43]

His disapproval of the use of power, understood as imposition and not as influence, extended to politics, leading him to regard this practical science as an unsatisfactory and secondary affair because it substituted real personal relationships with impersonal and ineffective bureaucracy. In the beginnings of the Oxford Movement, he had a severe disagreement with William Palmer, who opposed individual action and personal responsibility and wished for a committee or an association, with rules and meetings. Nothing could have been further from Newman's preferred way of doing things; he believed that "deliverance is wrought, not by the many but by the few, not by bodies but by persons."[44]

Regarding argumentation, Newman explained that when it is understood as a methodical process for the application of the rules of logic, it had a minimal reach and could only bring the individual to notional assent. To be effective, logical arguments need to be complemented by real ratiocination, which gives them a meaning beyond their letter and enables the person to reach conclusions above and beyond them. Newman called this capacity for going beyond the formality of an argument a living *organon* and personal gift, which cannot be contained in propositions. These cannot convey the details of any subject "with that rapidity and certainty which attend on the sympathy of mind with mind, through the eyes, the look, the accent [...]. The general principles of any study you may learn by books at home; but the [...] life which makes it live in us, you must catch all these from those in whom it lives already."[45]

The importance Newman placed on the eyes, the tone of voice, and the facial expression of the individual who wishes to be effective in his accompaniment of others is very telling and is what his parishioners remembered about him. Five decades after listening to Newman's sermons at St. Mary's, James Froude vividly recalled the following:

43.   *Camp*, 36.

44.   *Apo*, 135. Although what Newman valued most in the many projects he undertook were the people with whom he shared his mission, he had a deep antipathy towards bureaucracy. When he was rector of the Catholic University of Dublin, he proposed building the University Church with his own funds and not using university funds, to avoid going through a committee.

45.   *HS*, iii 8–9.

Greatly as his poetry had struck me, he was himself all that the poetry was, and something far beyond. I had then never seen so impressive a person. I met him now and then in private; I attended his church and heard him preach Sunday after Sunday; he is supposed to have been insidious, to have led his disciples on to conclusions to which he designed to bring them, while his purpose was carefully veiled. He was, on the contrary, the most transparent of men. He told us what he believed to be true.[46]

A few months after asking to be received into the Catholic Church, Newman detailed his experience regarding the human elements that accompanied his conversion: "The heart is commonly reached, not through the reason, but [...] by means of direct impressions, by the testimony of facts and events, by history, by description. Persons influence us, voices melt us, looks subdue us, deeds inflame us. Many a man will live and die upon a dogma: no man will be a martyr for a conclusion."[47] When he was asked about the reasons for his conversion, he answered:

I do not know how to do justice to my reasons for becoming a Catholic in ever so many words—but if I attempted to do so in few, and that in print, I should wantonly expose myself [...]. This I will not do. People shall not say "We have now got his reasons, and know their worth." No, you have not got them, you cannot get them, except at the cost of some portion of the trouble I have been at myself. You cannot buy them for a crown piece—you cannot take them in your hand at your will, and toss them about. You must

---

46.   Froude, *Short Studies on Great Subjects*, 4:278. In a similar note Leónce de Grandmaison remarked:

It is paradoxical of Newman's life and influence that before and after joining the Church, he essayed to trace out a *Via Media* which would set aside all excess and every extreme, and yet, that one can scarcely mention him without emotion. So direct is his grip on souls, and so inescapable is his method of reasoning that, like the arrows in Longfellow's poem, his shafts are shot off into space almost at random, only to be found one day still vibrating, fixed in the heart of some problem that has found its solution. (Leónce de Grandmaison, "John Henry Newman, Consideré Comme Maître," *Etudes*, no. 109 [1906]: 722, trans. by Boekraad and quoted in his *Personal Conquest of Truth According to Newman*, 116)

47.   *DA*, 293.

consent to *think* [...]. I am not assuming that my reasons are sufficient or unanswerable, when I say this—but describing the way in
which alone our intellect can be successfully exercised on the great
subject in question, if the intellect is to be the instrument of conversion. Moral proofs are grown into, not learnt by heart.[48]

This is the proper context in which to understand Newman's conviction
that in moral questions, egotism is true modesty. He believed that in moral
matters, a person could only speak for herself and could not place her experience as a law unto others.[49] However, by candidly sharing her experience, she
could enable others to make concrete their own propositions and reach real
assent. Newman was always willing to accompany others on their journey and
talk about his experience, as he did in his copious correspondence, but did
not offer a shortcut for his interlocutors. As an educator and pastor, Newman
helped others internalize principles and laws so as to apply them resourcefully
in their concrete situations.

The capacity to contrast and combine various pieces of data, theories,
and interpretations, to internalize them to transmit them, and to make an
impression on others, are essential qualities of the educator in Newman's
mind. He wrote that "if we wish to become exact and fully furnished in
any branch of knowledge which is diversified and complicated, we must
consult the living man and listen to his living voice."[50] Personal lectures
and accompaniment were Newman's preferred means of education since
he believed that "truth, a subtle, invisible, manifold spirit, is poured into the
mind of the scholar by his eyes and ears, through his affections, imagination, and reason; it is poured into his mind and is sealed up there in perpe-
tuity, by propounding and repeating it, by questioning and requestioning, by
correcting and explaining."[51]

When a professor limited himself to meeting students at formal engage-
ments and dispensing them with assignments, Newman believed that he had
not fulfilled his duty but rather "trotted on like a squirrel in his cage."[52] In
contrast, he regularly chose to meet his students outside of the established

48.   *LD*, xi 110 (1846).
49.   See *GA*, 384.
50.   *HS*, iii 8.
51.   *HS*, iii 14.
52.   *HS*, iii 75.

lectures, chapel, and academic gown and address their questions by opening his own mind and heart and giving testimony to the unifying principles of his own life. He did not offer them prefabricated answers but helped them ask the right questions and, by sharing his personal involvement with the same human quandaries, taught them to think. This allowed him to write that truth "has come down to us, not risen up among us, and is found rather than established."[53]

In summary, Newman believed that "with influence there is life, without it there is none; if influence is deprived of its due position, it will not by those means be got rid of, it will only break out irregularly, dangerously. An academical system without the personal influence of teachers upon pupils, is an arctic winter; it will create an ice-bound, petrified, cast-iron University, and nothing else."[54] These words can be applied not only to universities, but to any community whose members search for the truth, as "even with these few considerations before us, we shall find it difficult to estimate the moral power which a single individual, trained to practice what he teaches, may acquire in his own circle, in the course of years."[55] Newman's personal investment and influence over others was deeply fruitful. In a sketch Colin Wilson wrote in a book examining the lives and work of nine men who kept Christianity relevant in their times, he paid homage to Newman's influence in a poignant way:

> In the twentieth century, all the problems which Newman treats are still with us, and our civilisation declines steadily because they remain unsolved. Under the circumstances, Newman has one thing to teach us. It is [...] that the individual who understands the problems must attempt to bear them on his own shoulders. Even if he is completely alone, he must make the effort. Newman's example proves how great can be the influence of one man's attempt to shoulder the problems; his strength became the strength of a whole generation. If the twentieth century could produce even a few men of Newman's stature, the whole course of history might be changed.[56]

<hr>

53.   *HS*, ii 388.
54.   *HS*, iii 74.
55.   *US*, 94 (1832).
56.   Colin Wilson, *Religion and the Rebel* (London: Victor Gollancz, 1957), 230.

Conscience

Newman indeed was a significant influence on those around him, not only due to the clarity of his argumentation and the coherence of his testimony, but because he led others, through his words and example, to form their own conscience and rely on it. Speaking about matters of belief, he stated that "in these provinces of inquiry egotism is true modesty. In religious inquiry each of us can speak only for himself [...] he cannot lay down the law; he can only bring his own experiences to the common stock of psychological facts."[57] At a time when freedom of conscience was emerging as a novelty and was looked upon with suspicion by many in ecclesial and political settings, Newman argued that "obedience to our conscience, in all things, great and small, is the way to know the Truth."[58]

The *Letter to the Duke of Norfolk*, prompted by William Gladstone's criticisms of the decrees of the First Vatican Council and published in 1875 as a 150-page pamphlet, is Newman's best-known discussion of conscience. Therein, Newman describes it as "the aboriginal Vicar of Christ, a prophet in its informations, a monarch in its peremptoriness, a priest in its blessings and anathemas."[59] However, his doctrine of conscience underwent a gradual development throughout his life. Several sermons from his Anglican years dealt with the attributes and duties of conscience.[60] His *Essay on Development* and *The Idea of a University* refer to its formation, and *The Grammar of Assent* presents the fullest and most sophisticated account of its nature.

In addition to being central to Newman's intellectual interests, conscience had a crucial place in his vital trajectory. A few months before he asked to be received into full communion with the Roman Catholic Church, he wrote to his sister Jemima, "I am distressing all I love, unsettling all I have instructed or aided. I am going to those whom I do not know, and of whom I expect very little. I am making myself an outcast, and that at my age. Oh, what can it be but a stern necessity which causes this."[61] The necessity he referred to was that of following his conscience.

57.   *GA*, 384–85.

58.   *PS*, i 227 (1830).

59.   *Diff*, ii 248–49.

60.   See "Conscience and Its Use," in *Sermons 1824–1843*, ed. Clement McGrath, Placid Murray, and Vincent Blehl (Oxford: Clarendon Press, 1991–2012), v 236–42 (1825); "The Self-Wise Inquirer," in *PS*, i 215–27 (1830); "The Testimony of Conscience," in *PS*, v 237–53 (1838).

61.   *LD*, x 595 (1845).

While Newman's life and work are an excellent commentary on conscience, he does not present a systematic treatise of it in any of his writings. Rather, he identified and developed some of its dimensions and characteristics, which, if viewed on their own, can appear to be one-sided or even contradictory. Newman's doctrine of conscience presented a harmonious synthesis of its deeply personal and yet relational nature, understanding it to be both a moral sense and a sense of duty. In some instances, Newman spoke of conscience as a faculty of reason and in others as the voice of God, which is innate to the person and, at the same time, requires a thorough formation. Among the many descriptions of conscience Newman provided, these lines from the *Grammar* provide a comprehensive view:

> [Conscience] is a moral sense, and a sense of duty; a judgment of the reason and a magisterial dictate. [...] It is seated in the mind of the individual, who is thus his own law, his own teacher, and his own judge in those special cases of duty which are personal to him. It comes of an acquired habit, though it has its first origin in nature itself, and it is formed and matured by practice and experience; and it manifests itself, not in any breadth of view, any philosophical comprehension of the mutual relations of duty towards duty, or any consistency in its teachings, but it is a capacity sufficient for the occasion, deciding what ought to be done here and now, by this given person, under these given circumstances.[62]

Newman observed that, unlike in earlier times, in the nineteenth century, "when men advocate the rights of conscience [they mean] the right of thinking, speaking, writing, and acting, according to their judgment or their humour [...]. They do not even pretend to go by any moral rule, but they demand [...] for each to be his own master in all things."[63] He clearly distinguished the rights of conscience from the rights of self-will, which he deplored as a counterfeit never before heard of. He also argued that conscience was intrinsically relational, not individualistic: "Conscience is not a long-sighted selfishness, nor a desire to be consistent with oneself; but it is a messenger from Him, who, both in nature and in grace, speaks to us behind a veil."[64] He believed that the

62.   *GA*, 105, 354–55.
63.   *Diff*, ii 250.
64.   *Diff*, ii 248–49. Although pragmatism does not deal with topics such as conscience,

person is oriented towards relationship and communion, and if she stopped listening to her conscience, gave up her search for the truth, or delegated her decision-making to others, then she would lose her personality.[65]

Basing his reflections on this anthropological understanding, Newman did not present conscience as a faculty that determines the truth, but as the moral compass that points towards someone else, who as "Creator [...] implanted this Law, which is Himself, in the intelligence of all His rational creatures."[66] In his view, the person is not the author of her conscience, but the recipient of its dictates. In the words of Michael Buckley: "One found it [her conscience]—or, if you prefer, *one was found by it.* Conscience recognizes something or someone that is other."[67]

The universal sense of right and wrong, the awareness of transgression with its sense of guilt, and the enjoyment felt when one has done a good deed, led Newman to believe that conscience "implies a relation between the soul and a [*sic*] something exterior, and that, moreover, superior to itself; a relation to an excellence which it does not possess, and to a tribunal over which it has no power."[68] In Newman's anthropology, morality develops within the relationship between persons, and conscience is the meeting place of two self-evident beings—oneself and God, subjective truth and objective Truth. He portrayed this in his novel *Callista*, where the protagonist explains the following:

> I feel that God within my heart. I feel myself in His presence. He says to me, "Do this: don't do that." You may tell me that this dictate is a mere law of my nature, as is to joy or to grieve. I cannot understand this. No, it is the echo of a person speaking to me.

---

it promotes the understanding of the person's relational nature, and is in this way compatible with Newman's understanding of conscience.

65. See *PN*, 33. Newman felt for those who

> have no firm grasp of principles, are perplexed and lose their way every fresh step they take; they do not know what to think or say of new phenomena which meet them, of whatever kind; they have no view, as it may be called, concerning persons, or occurrences, or facts, which come upon them suddenly; they cannot form a judgment, or determine on a course of action; and they ask the opinion or advice of others as a relief to their minds. (*US*, 292 [1841])

66.   *Diff*, ii 246.

67.   Buckley, "Conscience and Atheism According to Newman," 83 (emphasis added).

68.   *US*, 18 (1830).

Nothing shall persuade me that it does not ultimately proceed from a person external to me. It carries with it its proof of its divine origin. My nature feels towards it as towards a person. When I obey it, I feel a satisfaction; when I disobey, a soreness—just like that which I feel in pleasing or offending some revered friend. So you see, Polemo, I believe in what is more than a mere "something." I believe in what is more real to me than sun, moon, stars, and the fair earth, and the voice of friends. [...] An echo implies a voice; a voice a speaker. That speaker I love.[69]

While revealing the existence of Another, conscience in Newman's understanding is also personal and requires the complete ownership of its premises and mandates. The individual is meant to judge by the action of his own mind, by his own lights and principles; these principles are not given as propositions but reached by abstraction from particular experiences.

In his last two years as an Anglican cleric, Newman sought to prevent others from leaving the Anglican Church without doing their own personal and lengthy discernment. He was adamant that they should work out their own reasons and follow their own path, as he believed that "conscience is nearer to me than any other means of knowledge. And as it is given to me, so also is it given to others; and being carried about by every individual in his own breast, and requiring nothing besides itself, it is thus adapted for the communication to each separately of that knowledge which is most momentous to him individually."[70] In the context of his own journey, Newman explained that "he who made us, has so willed that in mathematics indeed we should arrive at certitude by rigid demonstration, but in religious inquiry we should arrive at certitude by accumulated probabilities."[71] Although he did not state it explicitly, one can draw a parallel between the personal nature of conscience, as Newman understood it, and the Illative Sense, because it focuses on particular and concrete situations.

To summarize, conscience is the medium for the relation between the person and God, where she can hear his voice and answer in a uniquely

---

69.   *Call*, 314–15. In a letter to his publisher, Newman expresses the significance of this novel by stating that he does not think that "Catholics have ever done justice to the book; they read it as a mere story book." *LD*, xxvi 130 (1872).

70.   *GA*, 390.

71.   *Apo*, 292.

personal way. It is "a principle planted within us, before we have had any training, although training and experience are necessary for its strength, growth, and due formation."[72] The training of the conscience implies following good advice, reading edifying books, and acting upon experience. It presupposes that the person has fundamentally chosen generosity and has made a serious moral commitment to the good, which she displays not only on extraordinary occasions, but in day-to-day choices.

Patience, obedience, and an absolute regard for the truth are characteristic of Newman's understanding of the formation of conscience. Six years passed from the moment of his first doubts regarding the Anglican Church to the moment he asked to be received into the Roman Catholic Church. During this long period of discernment, he wrote to Catherine Froude that "time alone can turn a view into a conviction [...] It is possible in process of time to have a proposition so wrought into the mind, both ethically and by numberless fine conspiring and ever-recurring considerations [...] to command our obedience."[73]

In addition to having patience to discern God's voice correctly, the individual needs to be willing to obey it, since moral character is improved by acts of obedience. Even if it were mistaken, Newman claimed that conscience must be obeyed: "Certainly, I have always contended that obedience even to an erring conscience was the way to gain light, and that it mattered not where a man began, so that he began on what came to hand, and in faith—that any thing might become a divine method of Truth; that to the pure all things are pure, and have a self-correcting virtue and a power of germinating."[74] Newman wrote these words in the context of his discernment regarding whether to ask to be received into the Roman Catholic Church. He explained that even if he were mistaken in following his conscience in this particular step, God would be able to bring him to the truth through a circuitous route, as the only thing God asked of him is that he follow truth wherever it may lead him. In this regard, Newman often emphasized the priority of truth over moral virtues.[75]

---

72.   *Diff*, ii 248.

73.   *LD*, x 190 (1844).

74.   *LD*, x 190 (1844). See Buckley, "Conscience and Atheism According to Newman," 84.

75.   See Joseph Ratzinger, "Conscience and Truth," in *Benedict XVI and Cardinal Newman*, ed. Peter Jennings (Oxford: Family Publications, 2005), 46.

Although the person can never have absolute certainty regarding her decisions, Newman claimed that "the nearest approach to such certainty which is possible, would seem to be afforded by [...] this good understanding (if I may use such an expression) between the soul and its conscience."[76] If she chooses to disobey her conscience, it will be silenced, but not destroyed, since "man himself has not power over it [...] he did not make it, he cannot destroy it. He may silence it in particular cases or directions, he may distort its enunciations, but he cannot, or it is quite the exception if he can, he cannot emancipate himself from it. He can disobey it, he may refuse to use it; but it remains."[77]

In addition to relating conscience to a supernatural being, Newman grounded it in human nature, stating that it "has a legitimate place among our mental acts; as really so, as the action of memory, of reasoning, of imagination, or as the sense of the beautiful."[78] In the discernment of the particular truths that are most relevant for the fundamental questions of existence and for action in specific instances, he advocated for the joint action of reason and conscience. Considering conscience as a faculty of reason, Newman identified two dimensions: a judgment of reason, which he also called a testimony or moral sense; and a magisterial dictate, which he also called a sanction or sense of duty. He explained that while these two dimensions are distinct and call for separate consideration, they make up one indivisible act:

> Conscience has both a critical and a judicial office, and though its promptings, in the breasts of the millions of human beings to whom it is given, are not in all cases correct, that does not necessarily interfere with the force of its testimony and of its sanction: its testimony that there is a right and a wrong, and its sanction to that testimony conveyed in the feelings which attend on right or wrong conduct.[79]

Newman distinguished these two dimensions in his own discernment and showed how they have a different function: "My own convictions are

---

76.   *PS*, v 250 (1838).

77.   John Henry Newman, *Sermons Preached on Various Occasions* (London: Longmans, Green and Co., 1908), 64–65 (1856). See also *PN*, 53. Buckley explains that "if conscience is corrupted or misunderstood or deadened or neglected, there is nothing that can take its place." Buckley, "Conscience and Atheism According to Newman," 79.

78.   *GA*, 105. See also *PN*, 43.

79.   *GA*, 106.

as strong, as I suppose they can be—only it is so difficult to know whether it is a call of *reason* or of *conscience*. I cannot make out, if I am impelled by what seems clear to me, or by a sense of *duty*."[80] He understood that a call of reason would not be sufficient for his conversion, but a call of duty would, since it is "a voice, imperative and constraining, like no other dictate in the whole of our experience" and signifies what one must do in a specific circumstance.[81]

Another relevant theme in Newman's writings on conscience is its relationship with authority, which he details in his *Letter to the Duke of Norfolk*. Although Newman was invited three times to participate as an advisor in the First Vatican Council, he declined, wishing to avoid another public controversy. He considered that the decrees of the council were not timely, but he accepted them and avoided pronouncing himself until Gladstone condemned the doctrine of papal infallibility, asserting that as a consequence of this dogmatic definition Catholics would not be able to fulfill their civil duties. As he introduced his reply, Newman explained:

> When, then, Mr. Gladstone asks Catholics how they can obey the Queen and yet obey the Pope, since it may happen that the commands of the two authorities may clash, I answer, that it is my *rule*, both to obey the one and to obey the other, but that there is no rule in this world without exceptions, and if either the Pope or the Queen demanded of me an "Absolute Obedience," he or she would be transgressing the laws of human society. I give an absolute obedience to neither. Further, if ever this double allegiance pulled me in contrary ways, which in this age of the world I think it never will, then I should decide according to the particular case, which is beyond all rule, and must be decided on its own merits. I should look to see what theologians could do for me, what the Bishops and clergy around me, what my confessor; what friends whom I revered: and if, after all, I could not take their view of the matter, *then I must rule myself by my own judgment and my own conscience*. But all this is hypothetical and unreal.[82]

---

80.   *LD*, x 610 (1845).
81.   *GA*, 107.
82.   *Diff*, ii 243–44 (emphasis added).

Gladstone presented the morality of authority and the morality of conscience as two opposing models, constrained by the struggle with one another. However, Newman saw their tension as fruitful and lifegiving—indeed necessary for upholding the social system. Instead of choosing one over the other, as Gladstone or Manning did, Newman distinguished different realms of action: personal conscience and external authority.[83] He furthered his argument by dissolving the apparent clash between conscience and authority and explaining that these two principles do not hold jurisdiction in the same sense. He argued that the Pope's prerogative is engaged in general propositions, regards the domain of thought, and lies in speculative matters, while conscience is a practical judgment for action by a particular person in specific circumstances. He believed that "conscience has rights because it has duties"; therefore, it is meant to inform authority, while authority is meant to protect it.[84]

Newman claimed that he has "not known where to look for instances of his [the Pope's] actual interposition in our private affairs."[85] He also held that all rules have exceptions and explained that he would resolve conflicting situations by assessing their particular merits, aided by thorough consultation. In Newman's own words, conscience "is to be taken as a sacred and sovereign monitor, its dictate, in order to prevail against the voice of the Pope, must follow upon serious thought, prayer, and all available means of arriving at a right judgment on the matter in question."[86]

Although Newman did not articulate his doctrine on conscience systematically, he realized it in his own life. Amidst the decisions that guided his journey, one can see his conscience acting as a dynamism for truth, goodness, and charity. A letter to Louisa Simeon (1843–1895), which Newman wrote while he was working on *The Grammar of Assent*, presents a good synthesis of his beliefs on this topic:

---

83.   Henry Manning (1808–1892) was considered the representative of the party that held the ultramontane view. Though Newman's reply was prompted by Gladstone's pamphlet, it was just as much addressed to Manning since it espoused a *via media* against liberalism and ultramontanism—the left and the right.

84.   *Diff*, ii 250.

85.   *Diff*, ii 228.

86.   *Diff*, ii 257–58. See Walter Conn, "Newman on Conscience," *Newman Studies Journal* 6, no. 2 (2009): 94.

> To gain [...] starting points, we must in a parallel way, interrogate our hearts, and (since it is a personal, individual matter) our *own* hearts— interrogate our own consciences, interrogate, I will say, the God who dwells there. I think you must ask the God of Conscience to enable you to do your duty in this matter [...] and this with an earnest desire to know the truth and a sincere intention of following it.[87]

Fallibilism and Pluralism

In the words of Joseph Ratzinger, Newman's life and work can be understood as a prolonged commentary on the question of conscience.[88] Another angle for assessing his life's journey is his unwavering commitment to the truth. In an essay that compares Newman's philosophical method to that of the pragmatist Hilary Putnam, Newman was described as "a man so preternaturally sensitive to the nuances of his thought, so determined to set his ideas down with absolute precision, that his honesty became an excuse for his opponents to call him dishonest."[89] The accusation of dishonesty was precisely what prompted him to write his *Apologia* and explain with exquisite subtlety the development of his thought.

My argumentation so far has attempted to delve into Newman's life and writings and bring out the framework of his philosophical project. This encounter has revealed his deep commitment to the truth and has shown its consonance with Peirce's pragmatism. Vincent Blehl, the postulator for Newman's canonization cause, attributed his far-reaching influence to two factors: his sincerity and his earnest search for the truth.[90] Newman's writings also make it clear that he

> wrote with a particular context and particular controversies in mind, and so the contemporary reader should not expect to find in this nineteenth-century thinker a corpus of ready-made answers to our contemporary questions, concerns, and hermeneutical inquiries. As a result, the task is to work through the subtleties of Newman's

---

87.   *LD*, xxiv 276 (1869).

88.   See Ratzinger, "Conscience and Truth," 45.

89.   Joseph Bottum, "Hilary Putnam, 1926–2016," *The Washington Free Beacon* (blog), March 19, 2016, https://freebeacon.com/culture/hilary-putnam-1926-2016/.

90.   See Blehl, "The Intellectual and Spiritual Influence of Newman," 256.

thought, decipher possible connections, and show how insights from various disciplines contribute to a deeper understanding.[91]

The terms *fallibilism* and *pluralism* were coined after Newman's death, so it would be anachronistic to look for them in his works. Moreover, both terms can be understood in multiple senses, some of which would definitively be rejected by Newman. However, traces of both can be detected in his thought and can give his commitment to truth a particular relevance. In his *Essay on Development*, Newman elaborated on the nature of truth as follows: "That there is a truth then; that there is one truth; [...] that the search for truth is not the gratification of curiosity; that its attainment has nothing of the excitement of a discovery; that the mind is below truth, not above it, and is bound, not to descant upon it, but to venerate it; that truth and falsehood are set before us for the trial of our hearts."[92]

While firmly upholding the objectivity of truth, Newman explored its historical, pluralistic, personalistic, and—consequently—fallibilistic elements; this exploration allowed him to present a rich, nuanced, and resourceful understanding of truth, which built on the premise that "truth cannot change [and] what is once truth is always truth."[93] Regarding Newman's notion of the indefectibility of certitude, Ian Ker explains that

> this subjective confidence only reflects a *general rule* to which exceptions are always possible; Newman's concern, in his own words, is merely "to show, that, as a general rule, certitude does not fail" (*GA*, 221). Far from confusing indefectibility with incorrigibility, the latter of which does not entail the former, Newman proceeds immediately to enlarge upon but also to qualify this "inward assurance" [...]. The possibility of error is freely allowed.[94]

---

91.   Aquino and King, introduction to *The Oxford Handbook of John Henry Newman*, 2.

92.   *Dev*, 357.

93.   *GA*, 221.

94.   Ker, introduction to *The Grammar of Assent*, lxviii. Jamie Ferreira offers four possible ways of understanding the apparent inconsistency in Newman's analysis of the indefectibility of certitude, one of which is that his "continual qualifications of indefectibility effectively dissolve the claim altogether." Jamie Ferreira, *Doubt and Religious Commitment: The Role of the Will in Newman's Thought* (Oxford: Clarendon Press, 1980), 106.

In a similar way, Newman explained that the path of inquiry is circuitous and always perfectible. He understood that insights into truth are developments from concrete reasoning based on antecedent probabilities that take into account the individual's conscience, the community, and the guidance of authority.

Newman's philosophical principles are compatible with fallibilism when fallibilism is understood as a doctrine about the person as a cognitive agent. In *The Grammar of Assent*, he provided a thorough account of the certainty of faith that is consistent with fallibilism.[95] In a 1872 letter, Newman commented on a development of Church doctrine and admitted his uncertainty in these terms: "Now we are new born children [....] We do not know what exactly we hold—what we may grant, what we must maintain."[96] He conceded that the full consequences of what had been discovered would take time to come to light and would need to be adjusted through a gradual interchange between error and truth:

> There will be a general agitation of thought, and an action of mind upon mind. There will be a time of confusion, when conceptions and misconceptions are in conflict, and it is uncertain whether anything is to come of the idea at all, or which view of it is to get the start of the others. New lights will be brought to bear upon the original statements of the doctrine put forward; judgments and aspects will accumulate. [...] As time proceeds, one view will be modified or expanded by another, and then combined with a third [...]. The multitude of opinions formed concerning it in these respects and many others will be collected, compared, sorted, sifted, selected, rejected, gradually attached to it, separated from it, in the minds of individuals and of the community. [...] Thus in time it will have grown [...] according to its capabilities.[97]

In all his writings, from his *University Sermons* in the 1830s to his last works in the 1870s, Newman showed openness to fallibilism as a characteristic of

95.   See Dahm, "The Certainty of Faith," 144. Newman embraced fallibilism when it is predicated in relation to the subject who knows, not the object that is known, which is also the approach of Peircean pragmatism. See Susan Haack, "Fallibilism and Necessity," *Synthese* 41, no. 1 (1979): 54.

96.   *LD*, xxvi 59–60 (1872).

97.   *Dev*, 37.

human reason. Without using the term, he positively upheld fallibilism in opposition to the mechanical, cold, and fixed understanding of reason proposed by rationalism. For Newman, truth entailed "a combination of diversified aspects, with the suggestions and corrections of many minds, and the illustration of many experiences."[98] He wrote elsewhere that "there are no short cuts to knowledge; nor does the road to it always lie in the direction in which it terminates, nor are we able to see the end on starting. It may often seem to be diverging from a goal into which it will soon run without effort, if we are but patient and resolute in following it out."[99] In speaking about a road that diverges from its goal, or the need to make amendments along the way, Newman adopted the fallibilist claim that human knowledge can always be corrected, bettered, and augmented.

Describing a mature person as one who is aware of the relative validity of her convictions but can stand for them unflinchingly, Newman adopted the mission of providing tools for his contemporaries to grow in maturity; he also proposed a *via media* between skepticism and fundamentalism, which upheld a fallibilism and a cooperative pluralism. He believed that "the human mind is made for truth, and so rests in truth."[100] This approach supports the dialogue between thought and life and enables the rigor of philosophical reasoning to gain human depth and relevance, and thus to grow in fruitfulness.

Within the context of opening the door to scientific research in the Catholic University of Dublin, Newman wrote that "if we invite reason to take its place in our schools, we must let reason have fair and full play. [...] Great minds need elbow-room [for] thought. And so indeed do lesser minds, and all minds."[101] His openness to exploration and inquiry was opposed by some of his colleagues who were afraid of the possible errors to which free inquiry could lead; however, Newman believed that "when there is an honest purpose and fair talents, we shall somehow make our way forward, the error falling off from the mind, and the truth developing and occupying it."[102] Newman not only made room for tolerance and error, he also understood that they play a vital role in the acquisition of truth: "Error

98. *Dev*, 38.
99. *Idea*, 474.
100. *GA*, 221.
101. *Idea*, 475–76.
102. *GA*, 377.

may be said, without a paradox, to be in some instances the way to truth, and the only way."[103]

Newman's certainty that truth would be found through honest inquiry reflects his confidence in human reason and its potential. He was comfortable with the prospect of error not because he thought little of man, but because he thought much. He encouraged his congregation at St. Mary's to be courageous: "If we are intended for great ends, we are called to great hazards; and, whereas we are given absolute certainty in nothing, we must in all things choose between doubt and inactivity."[104] Newman preached these words in 1839, as he began his journey to the Roman Catholic Church. Six years later, and a couple months before taking the final step in this journey, he wrote: "I have always contended that [...] it mattered not where a man began, so that [...] any thing might become a divine method of Truth, that to the pure all things are pure, and have a self-correcting virtue and a power of germinating."[105] He recognized how his endeavors, which were aimed at the purification and strengthening of the Anglican Church, brought him closer to the truth, although in a very different direction than the one he was intending at the time.

Another aspect of fallibilism, which Newman recognized, is the cooperative and cumulative nature of the quest for truth. He wrote that "it is not often the fortune of any one man to live through an investigation; the process is one of not only many stages, but of many minds. What one begins another finishes; and a true conclusion is at length worked out by the co-operation of independent schools and the perseverance of successive generations."[106] The researcher is part of a community that extends through space and time. This reality brings forth the clear link between fallibilism and pluralism, since human experience occurs in a plural manner, and cannot be fully comprehended in an abstract or individualistic way. It can only be accessed through incarnated experiences, and only from that plural and yet personal vantage point can truth be discerned.

Grounded in realism and in his personal experience, Newman accepted diverse paths to the truth, which stem from different first principles and follow the methods of investigation proper to each science; he also under-

103. *Idea*, 474.
104. *US*, 215 (1839).
105. *LD*, x 190 (1844).
106. *Idea*, 474–75.

stood that these paths ultimately need to be completed by other inquirers in order to attain a comprehensive grasp of reality. As has been seen, comprehensiveness is a core aspect of Newman's understanding of truth: "It is the characteristic of our minds to be ever engaged in passing judgment on the things which come before us. No sooner do we apprehend than we judge, we allow nothing to stand by itself, we compare, contrast, abstract, generalize, connect, adjust, classify and we view all our knowledge in the associations with which these processes have invested it."[107]

Newman understood diversity as a place of encounter and developed a positive acceptance of a pluralist society. He observed that human realities can be considered from multiple angles that do not necessarily exclude one another, but can enrich one another and the broader reality. His views on pluralism do not imply the rejection of truth. On the contrary, his understanding of pluralism not only affirms that there are different ways of thinking about things but maintains that among them there are better and worse ways to do so and that through inquiry, experience, and dialogue, individuals can recognize the superiority of one opinion over another. The belief that theories are human creations and thus fallible, means that they must be corrected and improved as new evidence is discovered. Since reality has an unlimited number of aspects, truth cannot be exhausted by any particular claim but remains open to new formulations.

Another aspect of pluralism that is compatible with Newman's philosophy is the understanding that the highest good to be sought through inquiry is not diversity but dialogue. The goal of pluralism is not to present a multiplicity of options as a good in itself but to enable different sciences (or persons, or realities) to enter into a genuine conversation with one another. After expressing his refusal to make his own doctrinal views a necessary criterion for others to be recognized as "good Catholics," Newman concluded a letter by stating, "How strongly I advocate the maxim '*In necessariis unitas, in dubiis libertas, in omnibus caritas.*' "[108]

Considering the time in which he lived, Newman's advocacy for religious freedom, a core tenet of pluralism, is quite novel. He wrote to the Irish politician William Monsell (1812–1894), who had asked for his opinion on the benefits of having a religion upheld by the state:

107. *Dev*, 33.

108. *LD*, xxiii 190 (1867). "In essentials, unity; in doubtful matters, liberty; in all things, charity."

> There is so much corruption, so much deadness, so much hypocrisy, so much infidelity, when a dogmatic faith is imposed on a nation by law, *that I like freedom better.* [...] We see every where a new state of things coming in, and it is pleasant to believe one has reasons not to fear it, but to be hopeful about it, as regards the prospects of religion. It is pleasant not to be obliged to resist a movement, which is so characteristic of the age.[109]

Newman's understanding of liberal education is also related to his high regard for pluralism. The tension he recognized and assimilated between the discursive and nondiscursive elements of reasoning enabled him to establish a coherent foundation for pluralism, since he believed that the richness and subtlety of personal reasoning meant that the intellect would come to a variety of interpretations and would be able to recognize the harmony among them.

Newman's positive view of pluralistic doctrines reflects his admiration for the Fathers of the Church, who had a rich and paradoxical relationship with the culture that surrounded them and regarded the use of any of its resources as legitimate inasmuch as it was helpful to their cause. Newman had the courage to relate with the modern world with the same attitude of openness and trust, and to recognize elements of truth in non-Christian cultures. After listing more than ten such elements, he concluded that "from the beginning the Moral Governor of the world has scattered the seeds of truth far and wide over its extent; that these have variously taken root, and grown up as in the wilderness."[110]

In the *Idea,* Newman presented his assessment of the fruits that the embrace of a pluralistic view of reality can bring to a community: "Now every event has a meaning; they have their own estimate of whatever happens to them; they are mindful of times and seasons, and compare the present with the past; and the world, no longer dull, monotonous, unprofitable, and hopeless, is a various and complicated drama, with parts and an object, and an awful moral."[111] The beauty of diversity, grasped as in a polyphony, is also

---

109. *LD,* xx 477 (1863) (emphasis added).

110. *Ess,* ii 231. There is a striking resemblance between these words of Newman and the Second Vatican Council's revolutionary invitation to missionaries to non-Christian peoples: "Let them gladly and reverently lay bare the seeds of the Word which lie hidden among their fellows." Vatican Council II, *Ad gentes* (December 7, 1965), 11.

111. *Idea,* 133.

portrayed by Newman in his poem "The Dream of Gerontius" where he described heaven as "a grand mysterious harmony: It floods me, like the deep and solemn sound of many waters."[112] Newman understood that harmony presupposes difference and that differences are not to be feared but cherished. As an Anglican, he led the Church to a deeper appreciation for its Catholic roots, and as a Roman Catholic, he enriched the Church with lessons from the Anglican tradition, such as the education of the laity. Under his leadership, Catholics became more engaged with the broader society, which in turn was enriched and became a community of communities.

Although his life and writings were firmly rooted in the truth, Newman was aware that "truth is vast and far-stretching, viewed as a system; and, viewed in its separate doctrines, it depends on the combination of a number of various, delicate, and scattered evidences; hence it can scarcely be exhibited in a given number of sentences."[113] He was able to integrate his appreciation for the richness of truth at a personal and philosophical level while humbly recognizing his inability to grasp it in its totality. How he did so portrays a particular understanding of fallibilism and pluralism, which is consonant with the Peircean line of pragmatism and can be a great asset for a commitment to truth in today's world.

112. *VV*, 360.
113. *US*, 90 (1892).

Conclusion

John Henry Newman lived in a time of deep cultural change and had an immense influence upon his era. The assumptions that had held society together and served as the bedrock for religious belief were shaken by the scientific revolution and by the rise of democratic states in the nineteenth century. From his early years at Oxford, Newman was deeply involved in the undercurrents of thought that framed these revolutions and disputed tradition. He faced these challenges with eagerness to mature his own thought through study and dialogue both with others and with reality itself. Further, he did not limit himself to assessing the situation and finding his own way forward; he sought to offer practical pathways that could be useful to all—to those who had the benefit of an education as well as those who did not.

His intellectual environment prompted him to pay close attention to the way in which individuals actually reason, both in their everyday lives and when faced with complex transcendental questions. His observations and dialogue with his contemporaries led him to a nuanced understanding of reason, which found its most mature expression in the Illative Sense. He was not indifferent to the philosophical developments that surrounded him; whether he agreed with them or not, he sought to engage with their challenges and discern the elements that were consonant with a Christian view of the person and of the world. Richard Hutton, a contemporary of Newman who commented upon his works for over four decades, wrote of him: "No life known to me in the last century of our national history can for a moment compare with it, so far as we can judge of such deep matters, in unity of meaning and constancy of purpose."[1]

Newman's disagreement with Robert Peel's theory of liberal education (very popular at the time), which suggested that reason be limited to mathematical and scientific exercises meant to account for all human reality, is

---

1. Richard Hutton, *Cardinal Newman* (London: Methuen and Co., 1891), 250.

emblematic of his concern for the vindication of reason. Peel held that once every individual accepted a univocal principle of reason, all disagreements and conflicts would cease; Newman, on the other hand, believed that logic could not account for the totality of reason, since it is a personal faculty that is unique to each individual: "It is the mind that reasons, and that controls its own reasonings, not any technical apparatus of words and propositions."[2] Maintaining a nuanced understanding of reason, of its possibilities and limitations, Newman objected to rationalism and described it as an abuse of reason. He challenged those who, in an effort to safeguard religious belief, reduced its contents to propositions that could be scientifically proven, thus discarding the most cherished tenets of the faith.

The connection of liberalism in religion to rationalism is the ground for Newman's disapproval, which he described as his lifelong battle: "By Liberalism I mean false liberty of thought, or the exercise of thought upon matters, in which, from the constitution of the human mind, thought cannot be brought to any successful issue, and therefore is out of place."[3] Newman held that reason acts beyond its powers when it confines knowledge to those claims that can be empirically proven, and in this way, it reduces religion to a personal sentiment or opinion. While he denounced liberalism in religious matters, Newman clearly acknowledged what is good in liberalism: its assertion of the values of justice and truthfulness, its avowal of personal and social freedom, and its inclusion of a historical approach in religious inquiry. While endorsing dogma and tradition, Newman valued the suitability of the liberal movement for the advancement of social and political concerns. Terrence Merrigan explains that the key to unraveling the complexity of Newman's thought is found in "his ability to hold in tensile unity apparently opposite tendencies and concerns. Indeed, it is in the attempt at synthesis that Newman is most truly revealed."[4]

The nuances of Newman's philosophical principles are clearly seen in his discussion of skepticism and fundamentalism. Although these could be understood as opposing tendencies, Newman was accused of both during his lifetime, since he sought to defend the right of the uneducated person to believe in mysteries she cannot explain. He was called a skeptic because he accepted claims that were beyond reason and a fideist because he was open

2.   *GA*, 353.
3.   *Apo*, 288.
4.   Merrigan, "Newman and Theological Liberalism," 621.

to holding them as true. In finding his own way, Newman did not retreat into a fideist understanding of the certainty of faith, nor did he embrace a partial skepticism to make faith more palatable to his scientific-minded contemporaries. Rather, he showed that the scope and ways human reason is exercised encompass much more territory than logic alone, and he offered an insightful understanding of the operation of reason in concrete matters.

However, his rejection of dogmatic liberalism did not lead him to fundamentalism. He trod the path of inquiry by proposing a reasonable skepticism that discovers and discards what is contradictory in itself and thus allows truth to develop and occupy the mind. His proposal can be understood as a *via media* between two extremes: dogmatic subjectivism and objectivism. Newman held that truth is equally distant from both, and to defend the truth he expanded the dominant view of rationality so it could include that which is concretely lived, practical, and not strictly logical or scientific. He proposed admiration, trust, and love as the most effective safeguards for belief, all of which act *within* the person, not as impositions put upon her.

Even though Newman recognized the dangers in rationalism, liberalism, and skepticism, as well as the risks they posed for his contemporaries, he remained hopeful. In a letter to Emily Bowles he commented on the situation: "This is a way of things which, in God's own time, will work its own cure, of necessity; nor need we fret under a state of things, much as we may feel it."[5] He went on to describe how even though there are many obstacles to the propagation of the truth, the situation is less hostile than in ages past, and much good can be achieved with creativity and courage.

The study of Newman's creative and courageous ways of dealing with the philosophical questions he encountered shows that he has an undeniable place in the history of philosophy—the value of which we are just beginning to discover. The different angles from which he considered the possibilities and limitations of the intellect, advocating for the search for truth as a communal task while upholding the primacy of the individual conscience, provide us with fruitful avenues to continue to deepen our understanding of truth.

When studied alongside classical pragmatism—particularly the line that developed from the writings of Charles Peirce—Newman's insights take on special relevance. He can be considered a forerunner of pragmatism because he overcame the modern philosophy of his time by reconnecting to the

5. *LD*, xx 447 (1863).

Aristotelian tradition in a very similar way to how Peirce would fifty years later and to how the new pragmatists would a century after that. Further, he had similar intuitions to those that characterize pragmatism. Viewed side by side, these intuitions constitute a useful incentive and tool for strengthening our commitment to truth.

The conversation developed in this book between Newman and pragmatism also sheds light on pragmatism itself, showing that it is compatible with a realist metaphysics and epistemology. Further, it revealed some of the strengths of pragmatism, such as the way it upholds truth while incorporating the vulnerabilities of reason and how it offers substantial resources for the exercise of philosophy that can bear fruit if undertaken with an open mind and a trusting heart. The comparison of Newman's philosophical thought and the pragmatic tradition shows that

1. Although Newman was driven by one single objective—to follow the truth wherever it led him—some unjustly criticized him as duplicitous. As he grew in his understanding of the truth, he adjusted his course, displaying great humility and simplicity. While his intellectual qualities were remarkable, he knew and accepted their limitations and thus was guided not only by his reason but also by his conscience, and never ceased his lifelong journey of deepening his understanding of the truth. This shows that a commitment to the truth is a lifelong endeavor that is outwardly expressed in different ways in the different stages of one's life. It allows for flexibility and adaptation to life's changing circumstances, and above all, it allows for personal growth and development. If a person is committed to the truth, then she will necessarily change as she attunes her ideas and behaviors, ever more perfectly, to the truth she gradually discovers. Newman's commitment to truth as a lifelong undertaking is clearly coherent with Peirce's pragmatic maxim.

2. Newman lived his commitment to the truth not as an isolated or isolating endeavor, but in constant dialogue with others and with reality itself. He was fully aware of the social nature of the individual and recognized the importance of personal influence, while delicately respecting his own conscience and the consciences of his peers. All his works were written to provide answers to specific quandaries of specific people. It is precisely this engagement with others

and with reality that makes Newman's contributions so fruitful. Moreover, this shows that a commitment to the truth must be lived in constant dialogue. Although truth is a personal possession, it is not found through pure introspection, but through conversation, inquiry, and engagement with the external world. This search will be more successful if one connects with a variety of perspectives and opinions. While these perspectives may be diverse or even contradictory, they can enrich and deepen one's understanding of the truth, which by its nature is multifaceted, ever-expanding, and infinite. The classical pragmatists' call for inquiry to be carried out within a community is echoed clearly in Newman's views.

3. Newman believed that

> it is the very law of the human mind in its inquiry after and acquisition of truth to make its advances by a process which consists of many stages, and is circuitous. There are no short cuts to knowledge; nor does the road to it always lie in the direction in which it terminates, nor are we able to see the end on starting. [...] Moreover, it is not often the fortune of any one man to live through an investigation; the process is one of not only many stages, but of many minds. What one begins another finishes; and a true conclusion is at length worked out by the co-operation of independent schools and the perseverance of successive generations."[6]

These words from Newman show that a commitment to the truth is built on the understanding of the search for truth as a communal pursuit through time. The search for truth is more effective when it brings together people with diverse experiences who are willing and able to build upon what was previously discovered and who make their discoveries available to others, so that these discoveries can be enriched through further inquiry. This view of inquiry is fully compatible with pragmatism.

4. The basic idea behind Newman's Illative Sense is the understanding of the foundation of certainty as the accumulation of probabilities. To illustrate this principle, Newman used the image of a cord

6.   *Idea*, 474–75.

made up of many threads—each feeble in itself, but when bound together, as strong as an iron rod. Peirce used a remarkably similar image: he spoke of truth as a set of fibers that may be slender and fragile, but form a robust cable, provided that there are enough of them and they are tightly connected. This shows that a commitment to the truth entails the acknowledgement that certainty results from the accumulation of probabilities that, when put together, become irrefutable—and not that certainty results from the complete exclusion of every doubt. A person who is committed to the truth admits others' challenges and does not see them as a threat, but rather an opportunity for growth.

5. Newman wrote that different sciences are meant to complement and correct one another, without intruding into each other's respective fields of knowledge. He also recognized that principles that apply to one science do not necessarily apply to another; for instance, while he was very critical of liberalism in religion, he praised its effects in the cultural and political spheres, acknowledging that each sphere had a distinct object and methodology and was informed by different principles. This shows that a commitment to the truth embraces the unity and universality of knowledge while recognizing that each field is ruled by its proper methodology and must respect and aid the others. This does not imply independence, but rather interdependence among the sciences, which, when they work together, provide a fuller and more comprehensive picture of reality. Peirce's classification of the sciences evokes these same principles.

6. Newman was aware of the inherent limitations of human reason and recognized that in many instances error might be the only way to a truth that will eventually become clear. He invited his contemporaries to embrace difficulties as a pathway to truth and not to be disconcerted by detours in the process of inquiry. This shows that a commitment to the truth is compatible with fallibilism, when understood as a doctrine that concerns the person as a cognitive agent and her cognitive methods. A pragmatic understanding of fallibilism does not lead to the denial of the existence of truth; rather, it leads to its assertion, since the conviction that truth will eventually be found is the motive that keeps inquiry going.

7. Newman's life was a constant search for new and better ways to bring the truth to his contemporaries, with the awareness that each of them would need a personal approach to truth in order to reach real assent. Time and again, he expressed that notional assent was insufficient, and he sought to bring each person in her uniqueness closer to a commitment to the truth, thus opening the possibility to its plural understanding. This shows that a commitment to the truth is compatible with pluralism. Since reality is multifaceted and has an unlimited number of aspects, truth cannot be exhausted by any particular sphere of knowledge but remains always open to new formulations. In itself, the possibility of developing more accurate formulations, instead of denying truth, points to its existence, since it shows that there is an objective reality the formulations are approaching.

The insights Newman offers in his assessments of the philosophical quandaries he encountered and the means he proposed to help his contemporaries deal with them are still illuminating today. As we have seen, his work is compatible with the central tenets of classical pragmatism: a tradition that brings forth rich nuances for our understanding of rationality and truth. Newman wrote in 1875, "In centuries to come, there may be found out some way of uniting what is free in the new structure of society with what is authoritative in the old."[7]

The present project has sought to distill what is authoritative, authentic, and valuable in pragmatism, and—by placing it in dialogue with Newman—offer it as an asset to strengthen our commitment to truth in today's world. Not only through his writings, but especially through his actions, John Henry Newman has provided a clear, valuable, and relevant testimony of a life that integrates the light and shadows, harmonies and dissonances of our human existence and remains firmly and joyfully committed to the truth. May his witness strengthen us to do the same.

---

7. *Diff,* ii 268.

Bibliography

Works of J. H. Newman

[1824–59]¹ *Historical Sketches*. 3 vols. London: Longmans, Green and Co., 1909.

[1829–46] *Essays Critical and Historical*. 2 vols. London: Longmans, Green and Co., 1907.

[1830–45] *The Via Media of the Anglican Church*. 2 vols. London: Longmans, Green and Co., 1901.

[1833] *The Arians of the Fourth Century*. London: Longmans, Green and Co., 1908.

[1834–43] *Parochial and Plain Sermons*. 8 vols. London: Longmans, Green and Co., 1907–8.

[1836–66] *Discussions and Arguments on Various Subjects*. London: Longmans, Green and Co., 1907.

[1838] *Lectures on the Doctrine of Justification*. London: Longmans, Green and Co., 1908.

[1843] *Fifteen Sermons Preached before the University of Oxford*. London: Longmans, Green and Co., 1909.

[1843] *Sermons Bearing on the Subjects of the Day*. London: Longmans, Green and Co., 1902.

[1845] *An Essay on the Development of Christian Doctrine*. London: Longmans, Green and Co., 1909.

[1848] *Loss and Gain: The Story of a Convert*. London: Longmans, Green and Co., 1906.

[1849] *Discourses Addressed to Mixed Congregations*. London: Longmans, Green and Co., 1906.

---

1. The year or years in brackets represent the original year of publication. The year at the end of each entry is the edition used in this book.

This bibliography includes some sources that were cited in the original research but are not cited in this book.

[1850] *Certain Difficulties Felt by Anglicans in Catholic Teaching.* 2 vols. London: Longmans, Green and Co., 1901.

[1851] *Lectures on the Present Position of .Catholics in England.* London: Longmans, Green and Co., 1908.

[1855] *Callista.* London: Longmans, Green and Co., 1901.

[1856–66] *Sermons Preached on Various Occasions.* London: Longmans, Green and Co., 1908.

[1858] *The Idea of a University.* London: Longmans, Green and Co., 1907.

[1859] *On Consulting the Faithful in Matters of Doctrine.* Edited by John Coulson. New York: Sheed & Ward, 1961.

[1864] *Apologia pro Vita Sua.* Edited by Wilfrid Ward. London: Oxford University Press, 1913.

[1867] *Verses on Various Occasions.* London: Longmans, Green and Co., 1903.

[1870] *An Essay in Aid of a Grammar of Assent.* London: Longmans, Green and Co., 1903.

[1879] *Addresses to Cardinal Newman with His Replies (1879–81).* Edited by William Neville. London: Longmans, Green and Co., 1905.

[1885] "The Development of Religious Error." *The Contemporary Review* 48, no. 4 (1885): 457–69.

[1890] *Stray Essays on Controversial Points.* Printed by the author, 1890.

[1893] *Meditations and Devotions of the Late Cardinal Newman.* Edited by William Neville. London: Longmans, Green and Co., 1907.

[1896] *My Campaign in Ireland.* Edited by William Neville. Aberdeen: A. King & Co., 1896.

[1956] *Autobiographical Writings.* Edited by Henry Tristram. New York: Sheed & Ward, 1956.

[1970] *The Philosophical Notebook of John Henry Newman: The Text.* Edited by Edward Sillem. Louvain: Nauwelaerts, 1970.

[1976] *Theological Papers of John Henry Newman on Faith and Certainty.* Edited by Hugo de Achaval and Derek Holmes. Oxford: Clarendon Press, 1976.

[1978–2009] *Letters and Diaries.* Edited by Charles S. Dessain, Ian Ker, and Thomas Gornall. 32 vols. Oxford: Clarendon Press, 1978–2009.

[1979] *Theological Papers of John Henry Newman on Biblical Inspiration and on Infallibility.* Edited by Derek Holmes. Oxford: Oxford University Press, 1979.

[1991–2012] *Sermons 1824–1843.* Edited by Clement McGrath, Placid Murray, and Vincent Blehl. 5 vols. Oxford: Clarendon Press, 1991–2012.

General Bibliography

Abbagnano, Nicola. *Historia de la filosofía*. Translated by Juan Estelrich and J. Pérez Ballestar. 5 vols. Barcelona: Hora, 1994.

Abraham, William. "Revelation." In Aquino and King, *The Oxford Handbook of John Henry Newman*, 304–17.

Addams, Jane. *Twenty Years at Hull-House*. New York: Macmillan, 1912.

Alonso García, Gabriel. "J. H. Newman como autor filosófico." *Revista española de Teología* 61, no. 4 (2001): 505–9.

Altholz, Josef. *The Liberal Catholic Movement in England*. London: Burns & Oates, 1962.

Aquinas, Thomas. *Summa Theologica*. Translated by Fathers of the English Dominican Province. New York: Christian Classics, 1981.

Aquino, Frederick D. "The Craft of Teaching: The Relevance of Newman for Theological Education." *Christian Higher Education* 2, no. 3 (2003): 269–84.

———. *Communities of Informed Judgment: Newman's Illative Sense and Accounts of Rationality*. Washington, D.C.: The Catholic University of America Press, 2004.

———. "Externalism and Internalism: A Newmanian Matter of Proper Fit." *The Heythrop Journal* 51, no. 6 (2010): 1023–34.

———. "Philosophical Receptions of the *Grammar of Assent*, 1960–2012." In *Receptions of Newman*, 53–72. Oxford: Oxford University Press, 2015.

———. "The British Naturalist Tradition." In Aquino and King, *The Oxford Handbook of John Henry Newman*, 154–72.

———. "Epistemology." In Aquino and King, *The Oxford Handbook of John Henry Newman*, 375–93.

Aquino, Frederick, and Benjamin King, eds. *The Oxford Handbook of John Henry Newman*. Oxford: Oxford University Press, 2018.

Aristotle. *The Complete Works of Aristotle: The Revised Oxford Translation*. Edited by Jonathan Barnes. Translated by William Ross. Vol. 2. Princeton: Princeton University Press, 1984.

Arnold, Claus. "Newman's Reception in Germany: From Döllinger to Ratzinger." *The Newman Lecture at Oriel College*. Oxford, 2011.

Artz, Johannes. "Newman as Philosopher." *International Philosophical Quarterly* 16, no. 3 (1976): 263–87.

———. "Newman in Contact with Kant's Thought." *The Journal of Theological Studies* 31, no. 2 (1980): 517–35.

Athié, Rosario. *El asentimiento en J. H. Newman.* Cuadernos de Anuario Filosófico 141. Universidad de Navarra, 2001. https://dadun.unav. edu/bitstream/10171/5858/1/141.pdf.

Bacon, Michael. *Pragmatism: An Introduction.* Cambridge: Polity, 2012.

Barr, Colin. "Ireland." In Aquino and King, *The Oxford Handbook of John Henry Newman,* 48–69.

Barrena, Sara. "La creatividad en Charles S. Peirce." In *Charles S. Peirce (1839–1914): Un pensador para el siglo XXI,* 105–26. Pamplona: EUNSA, 2013.

Barrena, Sara, and Jaime Nubiola. "Una introducción a Charles S. Peirce." In *Charles S. Peirce (1839–1914): Un pensador para el siglo XXI,* 17–48. Pamplona: EUNSA, 2013.

———. "Abduction: The Logic of Creativity." In *Bloomsbury Companion to Contemporary Peircean Semiotics,* 185–203. London: Bloomsbury, 2019.

Barron, Robert. "John Henry Newman among the Postmoderns." *Newman Studies Journal* 2, no. 1 (2005): 20–31.

———. "John Henry Newman in Full." *Word on Fire* (blog), October 15, 2019. https://www.wordonfire.org/resources/article/john-henry-newman-in-full/25610/.

Barry, William. "John Henry Newman." In *The Catholic Encyclopedia.* Vol. 10. New York: The Encyclopedia Press, 1913.

Begley, Ronald. " 'To Diffident to Define': The Gentleman in Newman's *The Idea of a University.*" *Faith & Reason* 19, no. 4 (1993): 345–61.

Benedict XVI. "The Reasonableness of Faith in God." Address, Paul VI Hall, 2012.

Bernstein, Richard. *Beyond Objectivism and Relativism: Science, Hermeneutics, and Praxis.* Philadelphia: University of Pennsylvania Press, 1983.

———. *The Abuse of Evil: The Corruption of Politics and Religion since 9/11.* Cambridge: Polity, 2005.

———. *The Pragmatic Century: Conversations with Richard J. Bernstein.* Edited by Sheila Davaney and Warren Frisina. Albany: State University of New York Press, 2012.

Blehl, Vincent. "The Intellectual and Spiritual Influence of J. H. Newman." *The Downside Review* 111, no. 385 (1993): 251–57.

Boekraad, Adrian. *The Personal Conquest of Truth According to J. H. Newman.* Louvain: Nauwelaerts, 1955.

Borges, Jorge Luis. *Poesía Completa*. Edited by Sara Luis del Carril. Barcelona: Ediciones Destino, 2009.

Bottone, Angelo. "Newman and Wittgenstein after Foundationalism." *New Blackfriars* 86, no. 1001 (2005): 62–75.

———. *Philosophical Habit of Mind: Rhetoric and Person in John Henry Newman's Dublin Writings*. Bucharest: Zeta Books, 2010.

Bottum, Joseph. "Hilary Putnam, 1926–2016." *The Washington Free Beacon* (blog). March 19, 2016. https://freebeacon.com/culture/hilary-putnam-1926-2016/.

Brentano, Franz. *The Origin of the Knowledge of Right and Wrong*. Translated by Cecil Hague. Westminster: Archival Constable & Co., 1889.

Brightman, Edgar. "The Use of the Word Personalism." *The Personalist* 3, no. 4 (1922): 254–59.

Buchler, Justus. Introduction to *Philosophical Writings of Peirce*, by Charles S. Peirce. Edited by Justus Buchler, ix–xvi. New York: Dover Publications, 1955.

Buckley, Michael. "The Winter of My Desolation: Conscience and the Contradictions of Atheism According to John Henry Newman." In *Newman and Truth*, 67–109. Louvain: Peeters, 2008.

Cameron, James. "The Night Battle: Newman and Empiricism." *Victorian Studies* 4, no. 2 (1960): 99–117.

Cancela, Celesta. "Putnam and the Notion of 'Reality.' " In *Following Putnam's Trail: On Realism and Other Issues*, 9–16. Amsterdam: Rodopi, 2008.

Carballo, Robert. "Newman and the Transition to Modern Liberalism." *Humanitas* 7, no. 2 (1994): 19–41.

Century Dictionary, The. 8 vols. New York: The Century Company, 1889–1991.

Chadwick, Owen. *Newman: A Short Introduction*. Oxford: Oxford University Press, 2010.

Charles, Prince of Wales. "John Henry Newman: L'armonia della differenza." *L'Osservatore Romano*, no. 233 (2019): 1, 4.

Church, Richard. *The Oxford Movement*. London: Macmillan, 1922.

Clarke, William. "Review of *An Essay in Aid of a Grammar of Assent*." *The Athenaeum*, no. 2212 (1870): 379.

Collins, James. "Newman and Philosophy." In *Philosophical Readings in Cardinal Newman*, 1–33. Chicago: Henry Regnery Company, 1961.

Conn, Walter. "Newman on Conscience." *Newman Studies Journal* 6, no. 2 (2009): 15–26.

Copleston, Frederick. *A History of Philosophy*. 11 vols. New York: Doubleday, 1946–75.

Copleston, William. *Memoir of Edward Copleston, Bishop of Llandaff*. London: John Parker, 1851.

Corona, Marial. *Philosophy in Higher Education: A Study of J. H. Newman's* The Idea of a University. Madrid: Apeiron, 2019.

Cosgrove, Brian. " 'We Cannot Do without a View' John Henry Newman, William James and the Case against Scepticism." *Irish Theological Quarterly* 61, no. 1 (1995): 32–43.

Coulson, John. *Newman and the Common Tradition*. Oxford: Clarendon Press, 1970.

Crabbe, George. *The Poetical Works of George Crabbe*. Paris: A&W Galignani, 1829.

Cronin, John. "Cardinal Newman: His Theory of Knowledge." PhD diss., The Catholic University of America, 1935.

Crosby, John. "The 'Coincidentia Oppositorum' in the Thought and in the Spirituality of John Henry Newman." *Anthropotes* 6, no. 2 (1990): 187–212.

———. "Newman on Mystery and Dogma." In *John Henry Newman, Lover of Truth*, 37–60. Rome: Pontificia Universitas Urbaniana, 1991.

———. "John Henry Newman on Personal Influence." In *Personalist Papers*. Washington, D.C.: The Catholic University of America Press, 2004.

———. *The Personalism of John Henry Newman*. Washington, D.C.: The Catholic University of America Press, 2014.

———. "The Philosophical Legacy of John Henry Newman." *American Catholic Philosophical Quarterly* 94, no. 1 (2019): 1–3.

———. "What Newman Can Give Catholic Philosophers Today." *American Catholic Philosophical Quarterly* 94, no. 1 (2019): 5–26.

Cross, Lawrence. "John Henry Newman: A Father of the Church?" *Newman Studies Journal* 3, no. 1 (2006): 5–11.

Culler, Dwight. "Newman on the Uses of Knowledge." *The Journal of General Education* 4, no. 4 (1950): 269–79.

———. *The Imperial Intellect*. New Haven: Yale University Press, 1955.

Dahm, Brandon. "The Certainty of Faith: A Problem for Christian Fallibilists?" *Journal of Analytic Theology* 3, no. 1 (2015): 130–46.

Dawson, Christopher. "Newman's Place in History." In *Newman and Littlemore*, 32–36. Oxford: Salesian Fathers, 1945.

Denison, George. "Review of Newman's *Apologia pro Vita Sua*." *Church and State Review* 27, no. 5 (1864): 54–56.

Dessain, Charles. "Cardinal Newman on the Theory and Practice of Knowledge." *The Downside Review* 75, no. 239 (1957): 1–23.

———. *John Henry Newman.* London: Nelson, 1966.

Dewey, John. "The Need for a Recovery of Philosophy." In *Creative Intelligence: Essays in the Pragmatic Attitude,* 3–69. New York: Holt, 1917.

———. *Individualism Old and New.* London: Allen & Unwin, 1931.

———. *Logic: The Theory of Inquiry.* New York: Holt, 1938.

———. *The Later Works of John Dewey, 1925–1953.* Edited by Jo Ann Boydston. 17 vols. Carbondale, Ill.: Southern Illinois University Press, 2008.

Donne, John. *Devotions upon Emergent Occasions.* Ann Arbor, Mich.: University of Michigan Press, 1959.

Dulles, Avery. *John Henry Newman.* London: Continuum, 2009.

Dunne, Joseph. "Newman Now: Re-Examining the Concepts of 'Philosophical' and 'Liberal' in *The Idea of a University.*" *British Journal of Educational Studies* 54, no. 4 (2006): 412–28.

Ekeh, Ono. "The Phenomenological Context and Transcendentalism of John Henry Newman and Edmund Husserl." *Newman Studies Journal* 5, no. 1 (2008): 35–50.

Evans, Gillian. " 'An Organon More Delicate, Versatile and Elastic': John Henry Newman and Whately's Logic." *The Downside Review* 97, no. 328 (1979): 175–91.

Fann, Kuang. *Peirce's Theory of Abduction.* The Hague: Martinus Nijhoff, 1970.

Ferreira, Jamie. *Doubt and Religious Commitment: The Role of the Will in Newman's Thought.* Oxford: Clarendon Press, 1980.

———. *Scepticism and Reasonable Doubt: The British Naturalist Tradition in Wilkins, Hume, Reid and Newman.* Oxford: Clarendon Press, 1986.

Flamarique, Lourdes. "Enseñanza de la filosofía. Apuntes para la universidad del siglo XXI." *Pensamiento y Cultura* 11, no. 1 (2008): 95–112.

Fontrodona, Joan. *Ciencia y práctica en la acción directiva.* Madrid: Rialp, 1999.

Ford, John. "Newman Studies: Recent Resources and Research." *The Thomist* 46, no. 2 (1982): 283–306.

Frey, Reed. "*Cor ad Cor Loquitur*: The Philosophical Personalism of John Henry Newman." Master's thesis, University of Pittsburgh, 2015.

Froude, James. *Short Studies on Great Subjects.* 4 vols. London: Longmans, Green and Co., 1894.

Galecki, Sebastian. "Newman Versus Objectivism: The Context of Modern Rationalism, Legalism and 'Paper Logic.' " *Prace Naukowe Akademii* 12, no. 1 (2015): 27–39.

Garnett, Jane. "Joseph Butler." In Aquino and King, *The Oxford Handbook of John Henry Newman*, 135–53.

Gellius, Aulus. *Noctium Atticarum*.

Génova, Gonzalo. *Charles S. Peirce: la lógica del descubrimiento*. Cuadernos de Anuario Filosófico 45. Universidad de Navarra, 1997. https://dadun.unav.edu/handle/10171/9834.

Gold, Jeff. "Scholarly Practice Is HRD Research." In *Handbook of Research Methods on Human Resource Development*, 45–61. Cheltenham: Edward Elgar Publishing, 2015.

Grandmaison, Leónce de. "John Henry Newman, Consideré Comme Maítre." *Etudes* 109, no. 4 (1906): 721–50.

Grave, Selwyn. *Conscience in Newman's Thought*. Oxford: Oxford University Press, 1989.

Grenz, Stanley, and John Franke. *Beyond Foundationalism: Shaping Theology in a Postmodern Context*. Louisville: John Knox Press, 2001.

Griffin, John. "Cardinal Newman and the Origins of Victorian Skepticism." *Heythrop Journal* 49, no. 6 (2008): 980–94.

Gwynn, Denis. *A Hundred Years of Catholic Emancipation (1829–1929)*. London: Longmans, Green and Co., 1929.

———. "Father Dominic Barberi and Littlemore." In *Newman and Littlemore*, 37–42. Oxford: Salesian Fathers, 1945.

Haack, Susan. "Fallibilism and Necessity." *Synthese* 41, no. 1 (1979): 37–63.

———. "Descartes, Peirce and the Cognitive Community." *Monist* 65, no. 2 (1982): 156–81.

———. *Evidence and Inquiry: A Pragmatist Reconstruction of Epistemology*. Oxford: Blackwell, 1993.

———. "We Pragmatists: Peirce and Rorty in Conversation." In *Manifesto of a Passionate Moderate*, 31–47. Chicago: University of Chicago Press, 1998.

———. "Pragmatism." In *The Blackwell Companion to Philosophy*, 774–89. Malden: Blackwell, 2003.

———. "Pragmatism, Then and Now." *Pragmatism Today* 1, no. 2 (2010): 38–49.

———. "Five Answers on Pragmatism." *Journal of Philosophical Investigations* (Traviz) 12, no. 24 (2018): 1–14.

Habermas, Jürgen. "Richard Rorty's Pragmatic Turn." In *Rorty and His Critics*. Malden: Blackwell, 2000.

———. "Reflections on Pragmatism." In *Habermas and Pragmatism*, edited by Mitchell Aboulafia, Myra Bookman, and Catherine Kemp, 225–28. London: Routledge, 2002.

———. *Truth and Justification*. Translated by Barbara Fultner. Cambridge: Polity, 2003.

Hacking, Ian. "On Not Being a Pragmatist: Eight Reasons and a Cause." In Misak, *New Pragmatists*, 32–49.

Hamington, Maurice. "Jane Addams." In *The Stanford Encyclopedia of Philosophy*, edited by Edward Zalta. Updated May 23, 2018. https://plato.stanford.edu/entries/addams-jane/.

Harper, Gordon. *Cardinal Newman and William Froude: A Correspondence*. Baltimore: Johns Hopkins Press, 1933.

Harper, Thomas. "Dr. Newman's *Essay in Aid of a Grammar of Assent*." *The Month* 12, no. 6 (1870): 667–92.

Hastings, Adrian. "Newman as Liberal and Anti-Liberal." In *The Theology of a Protestant Catholic*, 116–32. London: SCM Press, 1990.

Hochschild, Joshua. "The Re-Imagined Aristotelianism of John Henry Newman." *Modern Age* 45, no. 4 (2003): 333–42.

Hookway, Christopher. *Truth, Rationality, and Pragmatism: Themes from Peirce*. Oxford: Clarendon Press, 2002.

Houser, Nathan. "Peirce's Contrite Fallibilism." In *Semiotics and Philosophy in Charles Sanders Peirce*, edited by Rossella Fabbrichesi and Susanna Marietti, 1–14. Newcastle: Cambridge Scholars Press, 2006.

Hughes, Brian. "The Contemplative Function of Theology within Liberal Education: Re-Reading Newman's *Idea of a University*." *Horizons* 32, no. 1 (2005): 7–25.

Hughes, Gerard. "Conscience." In *The Cambridge Companion to John Henry Newman*, 189–220. Cambridge: Cambridge University Press, 2009.

Hughes, Philip. "Newman and His Age." *The Dublin Review* 217, no. 435 (1945): 111–35.

Humphreys, Joe. "Pragmatism: A Philosophy That's as Sensible as It Is Unpopular." *The Irish Times*, October 24, 2017. https://www.irishtimes.com/culture/pragmatism-a-philosophy-that-s-as-sensible-as-it-is-unpopular-1.3260684.

Hütter, Reinhard. *John Henry Newman on Truth and Its Counterfeits*. Washington, D.C.: The Catholic University of America Press, 2020.

Hutton, Richard. *Cardinal Newman*. London: Methuen and Co., 1891.

Huxley, Thomas. *Lectures and Lay Sermons.* London: Dent & Sons, 1910.

Inge, William. "Cardinal Newman." In *Outspoken Essays,* 172–205. London: Longmans, Green and Co., 1926.

Jaki, Stanley. "Newman's Assent to Reality, Natural and Supernatural." In *Newman Today,* 197–227. San Francisco: Ignatius Press, 1989.

———. *Newman's Challenge.* Grand Rapids: Eerdmans Publishing, 2000.

James, William. "Remarks on Spencer's Definition of Mind as Correspondence." *Journal of Speculative Philosophy* 12, no. 1 (1878): 1–18.

———. "Philosophical Conceptions and Practical Results." *University Chronicle* 1, no. 4 (1898): 287–310.

———. "G. Papini and the Pragmatist Movement in Italy." *Journal of Philosophy, Psychology and Scientific Methods* 3, no. 13 (1906): 337–41.

———. *Pragmatism, a New Name for Some Old Ways of Thinking.* London: Longmans, Green and Co., 1907.

———. *Selected Papers on Philosophy.* London: Dent & Sons, 1918.

———. *The Letters of William James.* Edited by Henry James. 2 vols. London: Longmans, Green and Co., 1920.

John Paul II. *Fides et ratio.* Encyclical Letter. September 14, 1998.

———. "Letter on the Bicentenary of Newman's Birth." January 22, 2001.

Jost, Edward. "Newman and Liberalism: The Later Phase." *The Victorian Newsletter* 24 (1963): 1–6.

Ker, Ian. "Magisterium and Theologians." In *Verantwoordelijkheden in de Kerk Volgens John Henry Newman,* 33–46. Nijmegen: Dispuutgezelschap HOEK, 1981.

———. Introduction to *An Essay in Aid of a Grammar of Assent,* by John Henry Newman, xi–lxx. Edited by Ian Ker. Oxford: Clarendon Press, 1985.

———. Foreword to *An Essay on the Development of Christian Doctrine,* xvii–xxvii. Notre Dame: University of Notre Dame Press, 1989.

———. *The Achievement of John Henry Newman.* Notre Dame: University of Notre Dame Press, 1991.

———. "Newman's Standing as a Philosopher." *Proceedings of the American Catholic Philosophical Association* 78 (2004): 71–81.

———. "Newman on Education." *Studies in Catholic Higher Education* (blog). *The Cardinal Newman Society,* December 1, 2008. https:// cardinalnewmansociety.org/newman-on-education/.

———. *John Henry Newman: A Biography.* Oxford: Oxford University Press, 2010.

————. "Newman's *Idea of a University* and Its Relevance for the 21st Century." *Australian eJournal of Theology* 18, no. 1 (2011): 19–32.

Kerr, Fergus. " 'In an Isolated and, Philosophically, Uninfluential Way': Newman and Oxford Philosophy." In *Newman and the Word*, 155–79. Louvain: Peeters, 2000.

King, Benjamin. "The Church Fathers." In Aquino and King, *The Oxford Handbook of John Henry Newman*, 113–34.

Kingsley, Charles. "Review of Froude's *History of England*, Vols. VII and VIII." *MacMillan's Magazine* 9 (1864): 211–24.

Klaver, Jan. "The Apologia." In Aquino and King, *The Oxford Handbook of John Henry Newman*, 454–74.

Knitter, Paul. "Religious Pluralism and Religious Imagination." *Louvain Studies* 27, no. 3 (2002): 240–64.

Leggett, Don. "William Froude, John Henry Newman and Scientific Practice in the Culture of Victorian Doubt." *The English Historical Review* 128, no. 532 (2013): 571–95.

Lovejoy, Arthur. "The Thirteen Pragmatisms." *The Journal of Philosophy, Psychology and Scientific Methods* 5, no. 2 (1908): 29–39.

MacIntyre, Alasdair. *The Tasks of Philosophy: Selected Essays*. Cambridge: Cambridge University Press, 2006.

————. "The Very Idea of a University: Aristotle, Newman, and Us." *British Journal of Educational Studies* 57, no. 4 (2009): 347–62.

Magill, Gerard. "Newman on Liberal Education and Moral Pluralism." *Scottish Journal of Theology* 45, no. 1 (1992): 45–64.

————. "The Intellectual Ethos of John Henry Newman." In *Discourse and Context: An Interdisciplinary Study of John Henry Newman*, 1–11. Carbondale: Southern Illinois University Press, 1993.

Mainemelis, Charalampos. "When the Muse Takes It All: A Model for the Experience of Timelessness in Organizations." *The Academy of Management Review* 26, no. 4 (2001): 548–65.

Marchetto, Michele. "The Philosophical Relevance of John Henry Newman." *Louvain Studies* 35, no. 3 (2011): 315–35.

Maritain, Jacques. *The Person and the Common Good*. Translated by John Fitzgerald. New York: Charles Scribner's Sons, 1947.

McCarren, Gerard. "Development of Doctrine." In *The Cambridge Companion to John Henry Newman*, 118–36. Cambridge: Cambridge University Press, 2009.

McCarthy, Gerald. "A Via Media between Scepticism and Dogmatism? Newman's and MacIntyre's Anti-Foundationalist Strategies." *Newman Studies Journal* 6, no. 2 (2009): 57–81.

McInroy, Mark. "Catholic Theological Receptions." In *The Oxford Handbook of the Oxford Movement*, 495–516. Oxford: Oxford University Press, 2017.

Merrigan, Terrence. *Clear Heads and Holy Hearts: The Religious and Theological Ideal of John Henry Newman.* Louvain: Peeters, 1991.

———. "Newman and Theological Liberalism." *Theological Studies* 66, no. 3 (2005): 605–21.

———. "Myself and My Creator: Newman and the (Post-) Modern Subject." In *Newman and Truth*, 1–33. Louvain: Peeters, 2008.

———. "Conscience and Selfhood: Thomas More, John Henry Newman, and the Crisis of the Postmodern Subject." *Theological Studies* 73, no. 4 (2012): 841–69.

Merrigan, Terrence, and Geertjan Zuijdwegt. "Conscience." In Aquino and King, *The Oxford Handbook of John Henry Newman*, 434–53.

Meszaros, Andrew. "The Influence of Aristotelian Rhetoric on J. H. Newman's Epistemology." *Journal for the History of Modern Theology* 20, no. 2 (2013): 192–225.

Michael, Fred. "Two Forms of Scholastic Realism in Peirce's Philosophy." *Transactions of the Charles S. Peirce Society* 24, no. 3 (1988): 317–48.

Milburn, Joe. "Newman's Skeptical Paradox." *American Catholic Philosophical Quarterly* 94, no. 1 (2019): 105–23.

Miller, Edward. "Newman's *Idea of a University*: Is It Viable Today?" *Current Issues in Catholic Higher Education* 12, no. 1 (1991): 4–11.

———. Introduction to *Conscience the Path to Holiness: Walking with Newman*, 1–14. Newcastle: Cambridge Scholars Publishing, 2014.

Misak, Cheryl. *Truth, Politics, Morality: Pragmatism and Deliberation.* London: Routledge, 2000.

———. "C. S. Peirce on Vital Matters." In *The Cambridge Companion to Peirce*, edited by Cheryl Misak, 150–74. Cambridge: Cambridge University Press, 2004.

———. "Making Disagreement Matter: Pragmatism and Deliberative Democracy." *Journal of Speculative Philosophy* 18, no. 1 (2004): 9–22.

———. *Truth and the End of Inquiry: A Peircean Account of Truth.* Oxford: Clarendon Press, 2004.

———, ed. *New Pragmatists.* Oxford: Oxford University Press, 2007.

———. "The Reception of Early American Pragmatism." In *The Oxford Handbook of American Philosophy*, edited by Cheryl Misak, 197–223. Oxford: Oxford University Press, 2008.

———. "The Impact of Pragmatism." In *The Cambridge History of Philosophy, 1945–2015*, edited by Kelly Becker and Iain Thomson, 624–33. Cambridge: Cambridge University Press, 2019.

Mitchell, Basil. "Newman as a Philosopher." In *Newman after a Hundred Years*, 223–46. Oxford: Clarendon Press, 1990.

Mitchell, Cyprus. "The Pragmatism of John Henry Cardinal Newman." Master's thesis, University of Missouri, 1913.

Moore, Matthew. "Newman and Peirce on Practical Religious Certainty." In *Semiotics Yearbook*, 48–56. New York: Semiotic Society of America, 2008.

Morris-Chapman, Daniel. "Scepticism, Truth and Religious Belief in the Thought of John Henry Newman: A Contribution to Contemporary Debate." PhD diss., University of Bristol, 2014.

Mounier, Emmanuel. *Personalism*. London: Routledge, 1950.

Mozley, Thomas. *Reminiscences Chiefly of Oriel College and the Oxford Movement*. London: Longmans, Green and Co., 1882.

Mumford, Lewis. *My Works and Days: A Personal Chronicle*. New York: Harcourt Brace Jovanovich, 1979.

Myers, William. *The Thoughtful Heart: The Metaphysics of John Henry Newman*. Milwaukee: Marquette University Press, 2013.

Naulty, Reginald. "Newman's Dispute with Locke." *Journal of the History of Philosophy* 11, no. 4 (1973): 453–57.

Neumann, Jared. "Richard Whately's *Elements of Logic* and Its Popular Discontents." Accessed March 9, 2021. https://www.researchgate.net/publication/325177432_Richard_Whately's_Elements_of_Logic_and_Its_Popular_Discontents.

Newman, Jay. *The Mental Philosophy of John Henry Newman*. Waterloo, Ont.: Wilfrid Laurier University Press, 1986.

Newsome, David. "Newman and Oxford." In *Newman: A Man for Our Time*, 35–51. Harrisburg, Pa.: Morehouse, 1990.

Nicholls, David. "Conscience and Authority in the Thought of W. G. Ward." *The Heythrop Journal* 26, no. 4 (1985): 416–29.

Nichols, Aidan. *The Panther and the Hind: A Theological History of Anglicanism*. Edinburgh: T&T Clark, 1993.

Niiniluoto, Ilkka. *Truth-Seeking by Abduction*. Switzerland: Springer, 2018.

Nockles, Peter. "Oriel and the Making of John Henry Newman: His Mission as College Tutor." *British Catholic History* 29, no. 3 (2009): 411–21.

Norman, Edward. *Roman Catholicism in England.* Oxford: Oxford University Press, 1985.

Nubiola, Jaime. "Walker Percy y Charles S. Peirce: Abducción y lenguaje." *Analogía Filosófica* 12, no. 1 (1998): 87–96.

———. "La búsqueda de la verdad en la tradición pragmatista." *Tópicos*, nos. 8–9 (2001): 183–96.

———. "Peirce on Complexity." In *Sign Processes in Complex Systems*, 11–23. Dresden: Thelem, 2001.

———. "Pragmatismo y relativismo: una defensa del pluralismo." *Themata, Revista de Filosofía* 27 (2001): 49–57.

———. "The Law of Reason and the Law of Love." In *Process Pragmatism: Essays on a Quiet Philosophical Revolution*, edited by Guy Debrock, 39–50. Amsterdam: Rodopi, 2003.

———. "Abduction or the Logic of Surprise." *Semiotica* 153, no. 1 (2005): 117–30.

———. "The Classification of the Sciences and Cross-Disciplinarity." *Transactions of the Charles S. Peirce Society* 41, no. 2 (2005): 271–82.

———. "John Henry Newman y Charles S. Peirce: conexiones y afinidades." Paper presented at V Jornadas "Pierce en Argentina," Academia Nacional de Ciencias Buenos Aires, August 23–24, 2012.

———. "Pragmatism in the European Scene: The Heidelberg International Congress of Philosophy, 1908." *Rivista di Storia della Filosofia* 72, no. 3 (2017): 381–99.

Oakes, Edward. "Discovering the American Aristotle." *First Things* 38, no. 12 (1993): 24–33.

O'Connell, Marvin. "Newman: The Victorian Intellectual as Pastor." *Theological Studies* 46, no. 2 (1985): 329–44.

O'Regan, Cyril. "Newman's Anti-Liberalism." *Sacred Heart University Review* 12, no. 1 (1992): 83–108.

Pacchioni, Gianfranco. *The Overproduction of Truth: Passion, Competition, and Integrity in Modern Science.* Oxford: Oxford University Press, 2018.

Paternostro, David. "Newman and the Nones: St. John Henry Newman Can Help Us Understand Why Catholics Are Leaving the Church." *America* 222, no. 3 (2020): 32–34.

Pattison, Mark. *Memoirs.* London: Macmillan, 1885.

Peirce, Charles. "Review of Clark University, 1889–1899. Decennial Celebration." *Science* 11, no. 277 (1900): 620–22.

———. *Collected Papers.* Edited by Charles Hartshorne and Paul Weiss. 8 vols. Cambridge, Mass: Belknap Press, 1935–58.

———. *Writings of Charles S. Peirce: A Chronological Edition.* Edited by Max Fisch. 8 vols. Bloomington: Indiana University Press, 1982–2009.

———. *Historical Perspectives on Peirce's Logic of Science: A History of Science.* Edited by Carolyn Eisele. 2 vols. Berlin: Mouton, 1985.

———. *The Essential Peirce: Selected Philosophical Writings.* Edited by Nathan Houser and Christian Kloesel. 2 vols. Bloomington: Indiana University Press, 1992–98.

———. The Charles S. Peirce Papers. Harvard University Library Photographic Service.

Penelhum, Terence. *God and Skepticism: A Study in Skepticism and Fideism.* Boston: Reidel Publishing, 1983.

Pfau, Thomas. "Newman's Idea of Tradition." *Newman Studies Journal* 12, no. 2 (2015): 86–100.

Pieper, Josef. *Leisure, the Basis of Culture.* Translated by Gerald Malsbary. South Bend, Ind.: St. Augustine's Press, 1998.

Purcell, Edmund. *Life of Cardinal Manning, Archbishop of Westminster.* 2 vols. London: Macmillan, 1896.

Putnam, Hilary. *Reason, Truth and History.* Cambridge: Cambridge University Press, 1981.

———. *The Many Faces of Realism.* LaSalle, Ill.: Open Court Publishing Company, 1988.

———. *Pragmatism: An Open Question.* Oxford: Blackwell, 1995.

———. "Pragmatism and Realism." *Cardozo Law Review* 18, no. 1 (1996): 153–70.

———. "A Half Century of Philosophy, Viewed from Within." *Daedalus* 126, no. 1 (1997): 175–208.

———. *The Threefold Cord: Mind, Body, and World.* New York: Columbia University Press, 1999.

———. *Ethics without Ontology.* Cambridge, Mass.: Harvard University Press, 2004.

Quine, Willard. "Two Dogmas of Empiricism." *Philosophical Review* 60, no. 1 (1951): 20–43.

Ramelow, Anselm. "Knowledge and Normality: Bl. John Henry Newman's *Grammar of Assent* and Contemporary Skepticism." *Nova et Vetera* 11, no. 4 (2013): 1081–1114.

Raposa, Michael. *Peirce's Philosophy of Religion*. Bloomington: Indiana University Press, 1989.

Ratzinger, Joseph. *Introduction to Christianity*. San Francisco: Ignatius Press, 2004.

———. "Conscience and Truth." In *Benedict XVI and Cardinal Newman*, edited by Peter Jennings, 41–52. Oxford: Family Publications, 2005.

Richardson, Laurence. *Newman's Approach to Knowledge*. Herefordshire: Gracewing, 2007.

Robinson, James. "Newman's Use of Butler's Arguments." *The Downside Review* 76, no. 244 (1958): 161–80.

Rojas, William. "Filosofía e investigación en la universidad." *Franciscanum* 47, no. 140 (2005): 25–35.

Rorty, Richard. *Philosophy and the Mirror of Nature*. Princeton: Princeton University Press, 1979.

Rowell, Geoffrey. "The Ecclesiology of the Oxford Movement." In *The Oxford Handbook of the Oxford Movement*, 216–30. Oxford: Oxford University Press, 2017.

Ruggiero, Guido de. *The History of European Liberalism*. London: Oxford University Press, 1927.

Rupert, Jane. "Newman and Bacon." *The Downside Review* 118, no. 410 (2000): 45–70.

Rush, Fred. "Review of *The Phenomenology of Spirit* by Georg Hegel." *Notre Dame Philosophical Reviews* (blog). University of Notre Dame, August 27, 2018. https://ndpr.nd.edu/reviews/the-phenomenology-of-spirit/.

Sanks, T. Howland. "A Church That Can and Cannot Change: The Dynamics of Tradition." *Theological Studies* 76, no. 2 (2015): 298–310.

Schreiter, Robert. *Constructing Local Theologies*. New York: Orbis Books, 1985.

Scola, Angelo. *The Nuptial Mystery*. Translated by Michelle Borras. Grand Rapids: Eerdmans Publishing, 2005.

Seibert, Charles. "Charles Peirce's Reading of Richard Whately's *Elements of Logic*." *History & Philosophy of Logic* 26, no. 1 (2005): 1–32.

Seigfried, Charlene. *Pragmatism and Feminism: Reweaving the Social Fabric*. Chicago: University of Chicago Press, 1996.

Sherry, Patrick. "John Henry Newman and William Froude, F.R.S." *Heythrop Journal* 52, no. 3 (2011): 399–409.

Shields, Patricia. "The Community of Inquiry: Insights for Public Administration from Jane Addams, John Dewey and Charles S. Peirce." Paper presented at the Public Administration Theory Network, Portland, Ore., March 1999.

Short, Edward. *Newman and His Contemporaries*. New York: T&T Clark, 2011.

Sillem, Edward. *The Philosophical Notebook of John Henry Newman: General Introduction to the Study of Newman's Philosophy*. Louvain: Nauwelaerts, 1969.

Soames, Scott. "Analytic Philosophy in America." In *The Oxford Handbook of American Philosophy*, edited by Cheryl Misak, 449–81. Oxford: Oxford University Press, 2008.

Spiegelberg, Herbert. *The Phenomenological Movement, a Historical Introduction*. 2 vols. The Hague: Martinus Nijhoff, 1965.

Stephen, James. "Dr. Newman's *Apologia*." *Fraser's Magazine* 70, no. 417 (1864): 265–303.

Stephen, Leslie. "Dr. Newman's Theory of Belief II." *The Fortnightly Review* 22, no. 132 (1877): 792–810.

Stout, Jeffrey. "On Our Interest in Getting Things Right: Pragmatism without Narcissism." In Misak, *New Pragmatists*, 7–31.

Talisse, Robert, and Scott Aikin. *Pragmatism: A Guide for the Perplexed*. London: Bloomsbury, 2008.

Thagard, Paul, and Craig Beam. "Epistemological Metaphors and the Nature of Philosophy." *Metaphilosophy* 35, no. 4 (2004): 504–16.

Thureau-Dangin, Paul. *The English Catholic Revival in the Nineteenth Century*. London: Simpkin & Co., 1914.

Tillman, Mary K. "The Personalist Epistemology of John Henry Newman." *Proceedings of the American Catholic Philosophical Association* 60 (1986): 235–44.

———. "The Philosophic Habit of Mind: Aristotle and Newman on the End of Liberal Education." *Philosophical Inquiry in Education* 3, no. 2 (1990): 19–27.

Tolhurst, James. *The Church, a Communion: In the Preaching and Thought of John Henry Newman*. Herefordshire: Gracewing, 1988.

Toohey, John. "The *Grammar of Assent* and the Old Philosophy." *The Irish Theological Quarterly* 2, no. 8 (1907): 466–84.

Tracey, Gerard. Preface to *John Henry Newman: Sermons 1824–1843*, by John Henry Newman, vii–xi. Edited by Francis J. McGrath. Oxford: Clarendon Press, 1992.

Tristram, Henry. *Newman and His Friends*. London: Butler & Tanner Ltd., 1933.

Vatican Council II. *Ad gentes*. December 7, 1965.

Velez, Juan. *Passion for Truth: The Life of John Henry Newman*. Charlotte, N.C.: TAN Books, 2011.

Verbeke, Gerard. "Aristotelian Roots of Newman's Illative Sense." In *Newman and Gladstone Centennial Essays*, edited by James Bastable, 177–95. Dublin: Veritas Publications, 1978.

Walgrave, Jan. *Newman the Theologian: The Nature of Belief and Doctrine as Exemplified in His Life and Works*. New York: Sheed & Ward, 1960.

———. "The Rediscovery of Newman." *New Blackfriars* 49, no. 578 (1968): 518–27.

———. "Faith and Dogma in Newman's Theology." Translated by Edward Miller. *Newman Studies Journal* 15, no. 1 (2018): 44–55.

Walker, Leslie. *Theories of Knowledge*. London: Longmans, Green and Co., 1911.

Ward, Wilfrid. *The Life of John Henry Cardinal Newman Based on His Private Journals and Correspondence*. 2 vols. London: Longmans, Green and Co., 1912.

———. "Newman's Philosophy." In *Last Lectures*, 72–101. London: Longmans, Green and Co., 1918.

Westbrook, Robert. *Democratic Hope: Pragmatism and the Politics of Truth*. Ithaca, N.Y.: Cornell University Press, 2005.

Whately, Richard. *Easy Lessons on Christian Evidences*. London: John Parker, 1838.

———. *Elements of Logic*. New York: Sheldon & Company, 1848.

Williams, Bernard. *Truth and Truthfulness: An Essay in Genealogy*. Princeton: Princeton University Press, 2002.

Williamson, Timothy. "Realism and Anti-Realism." In *The Oxford Companion to Philosophy*, edited by Ted Honderich, 1808–12. Oxford: Oxford University Press, 2005.

Wilson, Colin. *Religion and the Rebel*. London: Victor Gollancz, 1957.

Young, George. *Daylight and Champaign*. London: Jonathan Cape, 1937.

Zuijdwegt, Geertjan. "Richard Whately's Influence on John Henry Newman's *Oxford University Sermons* on Faith and Reason (1839–1840)." *Newman Studies Journal* 10, no. 1 (2013): 82–95.

———. "Richard Whately." In Aquino and King, *The Oxford Handbook of John Henry Newman*, 196–216.

Index